Reinsurance Reference Guide

With Background Information on Commercial Insurance Policies, Captives, Risk Retention Groups, Purchasing Groups, Legal and more

YEAR 2012 EDITION
A BOOK FOR PROFESSIONALS AND NOVICES
BY
ALBERT P. AMATO

PURPOSE OF THIS BOOK

This book is for all those professionals involved in reinsurance, but can easily be used by others who upon occasion need to know an aspect of it. It's intended to be clear, concise, with examples to guide the reader. We want this to be a quick reference used often. We have included more than just reinsurance because those other topics come up during the course of that subject.

Reinsurance is no longer a stagnant industry; it's full of changes and innovations. However, most of the tried and true principles have endured. This book is an attempt to standardize many of those principles as well as add the recent changes.

Reinsurance is an outgrowth of insurance which originated in London. Reinsurance in the United States began around 1900 but did not really get going until the 1920's. It basically stayed a quiet and relatively small industry until the 1980's, then like so many things it roared ahead becoming huge compared to what it had been. Today, reinsurance remains a vital part of an insurer's overall strategy.

Please note

- In an effort to make explanations clear, we will refer to the insurance company as the *insurer* or *reinsured-company* rather than use the terms ceding company, cedant, reassured, ceding- insurer.
- All examples are fictitious names and circumstances.

Work in Progress

The author considers this manual a work in progress. For those readers having suggestions, revisions, or comments please send them on to amato@clfrates.net or aamato8809@aol.com 203-629-5600.

REINSURANCE REFERENCE GUIDE

ISBN 978-1-105-22986-2

Library of Congress

Acknowledgements

I wish to thank those who helped me with their expertise and support in an effort to create this work: Robert Enko, George Stoffel, Dan Labrie, David Dee, Gary Prestia, Don Bashline, Roger Rossiter and to Roger Beverage who inadvertently started this project when he asked me to do a reinsurance 101 talk. Thanks to the College of Insurance (now the School of Risk Management, Insurance and Actuarial Science) for generously allowing the author to use their library. A special thanks to Rod Frates for his support and friendship over the past twenty years.

TABLE OF CONTENTS

Section 1

BASIC CONCEPTS OF REINSURANCE

WHAT IS REINSURANCE?

Think of it as an insurance company buying insurance on some of the policies it issues from another company specializing in that type of transaction. That other company is a "re" insurance company. The insurance company is reinsured so they can be referred to as the reinsured company. They also can be referred to as reinsured, reassured, ceding insurer, ceding company, company or cedant. This book will use the term Reinsured- Company and insurer.

WHY DO INSURANCE COMPANIES NEED TO BUY REINSURANCE?

To limit their losing too much capital on policies issued. If an insurer sells 1,000 policies, each with a $1,000,000 policy limit (the amount it can pay on the policy), theoretically, it could lose $1,000,000 on each policy-total $1 billion. It's better to pass some potential risk to a reinsurance company (reinsurer). This will create financial stability.

Another reason to purchase reinsurance involves the regulation of the insurer by each state in which they do business. Insurance is regulated at the state level. States permit an insurer only to sell policies with a maximum policy limit of 10% of their surplus (net worth), unless the policies are reinsured. If an insurer has surplus of $100 million, then the maximum policy limit is $10 million; with proper reinsurance, it can increase that policy limit to a higher amount.

TWO BASIC METHODS OF REINSURANCE

(1) Facultative Reinsurance
(2) Treaty Reinsurance

(1) Facultative Reinsurance

This is specific reinsurance covering a single risk; the reinsurer is reinsuring one insured on a specific policy. Each facultative risk is submitted by the insurer to the reinsurer separately; they can accept or reject it. Facultative reinsurance is characterized by the reinsurer's right of rejection. Put another way, the reinsured company is under no obligation to offer the risk; the reinsurer is under no obligation to accept it if offered. If the reinsurer accepts the risk and the parties agree on all the details, it is bound and the reinsurer issues a certificate of reinsurance evidencing coverage, terms, conditions rates and reinsurance premium.

Example:

Reinsured Company	Mason Insurance Company
Policyholder (Insured)	Reland Corp, Phoenix, Arizona
Type of Insurance	Comprehensive General Liability

Facultative Reinsurance	$1,000,000 each occurrence x $1,000,000 each occurrence

(2) Treaty Reinsurance

This method of reinsurance requires the reinsured company and the reinsurer to formulate and eventually execute a Reinsurance Contract, which can also be referred to as the Agreement of Reinsurance or simply referred to as a "treaty." The reinsurer then covers all the insurance policies coming within the scope of that contract. The reinsurer is aware of the type of insurance policies issued (i.e., commercial automobile liability, commercial general liability, commercial property, etc.) but is not aware of any specific policy or insured.

The reinsurer is reinsuring a block or stream of business from the Reinsured- Company. For instance, Mason Insurance Company (fictitious name) enters into a reinsurance treaty to reinsure its commercial automobile liability, $500,000 each occurrence excess of $500,000 each occurrence for the period January 1 to December 31, 2009. Hundreds or even thousands of policies might be covered under this reinsurance treaty. The reinsurer cannot reject any specific policy; all policies written within the scope of the reinsurance contract are covered. Most reinsurers generate a majority of their premium income from treaty reinsurance.

TWO BASIC TYPES OF TREATY REINSURANCE
(1) Excess of Loss Treaty Reinsurance
(2) Proportional Treaty Reinsurance

(1) Excess Of Loss Treaty Reinsurance

This type of reinsurance is "excess" of a certain amount or attachment point or threshold. The reinsurer only pays a claim when it exceeds this attachment point or *excess* of the attachment point. For instance, on an excess of loss treaty $3,000,000 each occurrence "excess" $2,000,000 each occurrence, the claim must exceed $2,000,000 before the reinsurer pays, then it pays up to a maximum of $3,000,000. The abbreviation for excess is "x" or "xs;" therefore, in the reinsurance industry it would be written as $3,000,000 x $2,000,000 or $3,000,000 xs $2,000,000.

(2) Proportional Treaty Reinsurance
Most Common Form is Quota Share

The Reinsured- Company and the reinsurer pay losses in a stipulated proportion (percentage).

Example:

95/5 Quota Share Treaty
The 95 is a percentage (95%) referring to the reinsurer's share. The 5 is a percentage (5%) and refers to the Reinsured- Company share or retention

Loss		$10,000
Reinsurer pays	95%	$9,500
Reinsured- Company pays	5%	$500

The reinsurer is not excess of a certain amount.

The reinsurance premiums paid to the reinsurer are also in proportion; 95% for the reinsurer and 5% retained by the reinsured company, but after the Reinsured- Company has deducted its expenses to secure the business, and perhaps an override commission for profit. These deductions are called a ceding commission.

Original Gross Net Written Premium	$1,000,000
95% Ceded to Reinsurer	950,000
Deduct: Ceding Commission - 30%	285,000
Net Paid to Reinsurer	$665,000

Note: These are the Amounts Retained by Reinsured- Company

5% of 1,000,000	50,000
Ceding Commission	285,000
Total	$335,000

Section 2

SPECIFIC TYPES OF TREATY REINSURANCE

CASUALTY EXCESS OF LOSS REINSURANCE-LOWER LAYER (REFERRED TO AS WORKING LAYER)

This treaty attaches at a low level; therefore, the reinsurer is likely to have loss activity, and consequently the reinsurance premium could be substantial. The reinsurer may be exposed on almost all policies issued by the reinsured company, meaning when the Reinsured- Company issues a policy, its limit exposes the reinsurer to the possibility of loss. For instance, if policies are issued with limits of $250,000 or greater, then a reinsurer doing a layer $100,000 x $100,000 is exposed to loss on every policy issued.

Example:
Working layer, Reinsured- Company's retention is $100,000
$100,000 x $100,000

This treaty might have a profit commission; if the business ceded to the reinsurer is profitable, it will return a portion back to the insurer in the form of a profit commission. Working layer treaties will have sufficient actual loss data to be experience rated by the reinsurance actuary, often not the case with upper layers.

Casualty can mean commercial general liability, commercial auto liability, physician professional liability, hospital professional liability, directors and officers liability, workers compensation and much more. Casualty is often defined as all classes of insurance except property and referred to as long tail because of the long delays in reporting and settling claims. In recent years, there has been a movement to further define classes of insurance as property, casualty, and professional liability (physician professional liability, hospital professional liability, directors and officers liability, errors and omissions liability).

CASUALTY EXCESS OF LOSS REINSURANCE-UPPER LAYER OR HIGH LAYER

This type of reinsurance protects the reinsured company from an occasional large loss. The reinsurer is not exposed on every policy issued, and accordingly the reinsurance rate will reflect this reduced exposure.
Mason Insurance Company has $100 million in surplus and issues policies with limits up to $5,000,000. It has decided to purchase the following reinsurance above its $1,000,000 retention.
These treaties would be considered higher layers.
Reinsured- Company's retention is $1,000,000.
$2,000,000 x $1,000,000
$2,000,000 x $3,000,000
It is unlikely this type of excess of loss reinsurance will have a profit commission because it will be difficult for a reinsurer to accept a large amount of risk for a relatively small premium and return a portion of its premium in the form of a profit commission. This type of upper layer reinsurance often will not have sufficient loss data to be experience rated and therefore most likely will be exposure rated by the reinsurance actuary.

PROPERTY PER RISK EXCESS OF LOSS REINSURANCE

This reinsurance offers protection for each individual property risk written by the reinsured company. When an individual property claim exceeds an agreed upon attachment point, the reinsurance is triggered.

Example
$750,000 each risk, each loss x $500,000 each risk, each loss
Maximum any one occurrence $3,000,000
In this example we show the most the reinsurer will pay on any one occurrence is $3,000,000. Even though this reinsurance is covering individual property risks most treaties will contain a maximum amount of loss the reinsurer will pay for all claims from any one occurrence
Definition of each risk: All personal and commercial property and its contents covered by the Reinsured- Company's property policy issued to the named insured.

PROPERTY CATASTROPHE EXCESS OF LOSS REINSURANCE
This treaty reinsurance protects the reinsured company's *property retention* from an accumulation of numerous individual *property risk losses* caused by a single occurrence. An occurrence most likely causing an accumulation of individual property losses and covered by this type of reinsurance is a natural disaster such as a windstorm (including hurricanes and tornadoes), freeze, snow load, hailstorm, and earthquake. Flood is generally not covered or if it is very limited coverage is provided, and a few other types of events may be covered such as a riot or conflagration.

Example
The Reinsured- Company has a $500,000 retention on each property policy it issues. Hurricane Ashley (the occurrence) sweeps through an area in which the Reinsured- Company has issued many policies creating numerous individual losses; $6,000,000 of aggregated losses *within its $500,000 retention.* The company has property catastrophe excess of loss reinsurance ($25,000,000 each occurrence x $2,000,000 each occurrence for its own retention). Therefore, the company is only responsible for the first $2,000,000 of losses within its retention; the next $4,000,000 of losses is paid by the reinsurer.

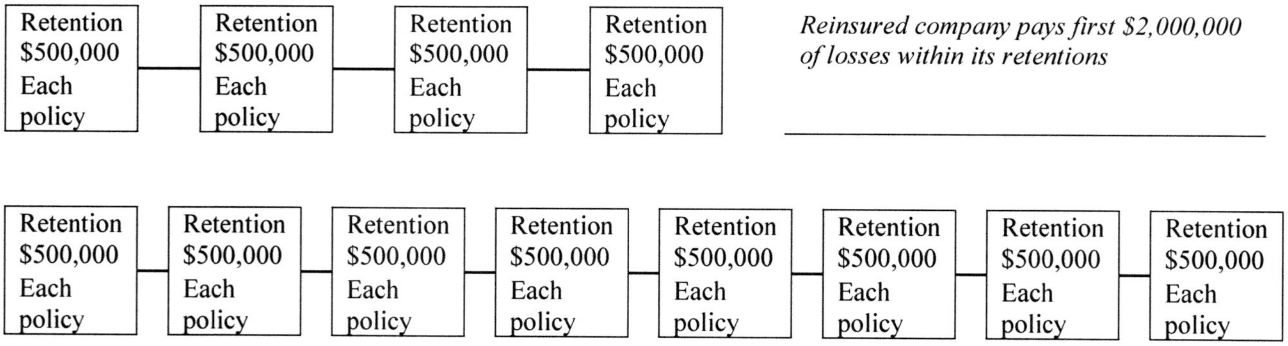

All the losses must be from Hurricane Ashley (the occurrence).

Reinsurer pays the next $4,000,000 of losses within the reinsured company retentions

Co-Reinsurance Participation

The reinsurer may require the Reinsured- Company to co-participate by taking a small percentage in the layers, such as 2.5% to 5.0%. In the example we use 2.5%.

i.e. 97.5% of $10,000,000 each occurrence x $2,500,000 each occurrence
The reinsurer has 97.5% of the layer and the reinsured company has 2.5%.

Property Catastrophe Excess of Loss Reinsurance "Layered"

This type of reinsurance usually requires a number of layers to be completed. Each layer will have its own reinsurance rate and premium.

First Layer

$3,000,000 each occurrence in respect to the Reinsured- Company's ultimate net property retention
Excess of
$2,000,000 each occurrence in respect to the Reinsured- Company's ultimate net property retention
Reinsurance Rate 2.50% of Gross Net Earned Premium Income
Annual Deposit $750,000 payable in two semi-annual installments
Annual Minimum $600,000

Second Layer

$5,000,000 each occurrence in respect to the Reinsured-Company's ultimate net property retention
Excess of
$5,000,000 each occurrence in respect to the Reinsured- Company's ultimate net property retention
Reinsurance Rate 1.75% of Gross Net Earned Premium Income
Annual Deposit $500,000 payable in two semi-annual installment
Annual Minimum $500,000

Third Layer

$10,000,000 each occurrence in respect to the Reinsured- Company's ultimate net property retention
Excess of
$10,000,000 each occurrence in respect to the Reinsured- Company's ultimate net property retention
Reinsurance Rate 1.50% of Gross Net Earned Premium Income
Annual Deposit $350,000
Annual Minimum $250,000

Fourth Layer

$25,000,000 each occurrence in respect to the Reinsured- Company's ultimate net property retention
Excess of
$20,000,000 each occurrence in respect to the Reinsured- Company's ultimate net property retention
Reinsurance Rate 1.25% of Gross Net Earned Premium Income
Annual Deposit $250,000 payable in two semi-annual
Annual Minimum $250,000

WEATHER EVENTS

Weather events can cause significant property losses and has the potential to create an accumulation of individual losses for an insurer and its reinsurer. These types of events pose a special problem for reinsurers in regard to when they start and when they end. Therefore all property catastrophe excess of loss reinsurance treaties will contain a definition in regard to the duration of the weather event for the purpose of defining the single loss occurrence, referred to as an "hours clause." It defines for reinsurance purposes when the weather event began and when it is considered ended. All individual losses sustained by the reinsured - company within that period of time are considered part of that single occurrence. Other events, such as riot and civil commotion, also have the potential to cause an accumulation of losses and therefore needs a definition of when it began and when it ended.

These are considered fairly standard hour clauses:

Windstorm, Hail, Tornado, Hurricane, Cyclone including Ensuing Collapse and Water Damage.
A loss occurrence shall be a sum of all individual losses sustained by the insurer during 72 consecutive hours. There is a movement in the industry towards (96) consecutive hours.

Riot, Civil Commotion, Vandalism, and Malicious Mischief
A loss occurrence shall be a sum of all individual losses sustained by the insurer during 72 consecutive hours.

Earthquake
A loss occurrence shall be a sum of all individual losses sustained by the insurer during 168 consecutive hours.

Freeze, Occasioned by Collapse, Breakage of Glass and Water Damage (caused by bursting of frozen pipes and tanks)
A loss occurrence shall be a sum of all individual losses sustained by the insurer during 168 consecutive hours.

EXAMPLE OF REINSURED- COMPANY (A) WITH PROPERTY PER RISK EXCESS OF LOSS REINSURANCE AND PROPERTY CATASTROPHE EXCESS OF LOSS REINSURANCE

Property Per Risk Treaties

First Layer $500,000 each risk x $500,000 each risk (retention) (Reinsurers occurrence limit $2,500,000)

Second Layer $4,000,000 each risk x $1,000,000 each risk (Reinsurance occurrence limit $12,000,000)

Third Layer $5,000,000 each risk x $5,000,000 each risk (Reinsurance occurrence limit $10,000,000)

Reinsured- Company maximum property policy for the individual risk $10,000,000. Reinsurance covers $9,500,000 of each policy.

Property Catastrophe Excess of Loss Treaties

First Layer 97.5% of $3,000,000 each occurrence x $2,000,000 each occurrence (Retention)
In respect to the company's retention, maximum any one risk retention $500,000.

Second Layer 97.5% of $10,000,000 each occurrence x $5,000,000 each occurrence
In respect to the company's retention, maximum any one risk retention $500,000.

Third Layer 97.5% of $10,000,000 each occurrence x $15,000,000 each occurrence
In respect to the company's retention maximum any one risk retention $500,000.

The treaty may have a minimum of two (2) risk warranty, meaning at least two (2) or more risks must be involved before the property catastrophe reinsurance will respond.
All property catastrophe treaties contain a maximum amount of loss the reinsurer will pay from any one occurrence.

CATASTROPHE MODELING

After Hurricane Hugo in 1989 and Hurricane Andrew in 1992, it became evident the insurance and reinsurance industry needed to make a better effort to predict their losses from such events. As a result of this need a few companies sprung up to do catastrophe modeling. A Reinsured-Company writing property uses limits and other relevant information categorized by zip code and the computer model predicts the liability loss from certain types of catastrophes. This assists the insurer in buying the correct amount of property catastrophe reinsurance. After Hurricane Katrina devastated New Orleans and the gulf coast in 2005 causing billions in insurance losses, it became evident models had to be further refined.

EXAMPLE OF A PROPERTY EACH RISK REINSURANCE AND PROPERTY CATASTROPHE REINSURANCE

The Reinsured- Company is issuing policies on property risks at different limits; this is just an illustration of some of those limits:

$10,000,000 policy limit each risk	$8,000,000 policy limit each risk	$6,000,000 policy limit each risk	$6,000,000 policy limit each risk	$7,000,000 policy limit each risk	Property each risk reinsurance will pay individual property claims excess of $500,000
$500,000 Retention	$500,000 Retention	$500,000 Retention	$500,000 Retention	$500,000 Retention	Property catastrophe reinsurance protects against an accumulation of losses with its $500,000 retention. It is willing to absorb the first (4) or $2,000,000

SURPLUS SHARE TREATY

This is a form of proportional treaty reinsurance used for property or marine risks. It's used when large limits are needed for individual risks. The Reinsured- Company and reinsurer quota share but do so at different percentages for each risk. The insurance underwriter determines the amount it wants to retain on each risk and reinsures the remaining amount. This type of reinsurance is characterized by the term "line." Reinsurance underwriters will formulate a 10 line surplus line treaty or a 5 line surplus line treaty. For each risk the Reinsured- Company determines its line or amount it will retain and the remaining amount or is reinsured. This is converted into a quota share percentage for each risk.

The treaty will have a minimum amount (line) the reinsured company must retain and a maximum amount or line reinsured.

Policy Limit	Reinsured Company Chooses Its Retention Amount or "Line"	Reinsurer Cession Amount or "Line"	Quota Share Percentages	
			Reinsured Company	Reinsurer
$100,000	$100,000	$0	100.00%	0.0%
$150,000	$100,000	$50,000	66.6%	33.3%
$250,000	$150,000	$100,000	60.0%	40.0%
$500,000	$200,000	$300,000	40.0%	60.0%
$900,000	$100,000	$800,000	11.2%	88.8%

Treaty Terms

Minimum retention $100,000 or 1 line.

Maximum cession to reinsurer $800,000 or 8 lines.

In this example the first column is "policy limit" which may be better than the term "risk" because reinsurers reinsure policies not risks.

The treaty will have a fixed ceding commission and could have a profit commission. A sliding scale ceding commission is never used.

STOP LOSS EXCESS OF LOSS AGGREGATE TREATY REINSURANCE

This treaty reinsurance protects the Reinsured- Company's retention from an accumulation of losses. These losses do not have to be from *one occurrence* but can be from all occurrences, events or accidents during the course of the year, as defined in the Agreement of Reinsurance.

A true stop loss would have the reinsurer paying unlimited claims after a certain attachment point. A true stop loss is basically unavailable because a prudent reinsurer will insist upon a maximum amount it will pay.

Example (1) Reinsured- Company retention is $250,000 each loss

Stop Loss, Excess of Loss Aggregate Treaty

For the Protection of the Reinsured's Aggregate Retention
$10,000,000 in the aggregate (reinsurer's maximum liability) excess of a 120% loss ratio (within the Reinsured Company's retention) for the annual period January 1, 2009 to December 31, 2009.

Explanation The reinsurer will pay up to $10,000,000 in claims when the reinsured company's loss ratio within its own retention exceeds 120%.

Example (2) Reinsured- Company retention $500,000 each loss

Stop Loss, Excess of Loss Aggregate Treaty

For the Protection of the Reinsured's Aggregate Retention
$5,000,000 in the aggregate excess of $5,000,000 in the aggregate. Annual period January 1, 2009 to December 31, 2009.

Explanation When claims within the company's retention exceed $5,000,000, the reinsurer is responsible for the next $5,000,000. These claims do not have to stem from one occurrence or loss event.

SEMI-AUTOMATIC REINSURANCE

(May be referred to as Semi-Automatic Treaty, Semi-Automatic Facultative, Semi-Obligatory)
This is a type of reinsurance combining some aspect of facultative reinsurance with treaty reinsurance. Basically, this is how it works: the specific risk ceded is known and declared to the reinsurer and the reinsurer accepts these risks on an "automatic" basis as long as the agreed upon criteria are met.

SURETY EXCESS OF LOSS TREATY REINSURANCE

Surety is a form of financial guarantee insurance and the Reinsured- Company is referred to as "the surety company." There are many types of bonds issued by the surety company. What they all have in common is they follow the obligation of the principal to the oblige. The date the loss is discovered fixes the "date of loss" regardless of when the events leading up to the loss took place. Excess of loss reinsurance can either be on a per bond basis (can be referred to as each bond) or it is often on a per principal basis (can be referred to as each principal).

PER PRINCIPAL OR EACH PRINCIPAL

In this type of coverage, the reinsurer is providing aggregate reinsurance coverage; the reinsurer is covering *a loss* from a collection of bonds as opposed to one bond.

All bonds involved in the loss are added together for a total loss under the treaty year in which the *loss was discovered*. The *losses discovered* date is used to determine the treaty year in which all the bonds collectively would be added together to determine the gross loss and then the reinsurers' loss.

Example

The principal in surety is the party which needs and obtains the bond for the benefit of the third party. For instance, construction contractor (A) is the lowest bidder to build a new wing of a public library in New Falls, Wisconsin. The town will require contractor (A) to give it a bond guaranteeing the job will be completed. The bond guarantees if contractor (A) is unable to complete the job the surety company will complete it or pay up to the limit of its bond. Most surety companies will issue a number of bonds to a single contractor because contractors have a number of jobs going simultaneously. Let's say contractor (A) has five (5) other jobs each with a bond issued by the same surety company. If contractor (A) becomes suddenly bankrupt the surety company has six (6) bonds in default. Per principal or each principal reinsurance would respond for such a loss.

Treaty Reinsurance:	$5,000,000 each principal x $500,000 each principal
Treaty Year:	1/1/09 – 12/31/09
Contractor (A) goes bankrupt on:	7/16/09 (the date of loss)

Date of Bond	Surety Company Bond Number	Bond Amounts Issued By Surety Company to Contractor (A)	Actual Loss Sustained By Surety Company
10/3/08	612	$750,000	$700,000
11/17/08	614	$600,000	$00
12/1/08	616	$250,000	$50,000
3/16/09	702	$600,000	$500,000
5/2/09	731	$300,000	$200,000
6/13/09	752	$250,000	$200,000
		Total	$1,650,000

The total loss for contractor (A) is $1,650,000; therefore the reinsurance would pay $1,150,000. All bonds for contractor (A), even those issued prior to the effect date of the reinsurance, get pulled together to calculate the reinsurance loss.

CESSION TREATY (CAN BE EXCESS OF LOSS OR QUOTA SHARE)

Used primarily for new books of business which are anticipated to develop slowly. The reinsurer using this method of reinsurance is trying to balance the relatively small premiums it will receive with the significant reinsurance limits it will provide. This method is often used for automatic facultative reinsurance.

The reinsurer is paid each time a policy issued exposes the reinsurance layer. A reinsurance actuary will promulgate the reinsurance cession factors applied to each policy limit. The reinsurer is exposed, arriving at a reinsurance premium cession. This type of reinsurance will not have a deposit premium or minimum premium.

Example
Cession Excess of Loss Treaty
$10,000,000 x $1,000,000
Effective January 1, 2009

Cession Factor Schedule

Original Policy Limit	Reinsurance Cession Factor
$1,000,000	None
$2,000,000	28.0%
$3,000,000	39.0%
$4,000,000	47.0%
$5,000,000	54.0%
$6,000,000	59.0%
$7,000,000	64.0%
$8,000,000	68.0%
$9,000,000	71.0%
$10,000,000	75.0%

Cession Excess of Loss Treaty
$10,000,000 x $1,000,000
Effective January 1, 2009

Original Policy Limits	Original Gross Premium	Reinsurance Cession Factor	Reinsurer Cession Premium
$2,000,000	$96,101	28.0%	$26,908
$3,000,000	$123,705	39.0%	$48,245
$4,000,000	$142,307	47.0%	$66,884
$5,000,000	$151,200	54.0%	$81,648
$6,000,000	$160,890	59.0%	$94,925
$7,000,000	$172,835	64.0%	$110,614
$8,000,000	$180,911	68.0%	$123,019
$9,000,000	$191,276	71.0%	$135,806
$10,000,000	$202,411	75.0%	$151,808

Notes:
(1) A cession treaty will have no minimum or deposit.
(2) This example does not have a ceding commission but another cession treaty may have a ceding commission.

Example

Cession 90/10 Quota Share Treaty
Maximum Policy Limit Ceded $2,000,000
Effective January 1, 2009

Cession Factor Schedule

Original Policy Limit	Reinsurance Cession Factor
$500,000	16.0%
$750,000	24.0%
$1,000,000	32.0%
$1,250,000	40.0%
$1,500,000	48.0%
$2,000,000	64.0%

Cession 90/10 Quota Share Treaty
Maximum Policy Limit Ceded $2,000,000
Effective January 1, 2009

Original Policy Limit	Original Gross Premium	Reinsurance Cession Factor	Gross Reinsurer Cession Premium	90% Ceded to Reinsurer	Less 30% Ceding Commission	Net Reinsurance Premium
$500,000	$75,211	16.0%	$12,034	$10,831	$3,249	$7,582
$750,000	$100,281	24.0%	$24,067	$21,660	$6,498	$15,162
$1,000,000	$125,351	32.0%	$40,112	$36,101	$10,830	$25,271
$1,250,000	$150,421	40.0%	$60,168	$54,151	$16,245	$37,906
$1,500,000	$172,984	48.0%	$83,032	$74,729	$22,419	$52,310
$2,000,000	$207,581	64.0%	$132,852	$119,567	$35,870	$83,697

LAYERING IN EXCESS OF LOSS REINSURANCE

A Reinsured- Company may want to buy significant amounts of excess of loss reinsurance, which means layering will be necessary. For various reasons, reinsurers may only want to participate at *different levels (layers)* on the reinsurance program. The different levels (layers) will also have different reinsurance rates.

Layering is always used in Excess of Loss reinsurance.

Example:
Mason Insurance Company issues a $5,000,000 policy
Mason's Retention is $200,000 per policy

Reinsurance Layered:		Reinsurance Rate of Subject Premium
First Layer Excess of Loss:	$300,000 x $200,000	15%
Second Layer Excess of Loss:	$500,000 x $500,000	10%
Third Layer Excess of Loss:	$1,000,000 x $1,000,000	5%
Fourth Layer Excess of Loss:	$3,000,000 x $2,000,000	2%

REINSURANCE PLACEMENT

For extensive reinsurance programs, a number of reinsurers may be needed in order to complete it. The reinsurers participating will each have a share.

Example Split among a Number of Reinsurers Participating

Applies to an excess of loss treaty or proportional treaty. In this example, six reinsurers are needed to complete the placement.

(1)	Reinsurer A	35%
(2)	Reinsurer B	25%
(3)	Reinsurer C	15%
(4)	Reinsurer D	10%
(5)	Reinsurer E	10%
(6)	Reinsurer F	5%
		100%

Example Excess of Loss Treaty Reinsurance/$600,000 x $400,000

In this example, three reinsurers are needed to complete the Excess of Loss Treaty Reinsurance, $600,000 x $400,000.

(1)	Reinsurer A	50%
(2)	Reinsurer B	30%
(3)	Reinsurer C	20%
		100%

Example 90/10 Quota Share

In this example, four reinsurers are needed to complete the 90/10 Quota Share Treaty.

		Each reinsurers share of the 90%
(1)	Reinsurer A	40%
(2)	Reinsurer B	40%
(3)	Reinsurer C	10%
(4)	Reinsurer D	10%
		100% (this is 100% of the 90%)

SPECIAL TREATY TERMS

INNER AGGREGATE DEDUCTIBLE

An inner aggregate deductible is sometimes placed in an excess of loss treaty to protect the reinsurer from claims it otherwise would be responsible for within the treaty. It should also assist in keeping reinsurance costs down. The amount of the deductible is determined in advance by the parties.

Example
Excess of Loss Treaty
$1,500,000 x $500,000
Inner aggregate deductible $1,500,000

Gross Loss	Reinsured Retention	Inner Aggregate Deductible	Loss Going Into Excess of Loss $1,500,000 x $500,000
$1,000,000	$500,000	<$500,000>	$0
$1,000,000	$500,000	<$500,000>	$0
$1,000,000	$500,000	<$500,000>	$0
$1,000,000	$500,000	$0	$500,000
$1,000,000	$500,000	$0	$500,000

The inner aggregate deductible in this example stopped (3) $500,000 losses from going into the excess of loss treaty $1,500,000 x $500,000.

CO-PARTICIPATION IN AN EXCESS OF LOSS TREATY

The Reinsured- Company takes a participation on the business ceded to the reinsurer. This is an additional retention. Reinsurers may insist on a co-participation to help guard against the reinsured adversely selecting against them. The amount of the co-participation may only be 2.5% to 5.0% but reinsurers feel if losing business is going to be ceded to them the reinsured will be forced to share in the poor results.

DISCOVERY PERIOD

The reinsurer may limit the time in which a claim can be introduced into the reinsurance layer; any claim after that is not covered.

Example:

Reinsurance Treaty:	$750,000 each occurrence x $250,000 each occurrence
Treaty Term:	12 Months - 1/1/08 to 12/31/08
Discovery Period:	36 months after expiration or 12/31/11

The Reinsured- Company has from 1/1/08 to 12/31/11 to introduce claims to the reinsurer for covered events in the period 1/1/08 to 12/31/08.

MAXIMUM ANY ONE LIFE (MAOL)

This is a "restriction" found in some Workers Compensation treaties. The reinsurer is limiting the amount of reinsurance coverage for any one life (worker). For instance, if the reinsurance treaty is $5 million per occurrence excess of $5 million per occurrence with a MAOL $5 million, this is what that means:
If one worker is involved in a single occurrence accident, with their total Workers

Compensation benefits (indemnity and medical) amount to $7 million, this treaty will not respond because the most it pays for any one life (worker) is $5 million. Therefore, by way of this example, you see this treaty is designed to respond only when "two (2) or more" workers are involved in the same occurrence accident. When purchasing such a treaty, it is important to know the limitations. If purchased, the reinsurance premiums should be significantly less than if purchased without this restriction.

SUNSET
A reinsurer may want to limit the number of years the Reinsured-Company can introduce a reinsurance claim into the treaty. This could be done via a "sunset."

Example: The reinsurance contract might say "the coverage provided in this agreement of reinsurance shall only apply to those losses where the Reinsurer has been provided with written notification of the loss by the Reinsured-Company within seven (7) years from the final day of this agreement."

RETROCESSIONAL REINSURANCE

This is when one reinsurer reinsures with another reinsurer (referred to as the retrocessional reinsurer or the retrocessionnaire). Each box shows the different names that can be used for the insured, insurer, reinsurer and retrocessional reinsurer.

INSURED
- Policyholder

INSURER (A)
- Reinsured- Company
- Insurance Company
- Company Reinsured
- Ceding Company
- Ceding Insurer
- Cedant
- Reinsured
- Reassured

The insurer (A) *cedes* reinsurance premiums to reinsurer (B), hence the term ceding insurer or ceding company. Reinsurer (B) is providing reinsurance to insurer (A).

REINSURER (B)
- Original Reinsurer
- Retrocedent

The reinsurer (B) is retroceding premium to retrocessional reinsurer (C).

RETROCESSIONAL REINSURER (C)
- Retrocessionnaire

Retrocessional reinsurer (C) is reinsuring reinsurer (B).

CONCEPT OF RETENTION

There is no exact formula to determine how much a Reinsured- Company should retain for its own account, referred to as its retention or net retention. It must make its own determination depending upon the size of their surplus, assets, current reserve adequacy, lines of insurance written, premium income, prior profitability, classes of insured, prior claims experience, expenses, the average policy limit, maximum policy limit, prior retentions, investment income philosophy, competition, availability, type and cost of reinsurance, insurance department regulations regarding maximum policy limit to surplus ratio and management's attitude and strategy toward retaining risk and protecting the surplus of the company.

Some Things to Consider

- A retention level must be chosen allowing sufficient premium to pay claims within that retention.
- The retention level will affect the amount of cash available for investment, a higher retention leaves more cash available for investment; a lower retention reduces the cash available.
- The retention level impacts the claims experience by cutting off the claim amount at the retention level thereby reducing fluctuations in financial results.
- The reinsurance must cover the maximum policy limit, if not the insurer will have a hidden retention only revealed after a loss exceeds the reinsurance.
- What will A.M. Best, the certified public accounting firm and the Reinsured- Company's actuaries say about a higher retention?

TYPES OF RETENTION

A Reinsured- Company's retention can be each risk, each policy, each occurrence, each claim or other structure.

When the Reinsured- Company has its retention structured in these ways it is retaining in some manner the first portion of each loss and above it has excess of loss reinsurance.

A Reinsured- Company's retention can be proportional (quota share) or Excess of Loss

Quota Share reinsurance goes up vertically. For instance, if it retained 20%, then it would retain $100,000 if the loss was $500,000 and it would retain $400,000 if the loss was $2,000,000.

Catastrophe or A Single Event Retention.

If a catastrophe occurs in an area in which a company has been issuing many policies there will most likely be numerous individual losses. The company is retaining a portion of those losses, therefore, it will have an accumulation of individual losses. Before such catastrophe occurs, the company must estimate its total loss from all its individual losses from a single catastrophe occurrence and then determine its retention and purchase reinsurance for the remainder of the exposure.

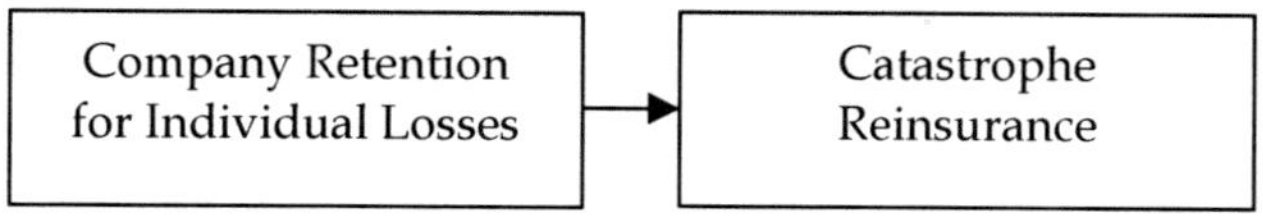

Retaining a Portion of Excess of Reinsurance.

A company can retain a percentage of its own excess of loss reinsurance layer. For instance, a company issues policies with a maximum limit of 10,000,000 and has a third reinsurance layer 5,000,000 x 5,000,000. It could chose to retain 15% of this layer i.e. place only 85% of it in the reinsurance market. One reason this would be done is to reduce the reinsurance cost for the third layer.

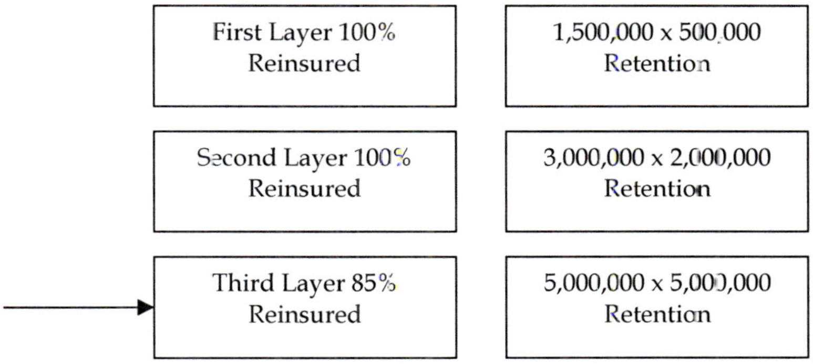

REINSURED- COMPANY'S RETENTION

One of the key ingredients for completing a reinsurance program with high quality reinsurers is a meaningful retention on the part of the Reinsured- Company, which will be viewed favorably by the potential reinsurer.

Reinsured-Company Retention	Maximum Policy Limit	Amount Reinsured	Reinsured Percentage	Reinsured Company Retention Percentage
50,000	10,000,000	9,950,000	99.5%	0.5%
100,000	10,000,000	9,900,000	99.0%	1.0%
250,000	10,000,000	9,750,000	97.5%	2.5%
500,000	10,000,000	9,500,000	95.0%	5.0%
1,000,000	10,000,000	9,000,000	90.0%	10.0%

It would be very difficult to complete a reinsurance program, whether excess of loss or quota share if the reinsured-company retains only 50,000 or 100,000 and cedes to reinsurers 99.5% or 99.0% of its maximum policy limit. If it could be completed, the reinsurance cost might be prohibitively high because the reinsurer is taking most of the risk.

EXCEPTION TO A MEANINGFUL RETENTION BY REINSURED-COMPANY

There are some instances when the reinsurer will approach the Reinsured- Company asking them to write a certain line of insurance, ceding almost all of the business to them. Such an arrangement would be done using a 99/1 quota share reinsurance treaty. In that case the Reinsured- Company has no meaningful retention in the business being written.

TERMINOLOGY

OFTEN USED	***EQUIVALENT***
Per Occurrence	Each Occurrence
Per Policy	Each Policy
Per Risk	Each Risk
Per Bond	Each Bond
Per Principal	Each Principal
Per Claim	Each Claim
Per Claim Per Policy	Each Claim, Each Policy
Insurer	Reinsured- Company, Reassured, Ceding -insurer, ceding company, Cedant. Insurance Company.

Section 3

WHAT TO LOOK FOR WHEN BUYING REINSURANCE

From a Buyer's Perspective

OVERALL GOALS

What are you trying to accomplish?

- Have you determined the proper retention for each line of insurance and buying reinsurance over that retention? What is your management's attitude toward risk taking?

- Buying reinsurance to increase maximum policy limit (capacity), does your reinsurance cover the maximum policy limit issued?

- Buying reinsurance to protect your net retention (sideways cover) from a catastrophe loss.

- Are you trying to satisfy insurance regulations which only permit the issuance of policies with a maximum limit equal to 10% of the insurer's surplus?

- Entering a new line of insurance, therefore a little uncertain of the results so reinsurance can reduce your exposure.

- Reducing your expense ratio with a quota share treaty with a significant overriding commission.

- You should always buy enough reinsurance to protect your company against a catastrophic loss. This is a must; a catastrophic loss not adequately covered can severely impair an insurer's surplus. You need to determine if your company is subject to an accumulation of claims from a single event which will cause a catastrophe loss. Catastrophe modeling must be done.

- Do you need to do a retention study? Does your retention need to be adjusted upward or downward because of inflation, economic outlook, or business mix? If the loss took place in 2006, how much more would it be in 2009? What is your business mix, projected business and economic conditions affecting your business?

- Are you buying reinsurance for a captive or a smaller company, with limited surplus, which usually means reinsurance is vital to its success?

- Do you need reinsurance to keep your surplus to net written premium ratio at 3 to 1 or better?

- Insurers with significant property writing will want to do a catastrophe model to estimate their losses in a catastrophe so they can buy the appropriate amount of property catastrophe reinsurance.

DETERMINE THE TYPE OF REINSURANCE TO FIT YOUR NEEDS

Excess of Loss or Quota Share

i.e.:

- Casualty Quota Share
- Casualty Excess of Loss
- Casualty Clash Cover
- Property Quota Share
- Property Per Risk Excess of Loss
- Property Catastrophe Excess of Loss
- Semi Automatic Treaty
- Stop Loss (if available)
- Facultative
- Other

BASIC ELEMENTS OF A REINSURANCE PROGRAM

- Security of Reinsurers:
    - Policyholder surplus
    - A.M. Best rating and size
    - Standard & Poor's rating
    - How many years they have been in business?
    - A reinsurer must be licensed, admitted, approved or accredited in the state the reinsured-company is domiciled. If not, they will need to meet the state's guidelines for non-admitted reinsurer. Such as supplying a letter of credit, a trust account or other mechanism to protect the Reinsured- Company.

- Do you want to establish criteria such as the reinsurer must have $250 million or more in surplus? Most reinsurers now have surplus exceeding $500 million.

- Are they part of a larger organization?

- What is their reputation for paying claims promptly?

- Are they willing to work with your organization?

- Price: What is the reinsurance costing you as a percentage of your gross original premium? How the reinsurer is paid, on a written premium basis or earned premium basis?

- Coverage: What is the reinsurance covering? How much coverage is there? Are there reinstatements, loss ratio caps or other limits on the amount of reinsurance coverage?

- Reinstatement of Reinsurer's Limit: If you have reinstatements, are they on a *paid* or *incurred* basis? Paid is more favorable to the buyer. If you have reinstatements requiring an additional premium (AP), how and when are they triggered? If there is calculation of an (AP), is it pro-rata for amount and time, which is to the benefit of the buyer, or is it 100% for time?

- Exclusions: What is your reinsurer excluding?

- Profit Commissions: Can you get some of your premiums returned without commuting the reinsurance?

- Basis of Reinsurance: How is your business reinsured? Each policy, each ultimate loss, each risk, each location, each occurrence, each claim, any one loss, each event, etc. The basis of reinsurance coverage needs to match the type of loss expected.

- Attachment of Reinsurer's Liability: How does the reinsurer attach itself to the business?
    - Losses occurring
    - Policies attaching, often referred to as risk attaching
    - Is it in force policies, renewal policies, new policies or all of these
    - Losses discovered, is it enforce, renewal and new?

- Defense Costs: How are allocated loss adjustment expenses (ALAE) handled within the treaty? Does it match the insurance policies your company is issuing? In reinsurance, ALAE can be handled as:
    - Part of the loss
    - Proportional, in addition to the loss

- Extra Contractual Obligations (ECO): How does reinsurance handle this within the reinsurer's limits or in addition to the reinsurers limit?

- Excess of Original Policy Limit (XPL Loss): How does reinsurance handle this?

- Declaratory Judgment Expenses: How does reinsurance handle this?

- Class Action Suits: How does reinsurance handle this? Do you need a clash cover and will the clash cover include or exclude class action suits.

FROM WHOM DO YOU BUY REINSURANCE – REINSURANCE INTERMEDIARIES OR DIRECT WRITING REINSURERS....No Pat Answers

Reinsurance Intermediary

- Places business with many reinsurers, receiving a commission which is deducted from the reinsurance premiums remitted to the reinsurer. In effect, the reinsurer pays the broker commission. This does not mean dealing with a direct reinsurer automatically means less expensive reinsurance because much of the work that would have been done by a reinsurance broker would have to be done by a direct reinsurer therefore could increase their cost. Each reinsurance agreement must be evaluated on its own.
- Advantage of another pair of eyes working with you, kind of like a Dutch uncle giving advice and championing your company.
- Should represent your best interest.
- Prepares a submission to be presented to the reinsurers.
- Prepares the reinsurance contract.
- All correspondence, accounting reports, and payments, go through the reinsurance broker.
- If called upon to pay a loss will collect from the reinsurers and remit to the Reinsured-Company.

Direct Reinsurer

- Security is excellent; there are relatively few direct reinsurers but they have large amounts of capital and surplus.
- You can talk directly to the reinsurer.
- They often want to do 100%. This could be an advantage or disadvantage depending on your viewpoint.
- They will use their own reinsurance contract.
- All correspondence, accounting reports, and payments are sent directly to the reinsurer.
- If called upon to pay a loss, will remit funds directly to Reinsured- Company.

HAVE YOU THOUGHT OF:

- Combining layers, sometimes you can spread a profit commission in the lower layer to the layer above which does not have it by combining the layers into one. Combining layers could create competition among reinsurers to stay on a reduced reinsurance program.
- Combining related lines of insurance into one reinsurance treaty.
- If you have a quota share which is continuously showing profits you might consider changing a fixed ceding commission to a sliding scale commission.
- Add profit commission to treaties where possible.
- Change no claim bonuses to a traditional profit commission.
- Change the reimbursement for extra contractual losses or losses in excess of the policy limits. If it is 80%, try to change it to 90%. If it is 90%, try to change it to 100%.

A FEW FINAL THOUGHTS TO THINK ABOUT:

- Buy as little reinsurance as you can to save your company money.
- Buy as much as you can when it's cheap and the terms are very favorable.
- Buy enough to protect your company from a catastrophic loss.
- Buy what you need to sleep at night.
- Make sure your company complies with state insurance regulations; think about your reinsurance in regard to your actuaries, outside auditors, S&P, A.M. Best.

HOW THE REINSURED- COMPANY CAN BEST COLLECT FUNDS FROM ITS REINSURER(S)

No one knows how good your reinsurance is until you need to collect losses. You also may need to collect a profit commission, no claims bonus, or premium adjustment. The Reinsured-Company along with the reinsurance intermediary should set the criteria to be a reinsurer on the reinsurance program. This should include the reinsurer's A.M. Best rating, S&P rating, surplus or net worth, years in business and their reputation for making timely payments. It is also important the reinsurance contract be thorough and correct and signed properly. Also important is the timely and accurate reporting of potential reinsurance claims and those in the beginning will be most likely in a loss reserve status. When the reinsurance treaty is up for renewal, the information reported to the reinsurer should also be reviewed for accuracy and should contain all the information the reinsurer would need to make an informed decision about renewal. In this way, should a dispute take place, the Reinsured-Company can make a case for it providing complete and accurate information throughout its relationship with the reinsurer.

Section 4

SUBMISSION TO REINSURER

The Reinsured- Company or its reinsurance intermediary will prepare a submission for the reinsurer to assist in their decision to underwrite and rate the business to be reinsured. We present a fairly comprehensive list; it is up to the reinsurance professional to pick and choose the ones needed for a specific submission.

BASIC FOR ALL REINSURANCE SUBMISSIONS

Corporate Information

Background of Reinsured-Company, such as years in business, A.M. Best and S&P ratings (if available), ownership, management, any re-organizations or recent events, how it acquires the business, direct writer, has its own agents, uses independent agents.

- Annual statement filed with states (yellow)
- Annual statement to shareholders
- 10K
- Proxy statement
- Corporate brochures
- Business plan

Financial Information

- Annual report to state insurance department (yellow cover)
- Certified Public Accountant's statement
- Investment advisor and philosophy

Actuarial Information

- Certification of claim reserves and loss study report
- Rates and rate study report

Marketing Information

- How will business be marketed and brought in? Directly to insureds, exclusive company agent force, independent agency force, managing general agents (MGA's), the Internet?
- Marketing brochures

Underwriting Information

- Anticipated premium volume (estimated subject premium)
- Type of business to be written
- Underwriting philosophy
- Underwriting guidelines
- Rating guideline
- Background of underwriters
- Policy form, endorsements and riders
- Application for each line of insurance
- Acquisition costs and expenses; breakout of those costs
- Do insureds have deductibles or SIR's
- Competition
- Territory

- Premium credit or dividend plans
- Rate of renewals

Claims Information
- All claims aggregated together
- All claims over a specific incurred amount (i.e. over 25,000, 50,000, 100,000)
- Open and closed claims
- Description of claims
- Triangles (losses paid, losses incurred, with and without ALAE, IBNR)
- Does the company handle its own claims or is there a third party administrator?
- Background of claims manager and staff
- Claims manual including company's policy on outside attorneys
- Number of claims handled per staff member
- Claims supervised by the ceding insurer? Are outside attorneys, adjusters and investigators employed on specific claims?
- Loss control and safety programs

Profile Information
- Policy limit profiles
- Risk profiles

Ratios
- Loss ratio of business reinsured
- Combined ratio of business reinsured
- Reinsurer loss ratio (if reinsurer has previously been on the reinsurance)
- Reinsurer combined (if reinsurer has previously been on the reinsurance)

Charts & Graphs
Some Suggestions:
- Growth of Premium
- Growth of Surplus
- Territories (states where business is to be written)
- Claim Activity

Expenses
- See Section "Deductions from Premiums"

Reinsurance Information
- Structure of reinsurance – excess of loss, quote share, clash cover, aggregate excess of loss, property catastrophe or other
- Experience of reinsurers on business reinsured (reinsurance premiums/losses incurred/open closed claims
- Estimated reinsurer's investment income, if they have already been on the reinsurance
- Placement slip or reinsurance contract (indicates type of reinsurance needed)
- Lines of insurance to be reinsured (i.e. commercial general liability, directors & officers, automobile liability, medical malpractice liability, property, etc.)
- Classes of business to be reinsured (i.e. banks, hardware stores, gas stations, various)
- Reinsured-company's attitude in regards to audits and visits by reinsurers, are they welcomed, does the reinsured-company consider them valuable.

Section 5

ATTACHMENT OF REINSURERS' LIABILITY

Policies Attaching (Risk Attaching)
Losses Occurring
Losses Discovered

It must be clear when a reinsurers liability starts and when it ends. There are three basic methods by which the reinsurer attaches itself to the Reinsured- Company.

POLICIES ATTACHING

Often this is called risk attaching, but a better term is *policies attaching* because it's the policies of the Reinsured- Company that are reinsured. The reinsurer attaches to each policy, paying losses emanating from those policies.

Example

Reinsurance treaty is effective 1/1/09 to 12/31/09; the reinsurer's liability attaches to policies issued between these dates. For instance, the reinsurer signs on to the treaty on a policies attaching basis (1/1/09 to 12/31/09). The reinsured company is issuing twelve-month policies. A policy is issued with the term 11/13/08 to 11/12/09 and a claim takes place under this policy. If this claim involves the reinsurance layer, the reinsurer is responsible for it, even though it may have a date of loss in 2009, because it is following the policy.

The Reinsured- Company is always issuing policies, so it must be defined as to which policies the reinsurer is attaching. Policies are either *inforce, renewal or new*.

Inforce: Those policies previously issued and in place (inforce) on the date the reinsurance is effective. In the example above, that would be policies already issued and in place at 1/1/09.

Renewal: Those policies coming up for renewal during the time the reinsurer is on. In our example that would be any policy renewing between 1/1/09 and 12/31/09.

New: New policies issued during the period the reinsurer is on. In our example that would be 1/1/09 to 12/31/09.

LOSSES OCCURRING

The reinsurer's liability is contained within the effective date of the treaty and the expiration date of the treaty. The loss must take place between these dates in order to trigger the reinsurance coverage. However, the loss does not have to be reported during this period; it only has to occur. The reinsurer is only responsible for losses taking place between the effective date of the treaty and the expiration date of the treaty.

Example

The treaty is 1/1/09 to 12/31/09; any loss taking place with a date of loss between these dates the reinsurer is responsible. The reinsurer is not following the policy but the calendar dates (1/1/09 to 12/31/09).

LOSSES DISCOVERED

This is essentially the same as losses occurring. The reinsurance follows the treaty's effective and expiration date. If the treaty is 7/1/09 to 6/30/10, any loss discovered between these dates is covered by the reinsurer.

SPECIFIC METHODS THE REINSURER REIMBURSES THE REINSURED-COMPANY FOR CLAIMS

Most Often Used

	Property	Liability	Workers Compensation	Surety	Marine
Each Location	X				
Each Insured Property	X				
Each Sum Insured	X				
Each Risk	X	X			
Each Occurrence	X	X	X		X
Each Event		X	X		X
Each Accident		X	X		
Each Incident		X			
Each Medical Incident		X			
Each Physician		X			
Each Policy		X			
Each Person		X	X		
Each Bond				X	
Each Principal				X	
Each Contractor				X	
Each Claim		X			
Each Insured		X	X		
Each Entity		X			

Note: Some treaties may say "per" instead of "each".

Section 6

REINSTATEMENT OF A REINSURER'S LIMIT

Excess of loss treaties most likely will have provisions to reinstate the reinsurers original limit. Up until 1986 most excess of loss treaties provided unlimited coverage, now most do not. Almost all excess of loss casualty and professional liability treaties have a limited number of times the reinsurer's original limit can be reinstated, which is to the benefit of the reinsurer because it places a limitation on their ultimate liability.

Reinstatement of the reinsurer's limit can be at no additional premium or additional premium or a combination. We present four (4) ways a treaty can be structured.

(1) Unlimited reinstatement of reinsurer's original limit at no additional reinstatement premium.

(2) Limited reinstatement of reinsurer's original limit at no additional reinstatement premium.

(3) Limited reinstatement of reinsurer's original limit at additional reinstatement premium, this provides the reinsurer with additional income to assist in off setting of poor experience.

(4) Limited reinstatement of reinsurer's original limit at a combination of no additional premium and additional reinstatement premium (i.e., first two (2) reinstatements of the original limit at no additional premium, third reinstatement of reinsurer's original limit at 100% additional premium pro rata for amount of limit reinstated, no consideration for the time reinstated.)

EXAMPLE OF THE REINSTATEMENT OF A REINSURER'S ORIGINAL LIMIT

A 500,000 x 500,000 treaty has four reinstatements, meaning the original limit can be reinstated *an additional* four times, (plus the original limit for a total of five.) The reinsurer will pay claims up to the original limit of 500,000 and four others, so the reinsurer can pay a total of five 500,000 claims totaling 2,500,000. The reinsurer pays the original limit plus the four reinstated limits. So, count the original limit as one and add the four reinstatements to it to get the total of five.

We omitted any reference to allocated loss adjustment expenses in this example. See the Defense Costs section in this book for further information on that topic.

TWO METHODS TO TRIGGER A REINSTATEMENT OF PREMIUM

Paid Claim Basis:	The reinstatement premium is paid to the reinsurer when a claim is actually paid by the reinsurer.
Incurred Claim Basis:	The reinstatement premium is paid to the reinsurer when the claim is reserved in the reinsurer's layer.

It's an advantage to the ceding insurer to pay the reinsurer reinstatement premiums on a Paid Claim Basis.

TWO METHODS TO CALCULATE THE REINSTATEMENT PREMIUM *(ADDITIONAL PREMIUM REFERRED TO AS AN A.P.)*

1. Pro rata for *amount of limits* reinstated, and no consideration for time.

   Most treaties are pro rata for *amount of limits* and 100% for *time*, which means *time* is not considered in the calculation.

2. Pro rata for amount of limits reinstated and pro rata for the *amount of time* remaining to reinstate the limit. Pro rating for *time* is rarely used because the loss or a series of losses often take place after the treaty's expiration or anniversary date. We are not recommending pro rata for *time* but if it was considered the only date that can be used in the calculation is the date of loss, not the date the claim was paid.

Treaty Term:	1/1/09 to 12/31/09
Date of Loss:	7/3/09
Date Claim Was Paid:	12/3/08 (not considered for purposes of calculating time)

   If time was pro rata it would be calculated from 7/3/09 to 12/31/09.

Example

REINSTATEMENT OF REINSURER'S ORIGINAL LIMIT AND REINSURER'S REINSTATEMENT PREMIUM

Excess of Loss Treaty	750,000 x 250,000
Final Subject Premium	10,126,911
Reinsurance Rate	8.75%
Annual Deposit Premium	$800,000 paid quarterly in advance
Ultimate Reinsurance Premium	$866,104
Treaty Term	1/1/09 to 12/31/09
Reinstatement Terms	2 free, 2 @ 50% additional premium each
Reinstatement Information	(A) Paid claim basis (B) Pro rata for amount (C) 100% for time (no consideration given for time)

Gross Loss Paid	Date of Loss	Reinsurer Share of Loss	Reinsurer's Limit	Reinsurer Remaining Limit After Loss	Amount of Limits to Be Reinstated	Reinstatement Premium
(1) 1,000,000	2/10/09	750,000	750,000	0	750,000	First reinstatement free

First loss eliminates the reinsurer original limit and is automatically reinstated at no additional premium

(2) 1,000,000	3/9/09	750,000	750,000	0	750,000	Second reinstatement free

Second loss eliminates the reinsurer reinstated limit and is automatically reinstated at no additional premium

(3) 1,000,000	6/14/09	750,000	750,000	0	750,000	Third reinstatement at 50% additional premium or $443,052.35

Third loss eliminates the reinsurer limit and is automatically reinstated at 50% additional premium, which is pro rated amount reinstated

(4) 650,000	7/3/09	400,000	400,000	350,000	400,000	Fourth reinstatement at 50% premium or $236,279.82

Four losses eliminate $350,000 of reinsurer's and 400,000 of limit need to be reinstated at 50% additional premium pro rated amount reinstated

Example

CALCULATION OF THE REINSTATED PREMIUM

The first and second reinstatements are at no additional premium

Third reinstatement at 50% additional premium

Step 1:	Calculate the Ultimate Reinsurance Premium	
	Final Subject Premium	10,126.91
	Reinsurance Rate	8.75%
	Ultimate Reinsurance Premium	886,104.71

Step 2: Convert the amount of limit reinstated into a percentage

750,000	. 750,000	=	100% of the reinsurers
Amounts of limits to be reinstated	. Reinsurers Limits		limit, needs to be reinstated

Step 3:	Ultimate Reinsurance Premium	886,104.71
	At 50% Additional Premium	443,052.35
	Pro rata for amount which in this case is 100%	= 443,052.35
Step 4:	The reinstatement premium is	443,052.35

Fourth Reinstatement Premium at 50% Additional Premium

Step 1:	Ultimate Reinsurance Premium	886,104.71

Step 2: Calculate The Amount Of Limit Reinstated Into A Percentage

400,000 . 750,000 = 53.33%

Step 3:	Ultimate Reinsurance Premium	886,104.71
	At 50% Additional Premium	443,052.35
	Pro rata for amount 53.33%	= 236,279.81
Step 4:	The reinstatement premium is	236,279.81

Example

REINSTATEMENT OF REINSURERS ORIGINAL LIMIT SCHEDULE

Box #1	Reinsurer's Original Limit 1,000,000
Box #2	Reinsurer's Limit 1,000,000 Can Be Reinstated First Reinstatement Free
Box #3	Reinsurer's Limit 1,000,000 Can Be Reinstated Second Reinstatement Free
Box #4	Reinsurer's Limit 1,000,000 Can Be Reinstated Third Reinstatement 50% Additional Premium Which is Pro Rated For The Amount of Limit Reinstated
Box #5	Reinsurer's Limit 1,000,000 Can Be Reinstated Fourth Reinstatement 50% Additional Premium Which is Pro Rated For The Amount of Limit Reinstated

Example

REINSTATEMENT OF LIMITS SCHEDULE

Original Limits	1,000,000 original limit	*Box #1*
Wilson claim reduces original limits from 1,000,000 to 813,514. At this point we are still in the original limit	1,000,000 Wilson claim – <u>186,470</u> Original limits remaining 831,530	*Box #1*
Stamford claim reduces 813,514 original limit adjusted to 0 and moves us into the one free reinstatement	Original limits remaining 813,530 Stamford claim – <u>1,000,000</u> original limits 0	*Box #1*
We currently have eaten into the one free reinstatement limit up to 186,470, but we still have remaining 813,530 of the free reinstatement.	free limit 1,000,000 - <u>186,470</u> remaining limits from the one free 813,530	*Box #2*

Example

If a reinstatement premium is triggered during the reinsurance term the deposit premium is used for the basis of calculation and when the ultimate reinsurance premiums are determined it is adjusted.

Excess of Loss Treaty	500,000 x 500,000
Reinsurance Rate	9.0%
Treaty Term	1/1/09 to 12/31/09
Reinsurance Terms	1 @ 100% additional premium
Reinsurance Information	(a) Paid claim basis (b) Pro rata for amount only, 100% for time

Section 7

HOW DEFENSE COSTS ARE HANDLED IN REINSURANCE

Types of Defense Costs

- Unallocated Loss Adjustment Expenses (ULAE)
- Allocated Loss Adjustment Expenses (ALAE)

UNALLOCATED LOSS ADJUSTMENT EXPENSES (ULAE)
These are the expenses not attributable to any specific claim. They are the in-house expenses of the insurer to carry on their day-to-day claim activities, such as salaries for employees and general office expenses. You might call these inside expenses. These expenses are almost always not covered by reinsurance treaties.

ALLOCATED LOSS ADJUSTMENT EXPENSE (ALAE)
These are the expenses directly linked to a specific claim, such as the fees for an outside attorney hired by the Reinsured- Company for a specific claim. You might call these outside expenses. They are almost always covered by reinsurance in some manner. Casualty business such as general liability, medical malpractice, errors and omissions liability, and directors and officer's liability will have much greater allocated loss adjustment expenses than the property lines of insurance.

HOW ALLOCATED LOSS ADJUSTMENT EXPENSES ARE HANDLED IN PROPORTIONAL REINSURANCE TREATIES (QUOTA SHARE)
Allocated Loss Adjustment Expenses (ALAE) are *added to the loss* to arrive at *one total loss* and then the Quota Share reinsurers share in the paying of that one total loss.

Example	*90/10 Quota Share:*		
		Loss:	500,000
		ALAE:	150,000
		Total:	650,000
Reinsurers' Share 90%:			585,000

HOW ALLOCATED LOSS ADJUSTMENT EXPESNSES (ALAE) ARE HANDLED IN EXCESS OF LOSS TREATIES
ALAE can be handled by two (2) basic methods:

Method (1) Part of the Loss: The ALAE is added to the loss to arrive at one total loss and therefore falls within the various excess of loss reinsurance layers. The reinsurer pays the loss plus ALAE.

See example (1)

Method (2) Proportional to the Loss and in Addition to the Reinsurer's Limit (Often referred to as Pro Rata in Addition to the Limit):

The reinsurer pays ALAE in the same proportion it pays the loss. If it pays 25% of the loss, it pays 25% of the ALAE. If the reinsurer's treaty limits are exhausted by the loss, the reinsurer pays ALAE *above* those exhausted limits.
In other words, the reinsurer can pay out its entire reinsurance limit by paying the loss and more if the ALAE takes it over the reinsurance limit. In other words, on the Excess of Loss treaty, 300,000 x 200,000, the reinsurer can pay 300,000 for the loss and its share of the ALAE.
See example (2)

Example (1):

ALAE: Part of Loss

Excess of Loss Reinsurance Treaties

		Reinsured-Company Retention	500,000 x 500,000	1,000,000 x 1,000,000	3,000,000 x 2,000,000
Loss	300,000				
ALAE:	200,000	500,000	0	0	0
	500,000				
Loss	425,000				
ALAE:	150,000	500,000	75,000	0	0
	575,000				
Loss	750,000				
ALAE:	300,000	500,000	500,000	50,000	0
	1,050,000				
Loss	1,800,000				
ALAE:	500,000	500,000	500,000	1,000,000	300,000
	2,300,000				
Loss	4,750,000				
ALAE:	1,000,000	500,000	500,000	1,000,000	3,000,000
	(1) 5,750,000				

Notes:

(1) The reinsurer does not pay out more than its limit. The remainder (750,000) has to be paid by the reinsured-company. A Reinsured-Company probably wouldn't buy a reinsurance treaty having ALAE as part of the loss unless its own policies had ALAE within the policy limits and theoretically, could not pay out more than the reinsurance protecting it. In other words, if it issued a 5,000,000 policy with ALAE within the limits, it shouldn't be paying 5,750,000, but a maximum of 5,000,000. We said this was theoretical; in the real world, courts may turn things upside down.

Example (2):

ALAE: Proportional to the loss and in addition to the reinsurer's limit.

Excess of Loss "Casualty" Reinsurance Treaties

		Reinsured Company		500,000 x 500,000		1,000,000 x 1,000,000		3,000,000 x 2,000,000	
		Retention	**ALAE**	**Loss**	**ALAE**	**Loss**	**ALAE**	**Loss**	**ALAE**
Loss	300,000	300,000	200,000	0	0	0	0	0	0
ALAE:	200,000								
	500,000								
Loss	425,000	425,000	150,000	0	0	0	0	0	0
ALAE:	150,000								
	575,000								

Reinsured-Company paid entire loss, so it pays the entire ALAE.

Loss	750,000	500,000	200,000	250,000	100,000	0	0	0	0
ALAE:	300,000	66.6%	66.6%	33.3%	33.3%				
	1,050,000								

Reinsured-Company paid 66.6% of loss and reinsurer paid 33.3% of loss, so reinsurer pays 33.3% of ALAE.

Loss	1,800,000	500,000	139,000	500,000	139,000	800,000	222,000	0	0
ALAE:	500,000	27.8%	27.8%	27.8%	27.8%	44.4%	44.4%		
	2,300,000								

Reinsured-Company paid 27.8% of loss and first layer reinsurer paid 27.8% of loss, so first layer reinsurer pays 27.8% of ALAE. Second layer reinsurer paid 44.4% of loss, so second layer reinsurer pays 44.4% of ALAE.

Loss:	4,750,000	500,000	105,000	500,000	105,000	1,000,000	210,000	2,750,000	580,000
ALAE:	1,000,000	10.5%	10.5%	10.5%	10.5%	21.0%	21.0%	58.0%	58.0%
	5,750,000								

Reinsured-Company paid 10.5% of loss and first layer reinsurer paid 10.5% of loss, so first layer reinsurer pays 10.5% of ALAE. Second layer reinsurer paid 21.0% of loss, so second layer reinsurer pays 21.0% of ALAE. Third layer reinsurer paid 58.0% of loss, so third layer reinsurer pays 58.0% of ALAE.

Note:
In each of the examples, the reinsurer paid its reinsurance limit *plus* ALAE.

WHAT TO CONSIDER WHEN CHOOSING THE METHOD TO HANDLE ALLOCATED LOSS ADJUSTMENT EXPENSE (ALAE) IN AN EXCESS OF LOSS REINSURANCE TREATY.

The most important item to consider is how the underlying insurance policy handles allocated adjustment expense.

(1) UNDERLYING POLICY PAYS THE LOSS LIMIT IN ADDITION TO THE ALLOCATED LOSS ADJUSTMENT EXPENSE

If the Reinsured- Company's policy will pay to the insured the loss limit and in addition allocated loss adjustment expense, then it is wise to structure ALAE in the excess of loss treaty as Method (2) which is proportional to the loss and in addition to the reinsurer's limit.

Why?

You need to cover the situation whereby the Reinsured- Company issues a policy for its maximum limit, let's say 5,000,000; you have reinsurance in place up to that maximum (5,000,000) and a loss is paid for $5,000,000 and ALAE is $250,000 or more. In this situation the reinsurer pays the loss and its portioned share of the $250,000 ALAE.

(2) UNDERLYING POLICY HAS THE LOSS AND ALAE WITH ITS LIMIT

If the Reinsured- Company's policy combines the loss and ALAE into one limit then it is possible to choose Method (1), part of the loss. This is advantageous to the Reinsured- Company because the entire ALAE above its retention will be covered by reinsurance. But when choosing this method you must be confident the underlying loss and ALAE will not exceed the reinsurance maximum treaty limit.

ALLOCATED LOSS ADJUSTMENT EXPENSES (ALAE) AND *LIABILITY INSURANCE POLICIES*

These expenses classified as allocated loss adjustment expenses (ALAE) can be broadly defined as those expenses the policy obligates the Reinsured- Company to incur to defend the insured and/or to settle the insured's claim.

.

OTHER ITEMS RELATED TO A SPECIFIC CLAIM WHICH NEEDS TO BE CONSIDERED FOR REINSURANCE COVERAGE

Declaratory Judgment Expense:	These are expenses related to bringing a declaratory action, which is usually brought by the insurer to determine policy coverage issues in regard to its insurance with its insured.
Prejudgment Interest Expense:	This is interest awarded by the courts Judgment for the benefit of the plaintiff which accrues from the date of the event.
Post Judgment Interest Expense:	This is interest which accrues to the benefit of the plaintiff while the case is on appeal.
Salvage:	Salvage is the remaining usable property that has some value after the insurance company settles all the claims, that insurer is entitled to the salvage. For reinsurance purposes salvage is handled exactly like subrogation.
Subrogation:	The Reinsured- Company has the right to seek *restitution* for a claim it paid on behalf of its policyholder *from another party*, who according to the reinsured company is responsible for that claim. In other words, a claim is paid by the insurer, then it turns around and sues those that it feels caused that claim in an effort to become whole again. It is rare that the Reinsured- Company collects 100% of the claim.
Extra Contractual Obligation:	Those obligations which are "extra contractual" meaning they are outside of the reinsurance contract unless specifically defined and included. The most likely source of an extra contractual obligation is when the insurer is sued for bad faith in regard to a claim such as failing to settle a claim, mishandling a claim or improper conduct related to a claim. Most reinsurance contracts cover some defined portion of extra contractual obligations.
Excess of Original Policy Limit:	A Reinsured- Company may be required by a court award to pay a loss that exceeds its original policy limit. This usually comes about when the Reinsured- Company is found to have acted in bad faith by failing to adequately consider the interest of the insured by not settling the claim within the original policy limit. Most reinsurance contracts will cover a loss in excess of the original policy limit under agreed upon circumstances.

Section 8

SUBROGATION AND SALVAGE

SUBROGATION IN LIABILITY REINSURANCE

The insurer has the right to seek *restitution* for a claim it paid on behalf of its policyholder *from another party*, who according to the insurer is responsible for that claim. In other words, a claim is paid by the insurer, then it turns around and sues those it feels caused the claim in an effort to become whole. It is rare the insurer collects 100% of the claim.

How is subrogation handled in reinsurance treaties? If the reinsurer has paid the loss, it is entitled to be *reimbursed first* from subrogation recoveries. The theory behind paying the reinsurer first, is that there would not have been a reinsurance claim in the first place if subrogation was immediately applied to the claim.

Example:	Ground Up Claim:	1,000,000
	Reinsurance Layer:	500,000 x 500,000
	Reinsurer Pays:	500,000
	If we introduce subrogation:	
	Ground Up Claim:	1,000,000
	Subrogation:	600,000
	Claim:	400,000
	Reinsurance Layer:	500,000 x 500,000
	Reinsurer Pays:	0

Paying of Subrogation To Reinsurers In Reverse Order
Subrogation recoveries are paid "first" to the reinsurers who paid the claim "last". In other words, the third layer reinsurers are paid subrogation before the second layer reinsurers.

SALVAGE IN PROPERTY REINSURANCE

Salvage is the remaining usable property that has some value after the insurance company settles all the claims, that insurer is entitled to the salvage. For reinsurance purposes salvage is handled exactly like subrogation. Salvage recoveries are paid *first* to the reinsurers who paid the claim *last.*

Section 9

COMMUTATION

Commuting the reinsurance or commuting a specific reinsurer means the Reinsured- Company and the reinsurer have reached a mutually acceptable method to relieve the reinsurer of some or all of its obligations which is almost always in regard to claims or potential claims in the reinsurers layer. The practice of commuting a reinsurer's liability basically started in the 1980's. It is not often done but there is nothing unusual about it.

PAYMENTS TO REINSURED COMPANY

All commutations have the reinsurer paying the Reinsured- Company a sum for the right to be relieved (commuted) of its obligations for existing claims, future claims, or incurred but not reported claims. The amount the reinsurer returns is mutually agreed upon.

BASIC COMMUTATION METHODS

(I) Only the reinsurer's existing claim reserves are commuted. There is a schedule and only those specific claims on the schedule are commuted.

Each claim reserved by the reinsurer is evaluated. The reinsurer pays the Reinsured- Company a discounted amount for those reserves and because it is accelerating the payment, it is commuted from further liability on those claim reserves. For instance, if the claim reserves total $3,000,000, it might pay $2,600,000 and it would be relieved of all liability for those claims. It would continue to be on risk for all new claims that could develop.

(II) The reinsurers existing case reserves are commuted. There is no schedule because when the parties agree on an amount all existing claim reserves are commuted.

(III) Only the reinsurers incurred but not reported (IBNR) is commuted.

(IV) Commuting all the reinsurer's liability:
The reinsurer returns an agreed upon amount to be 100% relieved of all its past, existing and future reserves, including late developing claims, claims closed in the past that could be reopened, and incurred but not reported (IBNR) claims. This is the only method of commuting that the reinsurer is guaranteed not to go back and pay any claims.

(V) Non-Standard Method:
This method has the reinsurer returning a portion of the reinsurance premium previously paid to them. In return the reinsurer is relieved of all of its claim obligations. This can only be done on a profitable treaty in which the reinsurer wants to guarantee a portion of that profit and clear its books.

(VI) Profit Commission:
Some reinsurance treaties have a profit commission and when the reinsurer pays it they are commuted of all future obligations. Most reinsurance treaties do not have this commutation requirement but a few do.

(VII) No Claims Bonus:
Some reinsurance treaties have a no claims bonus and when the reinsurer pays that no claims bonus they are commuted of all future obligations.

BEFORE COMMUTING YOU MIGHT WANT TO THINK ABOUT:

- Should the Board of Directors be informed reinsurance coverage is being discontinued by the commutation?

- What form are the underlying insurance policies reinsured, occurrence claims made, or losses discovered.

- Does the business written have a lengthy lag from the time a policy is issued to the time claims are reported?

- How will commuting reinsurers affect your actuarial reserve reports? What will your Certified Public Auditors think, A.M. Best or perhaps insurance departments?

- Is there any risk to the Reinsured- Company in commuting?
  There is always some risk, which is the claim reserves may have unanticipated severe loss development and the amounts received from commuting are insignificant compared to the final payments.

Sample

COMMUTATION AGREEMENT
EFFECTIVE _______

ARTICLE 1

SCOPE OF AGREEMENT The terms of this Commutation Agreement, (hereinafter referred to as "Agreement") shall determine the rights and obligations of the parties.

This Agreement constitutes the entire Agreement between the parties related to the subject matter of this Agreement, which may not, except by written amendment executed and agreed to by the parties, be amended or modified.

The rights, duties and obligations, set forth herein, shall inure to the benefit and be binding upon the parties hereto and their predecessors and successors.
This Agreement shall be governed by and construed in accordance with the laws of _____ ______.

ARTICLE 2

PARTIES TO AGREEMENT The Agreement is made effective _________ by and between ____________(hereinafter referred to as the "Reinsured- Company") and _____________ ______ (hereinafter referred to as the "Reinsurer").

ARTICLE 3

BUSINESS COMMUTED WHEREAS, the parties hereto have entered into one or more reinsurance agreements in which the Reinsurer has reinsured certain liabilities of the Reinsured-Company.

Whereas, the parties hereto now wish to fully and finally settle and commute all liabilities and obligations of the Reinsurer under such reinsurance agreements.

THEREFORE, in consideration of the covenants set forth herein and the payment to be made hereunder, the parties agree as follows:

ARTICLE 4

DEFINITION – "Reinsurance Agreements" as used herein shall mean all reinsurance agreements which have been entered into between the Reinsured- Company, as ceding insurer, and the Reinsurer, as reinsurer, listed in Exhibit 1 attached hereto an incorporated herein.

ARTICLE 5

PAYMENT TO REINSURER Upon execution of this Agreement, the Reinsurer shall pay the Reinsured -Company the sum of $______________.

ARTICLE 6

RELEASE In consideration of the payment the Reinsurer hereby release and discharges the Company for all obligations under the Reinsurance Agreement(s). The Company hereby irrevocably and unconditionally releases the Reinsurer from any and all liability past, existing and future whether known or unknown, discovered or undiscovered whether reported or unreported by reason of but not limited to a claim or claims, debt, demand, courses of action, contracts, promises, judgments, whatsoever arising under or in respect of the Reinsurance Agreements.

IN WITNESS WHEREOF, the parties have executed this *Agreement* by their respective authorized officers.

Date:____________________

By the Reinsured- Company:

____

Date:__________________________

By the Reinsurer:

____

Section 10

NOTICE OF CANCELLATION IN TREATY REINSURANCE

Treaty reinsurance contracts are sometimes written for an unlimited duration and then provide for cancellation by either party with sixty (60) or ninety (90) days written notice prior to the treaty's anniversary date. Some treaties can be cancelled at any time with sixty (60) to ninety (90) days written notice. The treaty may require that the notice be delivered by registered mail.

Example
Treaty is on an Unlimited Basis and provides for Cancellation with written notice at least (90) days before the upcoming treaty's Anniversary.

Commencement And Termination Article In The Reinsurance Contract (Also Referred To As The Agreement of Reinsurance):
This Agreement shall incept 12:01 a.m. Eastern Standard Time January 1, 2009 and shall remain in force for an indefinite period, but either party shall have the right to cancel at anniversary, January 1, 2010, or any subsequent January 1 anniversary by giving at least ninety (90) days written notice.

<u>Example of Notice Of Cancellation That Can Be Sent By The Reinsured-Company Or Reinsurer:</u> Mason Insurance Company
Excess of loss treaty 750,000 xs 250,000
Reference number 10078/00

Dear Ms. Gwynne Vik:

In accordance with the cancelation provision of the above captioned treaty, we hereby give Notice of Cancellation effective January 1, 2010. This notice is being sent to allow a sufficient time to properly evaluate this treaty prior to its anniversary.

Sincerely,

Example
Treaty is on an Unlimited Basis and provides for Cancellation at any time with (90) Days Written Notice Delivered By Registered Mail.

<u>Commencement And Termination Article In The Reinsured Contract (Referred To As Agreement):</u>
This Agreement shall continue until termination by mutual consent, or by either party giving to the other not less than (90) days written notice, delivered by registered mail, stating the termination date.

RE: GVA Insurance Company
Excess of loss treaty 500,000 xs 500,000
Reference number 730010/01
Sent by Registered Mail #336 437-703

Dear Mr. Harold Wilson:

In accordance with the terms and conditions of the above captioned treaty, we hereby give Notice of Cancellation effective October 1, 2010.

Sincerely,

<u>Is there a "Provisional" Notice of Cancellation?</u>
Parties to reinsurance contracts will often mention in the Notice of Cancellation or in a separate letter that the Notice is provisional and they look forward to renewal information. In effect they do not really want to come off the treaty. Their intention is to renew, perhaps with different terms, after they have time to review the renewal information. We want to bring in a note of caution, because reinsurance treaties do not provide for a "provisional" Notice of Cancellation. It is either cancelled or not. If either party renders a Notice of Cancellation it is binding, in order to renew both parties must agree to that renewal. For instance, if a reinsurer sends in a Notice of Cancellation and then later decides to rescind it and renew, it shall have to do so with the permission of the Reinsured- Company. It cannot unilaterally withdraw its notice of cancellation.

The reason reinsurance treaties are usually written on an unlimited basis is that from the 1930's to about 1980, insurers and reinsurers had incredibly long relationships, often lasting a decade or more with little change. Management's attitude during this period was relationship driven and simply there weren't many reinsurance companies. Also the economy was not as dynamic in changing as it has been in the last 20 years. Now companies are transaction driven or where can I get the best deal. Therefore almost all treaties written on an unlimited basis will have one of the parties sending a notice of cancellation annually.

Section 11

RATING OF EXCESS OF LOSS REINSURANCE TREATIES BY THE REINSURER

There are four (4) basic methods reinsurers use to rate excess of loss treaties, which determine the reinsurance premium.

FOUR BASIC METHODS

(1) Flat Rate or Fixed Reinsurance Premium
(2) Rated
(3) Retrospectively Rated (Swing rate)
(4) Cession Basis

(1) Flat Rate or Fixed Reinsurance Premium

In this method there are no rates, just a fixed reinsurance premium.

Example: 1,000,000 x 1,000,000 treaty has a fixed reinsurance premium of $450,000. This premium is not increased or decreased in anyway regardless of the subject premium.

(2) Rated

In this method a rate is applied to the subject premiums.

The rate times the subject premium equals the ultimate reinsurance premium. Almost all *rated* treaties have a minimum reinsurance premium and a deposit reinsurance premium.

(3) Retrospectively Rated

This method uses the loss experience produced in the treaty to determine the ultimate reinsurance rate, which is then used to calculate the ultimate reinsurance premium, subject to the treaty's minimum and maximum rates.

Two types of Retrospectively Rated Methods

(I) Losses Incurred Loaded divided by the final subject premium equals the ultimate reinsurance premium, subject to the treaty's minimum and maximum rates.
(II) Losses Incurred Loaded Plus the Minimum Reinsurance Premium divided by the final subject premium equals the ultimate reinsurance premium, subject to the treaty's minimum and maximum.

Most retrospectively rated treaties are written for three years. The amounts are accumulated each year and a final calculation is done at the end of all three years combined.

In effect, the reinsured company pays (in the form of reinsurance premiums) the equivalent of its own losses up to the maximum reinsurance premium (rate).

(I) Losses Incurred Loaded Formula Steps:

(a) Losses Incurred

(b) Losses Incurred x Loading Factor = Losses Incurred Loaded

(c) Losses Incurred Loaded ÷ Subject Premium = Ultimate Reinsurance Rate (subject to the minimum and maximum)

(d) Ultimate Reinsurance Rate x Subject Premium = Ultimate Reinsurance Premium

(II) Losses Incurred Loaded Plus Minimum Reinsurance Premiums Formula Steps:

(a) Losses Incurred

(b) Losses Incurred x Loading Factor = Losses Incurred Loaded

(c) Losses Incurred Loaded Plus Minimum Reinsurance Premium ÷ Subject Premium = Ultimate Reinsurance Rate (subject to the minimum and maximum)

(d) Ultimate Reinsurance Rate x Subject Premium = Ultimate Reinsurance Premium.

(4) Cession Basis

This method is used when it is anticipated the reinsurance premium will be relatively small compared to the reinsurance limit. The reinsurer will be paid each time an original policy limit exposes the reinsurer. Cession factors are actuarially arrived at by the reinsurer; these factors are used to determine the reinsurance premium or cession.

Example (1)

FLAT RATE OR FIXED REINSURANCE PREMIUM

Gross Net Written Premium Income	8,937,412
Less: Facultative Reinsurance Premiums	606,753
Adjusted Gross Net Written Premium Income	8,330,659
Rate	None
Ultimate Reinsurance Premium	650,000
Minimum and Deposit	Not applicable
Due Reinsurer	Not applicable

Example (2)

RATED

Premium Adjustment

Gross Net Written Premium Income	10,612,897
Less: Facultative Reinsurance Premiums	356,714
Adjusted Gross Net Written Premium Income	10,256,183
Rate	9.0%
Ultimate Reinsurance Premium	923,056
Minimum and Deposit	900,000
Due Reinsurer	$23,056

Example (3)

RETROSPECTIVELY RATED TREATY

Losses Incurred Loaded
Divided By Final Subject Premium Equals Ultimate Reinsurance Premium
(Subject to Minimum and Maximum)

Treaty:	Excess of Loss 1,000,000 x 1,000,000
Estimated Subject Premium (Determined before the treaty starts):	10,000,000
Final Subject Premium (Determined at the end of the treaty):	10,358,781
Losses Incurred Loading Factor:	100/75ths or 133.3%
Schedule of Rates:	Minimum Rate 5.00% Provisional Rate 10.00% (Determines the Deposit Premium) Maximum Rate 15.00%
Deposit Premium:	\$800,000 payable quarterly at \$200,000 per quarter (10% of the estimated subject premium, at 80%)

Various Losses Incurred Scenarios	Losses Incurred	Losses Incurred Loaded by 133.3%	Losses Incurred Loaded ÷ Final Subject Premium	Ultimate Reinsurance Rate	Ultimate Reinsurance Premiums	Less Deposit	Net Due Reinsurer	Net Due Company
(1)	.00	.00	.00 ÷ 10,358,781 = .00	5.00 min	517,939 min	800,000		282,061
(2)	386,439	515,239	515,239 ÷ 10,358,781 = 4.97	5.00 min	517,939 min	800,000		282,061
(3)	717,212	956,259	956,259 ÷ 10,358,781 = 9.23	9.23	956,612	800,000	156,612	
(4)	1,059,781	1,413,006	1,413,006 ÷ 10,358,781 = 13.64	13.64	1,412,938	800,000	612,938	
(5)	1,562,485	2,083,261	2,083,261 ÷ 10,358,781 = 20.11	15.00 max	1,553,817 max	800,000	753,817	

Example (4)

RETROSPECTIVELY RATED TREATY

Losses Incurred Loaded Plus Minimum Reinsurance Premium
Divided By Final Subject Premium Equals Ultimate Reinsurance Premium
(Subject to Minimum and Maximum)

Treaty:	Excess of Loss 500,000 x 500,000
Estimated Subject Premium (Determined before the treaty starts):	8,000,000
Final Subject Premium (Determined at the end of the treaty):	8,312,000
Loses Incurred Loading Factor:	100/80^{ths} or 125.0%
Schedule of Rates:	Minimum Rate 3.00% Provisional Rate 6.00% (Determines the Deposit Premium) Maximum Rate 9.00%
Deposit Premium:	$384,000 payable quarterly at $96,000 per quarter 6% of the estimated subject premium, at 80%

Various Losses Incurred Scenarios	Losses Incurred	Losses Incurred Loaded by 125.0%	Minimum Reinsurance Premium 3.0%	**Losses Incurred Loaded Plus Minimum Reinsurance** Premiums ÷ Final Subject Premium
(1)	.00	.00	249,360	249,360 ÷ 8,312,000 = 3.00 min
(2)	211,611	264,514	249,360	513,874 ÷ 8,312,000 = 6.18
(3)	301,482	376,852	249,360	626,212 ÷ 8,312,000 = 7.53
(4)	782,015	977,519	249,360	1,226,879 ÷ 8,312,000 = 14..76

Various Losses Incurred Scenarios	Ultimate Reinsurance Rate	Ultimate Reinsurance Premiums	Less Deposit	Net Due Reinsurer	Net Due Company
(1)	3.00 min	249,360 min	384,000		134,640
(2)	6.18	513,682	384,000	129,682	
(3)	7.53	625,894	384,000	241,894	
(4)	9.00 max	748,080 max	384,000	364,080	

Example (5)

3 YEAR RATING BLOCK
RETROSPECTIVELY RATED TREATY

Losses Incurred Loaded

Divided By Final Subject Premium Equals Ultimate Reinsurance Premium (Subject to Minimum and Maximum)

Treaty:	Excess of Loss 750,000 x 250,000
Losses Incurred Loading Factor:	100/80ths or 125.0%
Schedule of Rates:	Minimum Rate 2.50% Provisional Rate 5.00% (Determines the Deposit Premium) Maximum Rate 10.00%

YEAR 1

Estimated Subject Premium (Determined before the treaty starts):	7,000,000
Final Subject Premium (Determined at the end of the treaty):	7,239,611
Deposit Premium:	$280,000 payable quarterly at $70,000 per quarter 5% of the estimated subject premium, at 80%

Losses Incurred	Losses Incurred Loaded by 125.0%	Losses Incurred Loaded ÷ Final Subject Premium	Ultimate Reinsurance Rate	Ultimate Reinsurance Premiums	Less Deposit	Net Due Reinsurer	Net Due Company	Total Paid Reinsurer
400,000	500,000	500,000 ÷ 7,239,611 = 6.90	6.90	499,533	280,000	219,533	-	499,533

Example (5) Continued

YEAR 2

Estimated Subject Premium (Determined before the treaty starts):	7,200,000		
Final Subject Premium (Determined at the end of the treaty):	7,622,909		
Cumulative Final Subject Premium(s)	Year (1)	7,239,611	
	Year (2)	7,622,909	
		14,862,520	
Deposit Premium:	$345,000 payable at $86,250 per quarter. Provisional rate adjusted upward to 6% because first ultimate reinsurance premium was $499,533; Reinsurer and Company agreed to this. 6% of the estimated subject premium at 80% is *new deposit.*		

	Losses Incurred	Losses Incurred Loaded by 125.0%	Losses Incurred Loaded ÷ Final Subject Premium	Ultimate Reinsurance Rate	Ultimate Reinsurance Premiums	Less Previously Paid to Reinsurer	Net Due Reinsurer	Net Due Company	Total Paid Reinsurer
Year (1)	400,000					499,533			
Year (2)	600,000					345,000			
Cumu-lative	1,000,000	1,250,000	1,250,000 ÷ 14,862,520 = 8.41	8.41	1,249,938	844,533	405,405	-	1,249,938

Example (5) Continued

YEAR 3

FINAL ADJUSTMENT FOR ALL 3 YEARS COMBINED

Estimated Subject Premium (Determined before the treaty starts):	7,500,000	
Final Subject Premium (Determined at the end of the treaty):	7,44,813	
Cumulative Final Subject Premium(s)	Year (1)	7,239,611
	Year (2)	7,622,909
	Year (3)	7,422,813
		22,285,333

Deposit Premium: $420,000 payable at $105,000 per quarter. Provisional rate adjusted upward to 7% by mutual agreement; 7% of the estimated subject premium at 80% is *new deposit.*

	Losses Incurred	Losses Incurred Loaded by 125.0%	Losses Incurred Loaded ÷ Final Subject Premium	Ultimate Reinsurance Rate	Ultimate Reinsurance Premiums	Less Previously Paid to Reinsurer	Net Due Reinsurer	Net Due Company	Total Paid Reinsurer
Year (1)	400,000								
Year (2)	600,000								
Year (3)	450,000								
Cumu-lative	1,450,000	1,812,500	1,812,500 ÷ 22,285,333 = 8.13	8.13	1811,798	1,249,938	561,860	-	1,811,798

Example (6)

Cession Basis
5,000,000 x 1,000,000
Effective January 1, 2009

Cession Factor Schedule

Original Policy Limit	Reinsurance Cession Factor
1,000,000	None
2,000,000	28.0%
3,000,000	37.0%
4,000,000	49.0%
5,000,000	54.0%
6,000,000	59.0%

Cession Basis
5,000,000 x 1,000,000
Effective January 1, 2009

Policy Number	Original Policy Limit	Original Gross Premium	Reinsurance Cession Factor	Reinsurer Cession Premium
78413	3,000,000	$161,898	37.0%	$59,902
80310	2,000,000	$140,089	28.0%	$39,225
80362	3,000,000	$159,216	37.0%	$58,910
80411	4,000,000	$170,811	49.0%	$83,698
81016	5,000,000	$179,216	54.0%	$96,776
81712	6,000,000	$184,111	59.0%	$108,625

The reinsurer is only exposed on original policy limits of 1,000,000 or greater; therefore it only is paid on those policies.

Section 12

CEDING COMMISSION IN EXCESS OF LOSS TREATY

At one time no excess of loss treaty would have a ceding commission, now more and more of them do. The function and justification for a ceding commission is that whenever reinsurance premium is ceded to the reinsurer a corresponding percentage of expense can be deducted and reduce the insurer's (ceding insurer) expenses leaving the expense ratio neutral. If a higher ceding commission can be obtained the expense ratio can be lowered.

Example
Insurer has three (3) excess of loss treaties with reinsurance premiums totaling $2,000,000. Its expenses prior to any reinsurance are 30%.

REVIEW OF REINSURANCE
With or without the ceding commission the reinsurer is to be paid $2,000,000.

Without Ceding Commission		With Ceding Commission of 30.0%		
Gross Reinsurance Premium	2,000,000	Gross Reinsurance Premium		2,857,142
Less Ceding Commission	00	Less Ceding Commission	30.0%	857,142
Net Reinsurance Premium Paid to Reinsurer	2,000,000	Net Reinsurance Premium Paid to Reinsurer		2,000,000

Statutory Financial Statement of Insurer

Before Reinsurance		Before Reinsurance	
Original Gross Net Premium	10,000,000	Original Gross Net Premium	10,000,000
Expenses 30%	3,000,000	Expenses 30%	3,000,000
Expense Ratio	30.0%	Expense Ratio	30.0%

After Reinsurance Transaction		After Reinsurance Transaction	
Original Gross Net Premium	10,000,000	Original Gross Net Premium	10,000,000
Less Reinsurance Premium	2,000,000	Less Reinsurance Premium	2,857,142
	8,000,000		7,142,858
Expenses	3,000,000	Expenses	3,000,000
Less Ceding Commission	00	Less Ceding Commission	857,142
	3,000,000		2,142,858
Expense Ratio	37.5%	Expense Ratio	30.0%
	3,000,000 divided by 8,000,000		2,142,858 divided by 7,142,858

In order to accommodate a 30.0% ceding commission the reinsurance premium is grossed up to 2,857,142 (2,000,000 divided by reciprocal of 30.0% or 70.0% = 2,857,142).

Section 13

PROFIT COMMISSION

Profit commissions can be in excess of loss or quota share treaties. The profit commission paid by the reinsurer to the Reinsured- Company is a portion of the overall profit the reinsurer realized on the treaty. Looked at another way, you can say the reinsurer is returning a portion of the reinsurance premium because its experience has been profitable.

PROFIT COMMISSIONS IN EXCESS OF LOSS TREATIES

Generally, profit commissions are only put in the lower layers of excess of loss treaties because the layers above have much smaller premiums. A reinsurer cannot afford to take a risk on a higher layer where it can have a significant loss for a relatively small premium, and at the same time return premiums in the form of a profit commission if it does not have those losses. The profit commission is a "double edged sword." If there is a profit commission in a treaty, the reinsurance rate may not easily be lowered because the reinsurer must consider the potential return of premiums. On the other hand, you could not just eliminate the profit commission and get the lower rate because that assumes the reinsurer will have no claims.

Example	Treaty 500,000 x 500,000	Most likely the only treaty of the three here that would have a profit commission would be the 500,000 x 500,000
	1,000,000 x 1,000,000	
	3,000,000 x 2,000,000	

PROFIT COMMISSIONS IN QUOTA SHARE TREATIES

Profit commissions can be placed in quota share treaties and they work similar to profit commissions in excess of loss treaties.

DEFICITS CARRIED FORWARD

All this means is if the profit commission calculation produces a deficit, it is *carried forward* into the next calculation. This allows the reinsurer to bring deficits into future profit commission calculations.

Is a reinsurer who goes on a treaty *after* the deficit was created entitled to have the deficit carried forward into their profit commission formula, thereby returning less profit to the reinsured company? In our opinion, no. They did not incur the deficit so it should not be carried into their calculation. However, it is often done because it's more convenient than calculating it separately. However, with the use of computers it should be achievable.

NO CLAIMS BONUS IN EXCESS OF LOSS TREATIES

The reinsurer will return to the Reinsured- Company reinsurance premium if there are absolutely no claims incurred for which the reinsurer is responsible. If the Reinsured- Company accepts the no claim bonus then it has guaranteed to the reinsurer there will be *no claims*, in effect the reinsurer is commuted from all liability. Therefore, it is extremely important for the ceding insurer to understand the concept of a no claims bonus. No claims bonus will only be found in excess of loss treaties.

Example (1)

Neptune Insurance Company
Profit Commission
1/1/09 – 12/31/09
Casualty Excess of Loss Treaty
1,500,000 x 500,000

Income:	
Reinsurance Premium	2,000,000
Outgo:	
Claims Paid	152,000
Claims Reserved	320,000
Reinsurers Home Office Expense (5% of reinsurance premium)	100,000
Total	572,000
Profit:	1,428,000
Profit Commission 30%	$428,400 (Due Neptune Insurance Company)

Example (2)

Neptune Insurance Company
Profit Commission
1/1/09 – 12/31/09
Casualty Excess of Loss Treaty
500,000 x 500,000

Income:	
Reinsurance Premium	1,000,000
Outgo:	
Claims Paid	600,000
Claims Reserved	900,000
Reinsurers Home Office Expense (5% of reinsurance premium)	50,000
Total	1,550,000
Deficit:	(550,000) (This profit commission formula did not produce any profit for the reinsurer but created a deficit)
Profit Commission 30%	NONE

Note:
If the treaty states "deficits carried forward" then the (550,000) would be included in the next years calculation but only in regard to this treaty. See example 3.

Example (3)

Neptune Insurance Company
Profit Commission
1/1/09 – 12/31/09
Casualty Excess of Loss Treaty
500,000 x 500,000

Income:	
Reinsurance Premium	1,200,000
Outgo:	
Claims Paid	150,000
Claims Reserved	300,000
Reinsurers Home Office Expense (5% of reinsurance premium)	60,000
Total	510,000
Profit:	690,000
Deficit Carried Forward (from period 1/1/08 – 12/31/08):	(550,000)
Adjusted Profit:	140,000
Profit Commission 30%	$42,000

Section 14

PREMIUM ADJUSTMENT

Excess of loss treaties will usually be on a *rated basis*, which means there is a rate applied to the final subject premium to produce a final reinsurance premium at the end of the year. However, reinsurers don't want to wait until the end of the year to get paid their premiums, so a *deposit* is usually paid to them quarterly and adjusted at the end of the year. The statement rendered at the end of the year is called a premium adjustment.

EXAMPLE (1)

NEPTUNE INSURANCE COMPANY
EXCESS OF LOSS REINSURANCE TREATY
500,000 x 500,000
PREMIUM ADJUSTMENT
JANUARY 1, 2009 TO DECEMBER 31, 2009

Subject Premium: Original Gross Net Written Premium Income (OGNWPI):	10,436,312
Adjustment to OGNWPI (allowed per the treaty, if any):	(60,814)
Final Subject Premium:	10,375,498
Reinsurance Rate:	6.25%
Final Reinsurance Premium:	$648,469
Annual Deposit: ($125,000 x quarterly payments)	500,000
Due Reinsurer:	$148,469

Notes:

- In this example, an additional $148,469 is due the reinsurer.
- The deposit of $500,000 is arrived at prior to the inception of the treaty and is usually 80% of the estimated final reinsurance premium.
- When original gross net written premium income used for an excess of loss treaty most likely the reinsurers liability is on a risk attaching basis (we like the term policies attaching better).
- Most premium adjustment statements will have some adjustment of the subject premium such as facultative reinsurance premiums, return premiums, cancellation premiums.

EXAMPLE (2)

NEPTUNE INSURANCE COMPANY
EXCESS OF LOSS REINSURANCE TREATY
750,000 x 250,000
PREMIUM ADJUSTMENT
JANUARY 1, 2009 TO DECEMBER 31, 2009

Most treaties will also have a minimum reinsurance premium in addition to the deposit. The minimum may apply and therefore stops the reinsurer from returning premiums.

Subject Premium: Original Gross Net Written Premium Income (OGNWPI):	15,416,732
Adjustment to OGNWPI (allowed per the treaty):	(174,892)
Final Subject Premium:	15,241,840
Reinsurance Rate:	8.00%
Final Reinsurance Premium:	$1,219,347
Annual Deposit Premium:	1,500,000
Due Neptune Ins. Co. (before minimum is applied):	$280,653
Minimum Reinsurance Premium:	1,500,000
Final Amount Due Neptune Insurance Co.:	None

Notes:

- In this example, the minimum of 1,500,000 stops a return premium to Neptune Insurance Co.
- Most treaties will have a minimum the same as the deposit.
- When original gross net written premium income used for an excess of loss treaty most likely the reinsurers liability is on a risk attaching basis (we like the term policies attaching better).

EXAMPLE (3)

NEPTUNE INSURANCE COMPANY
EXCESS OF LOSS REINSURANCE TREATY
750,000 x 250,000
PREMIUM ADJUSTMENT
JANUARY 1, 2009 TO DECEMBER 31, 2009

Subject Premium: Earned Premium	16,189,334
Adjustment to Earned Premium:	(52,793)
Final Subject Premium:	16,136,541
Reinsurance Rate:	7.50%
Final Reinsurance Premium:	1,210,241
Annual Deposit Premium:	1,000,000
Minimum Reinsurance Premium:	1,000,000
Due Reinsurer.:	$210,241

Notes:

- Most treaties will have a minimum the same as the deposit.
- When premiums earned is used for an excess of loss treaty most likely the reinsurers liability is on a losses occurring basis.

Section 15

CASUALTY CLASH REINSURANCE

(May also be known as casualty contingency excess of loss or casualty catastrophe excess of loss)

This is a form of treaty reinsurance intended to cover rare *casualty* loss occurrences.

ORIGINAL DEFINITION

In its original and *purest* form, casualty clash-reinsurance covers casualty claims arising from *two or more of the Reinsured- Company's casualty policies* which become involved in the "same common casualty loss occurrence" before triggering the clash reinsurance. The policies can be issued to two different insureds or the same insured could have more than one policy (i.e., covering two different lines of insurance such as automobile liability and general liability). The term "clash" is referring to casualty policies clashing or coming together.

EVOLVING AND EXPANDING REINSURANCE

Casualty clash-reinsurers over the years have expanded coverage to enhance its value, now Clash-reinsurance treaties cover some *unusual casualty* loss occurrences when only *one policy* is involved. These are loss occurrences stemming from an extra contractual obligation claim, excess of an original policy limit claim, run away loss adjustment expense claim or a claim involving stacking of limits most likely coming from automobile uninsured motorist and underinsured motorist. The similarity with pure casualty clash-reinsurance is these types of claims are also rare.

The New Purpose of Casualty Clash Reinsurance is to Protect the Reinsured - Company's Retention (sideways reinsurance) and providing Additional Limits Above the Underlying Reinsurance (vertical reinsurance)

(I) Protecting the Reinsured- Company's Retention.
Casualty clash reinsurance covers casualty claims arising from two or more of the Reinsured- Company's casualty policies which become involved in the same common casualty loss occurrence resulting in the Reinsured- Company having more than one claim in their retention. The purpose of casualty clash-reinsurance is to provide reinsurance protection to the Reinsured- Company's retention; this can be referred to as sideways reinsurance.

(II) Additional Reinsurance Limits Above the In Place Vertical Reinsurance.
Casualty clash-reinsurance purpose here is to provide additional reinsurance limits in respect to rare casualty claims exceeding the underlying vertical reinsurance in place. These casualty claims arise from (a) two or more of an Reinsured- Company's policies coming together in a casualty loss occurrence creating a claim greater than the vertical reinsurance in place, (b) an extra contractual obligation claim, (c) excess of original policy limits claim, (d) runaway loss adjustment expense claim, (e) a claim stemming from a policy issued with statutory (unlimited) limits, and (f) a situation where policy limits stack (most likely from an automobile policy).

WARRANTIES and DEFINITIONS in CASUALTY CLASH TREATIES.
The treaty is not design to cover standard casualty claims; therefore there will be warranties in the treaty to protect the reinsurer.

It is extremely important to have in the casualty clash-reinsurance contract full and complete definitions on what is exactly being covered by the reinsurer.

CLASS ACTION SUITS
Casualty clash-reinsurance was not intended to cover class-action lawsuits however it might be possible to structure a reinsurance agreement to cover such events

We describe here five (5) aspects of casualty clash reinsurance. All five may be combined into one treaty, but for the purpose of clarity we have separated them. Each one of these aspects either protects the insurer's retention (sideways reinsurance) or provides additional reinsurance to the Reinsured- Company's vertical reinsurance program.

(Aspect 1) Protecting the Reinsured- Company's Retention (Sideways Reinsurance). Two Policy Warranty

A casualty clash-reinsurance treaty protects the Reinsured- Company's "retention" when it has an accumulation of casualty claims (two or more) related to the same *common loss occurrence and* these claims involve two or more of the company's insurance policies.

If each claim has a separate retention, the Reinsured- Company will have a significant loss (within its retention) from the common loss occurrence.

This type of casualty clash-reinsurance is designed to attach after a certain number of retentions and is similar to a property catastrophe reinsurance treaty.

(Aspect 2) Protecting Against Claims, Exceeding the Reinsured- Company's (Vertical Reinsurance) Program

Two Policy Warranty

Here is one example of this type of casualty clash-reinsurance protection: the Reinsured- Company's vertical reinsurance program is on an each occurrence basis, and the Reinsured- Company's maximum policy limit matches this each occurrence reinsurance. It's possible that two or more of the Reinsured- Company's policies issued to different insureds or to the same insured are involved in the same common casualty loss occurrence producing claims exceeding the Reinsured- Company's each occurrence vertical reinsurance.

This type of clash cover would attach excess of the vertical (each occurrence reinsurance) and excess of a maximum any one-policy limit providing casualty clash-reinsurance. Therefore, it would take two or more policies to trigger the clash-reinsurance.

(Aspect 3) Protecting Against Claims Exceeding the Reinsured- Company's (Vertical Reinsurance) Program for Claims Involving an Extra Contractual Obligation (ECO) Award, Excess of Original Policy Limit (XPL) Award or Runaway Loss Adjustment Expense (Indemnity is Not Covered).

One Policy Can Be Involved.
This type of clash *does not* have a two-policy warranty. It will cover just one of the Reinsured- Company's policies involved in one claim, which exceeds the vertical reinsurance in place. The claim *must* be one that has an extra contractual award, excess of original policy limit award or runaway loss adjustment expense from a single claim. Indemnity is not covered.

(Aspect 4) Protecting Against Claims Exceeding The Reinsured- Company's Vertical Reinsurance Program When the Reinsured- Company Issues Policies with Statutory (Unlimited) Limits.
One Policy Can Be Involved.
Coverage for worker's compensation and employers' liability would have two or more claimants or two or more employee's warranty.
Another area casualty clash-reinsurance would cover is when the Reinsured- Company issues policies having statutory (unlimited) limits, such as the medical expenses in a worker's compensation policy, and in some states worker's compensation has unlimited benefits and unlimited employers liability limits, and in at least one state the medical section of the automobile policy has statutory (unlimited) limits. A single policy such as these could produce a loss greater than the vertical reinsurance the Reinsured- Company has in place, which then would be covered by clash reinsurance. Indemnity is not covered. In regard to worker's compensation, the reinsurer will require two or more claimants to be involved in the same common loss occurrence. Some reinsurers might structure it slightly different by requiring two or more employees to be involved in the same common loss occurrence.

(Aspect 5) Protecting Against Claims Exceeding the Reinsured- Company's (Vertical Reinsurance) When One Policy Is Stacked on Top of Another; Permitted by Statute in a Few States (i.e. auto uninsured motorist and underinsured motorist).
Certain states have statutes permitting policy limits (with respect to auto uninsured motorist and underinsured motorist) to be added together (stacked one on top of the other) producing a loss greater than the Reinsured- Company's vertical reinsurance program. This could also be covered by clash-reinsurance. For instance, an insured may have three (3) automobiles; each has coverage for limits of 500,000. Some states permit all three to be added together to cover a serious claim, therefore producing one total limit of 1,500,000. Clash-reinsurance could cover this claim above a certain attachment point. Some states may permit uninsured and underinsured motorist limits to be added to primary limits which is another potential stacking of limits for one serious claim.

EXAMPLE OF A CASUALTY CLASH-REINSUARNCE TREATYCOVERING THE FIVE ASPECTS.

Neptune Insurance Company Casualty Clash-Reinsurance Treaty

Section (A) *Protecting the Reinsured- Company's Retention – Two Policy Warranty*

5,000,000 each common occurrence excess of 1,000,000 each common occurrence in respect to the reinsured's retention.

Section (B) *Providing Additional Reinsurance Limits*
5,000,000 excess of reinsured's underlying reinsurance Schedule (A) or 1,000,000 whichever is greater in respect to:

- Two or More Policies in the Same Loss Occurrence Claim
- Extra Contractual Obligation Claim (100%)
- Excess of Original Policy Limit Claim (100%)
- Runaway Loss Adjustment Expense Claim
- Policies with Statutory (unlimited) Limit Claim
- Stacking of Limits Claim

Underlying Reinsurance Schedule (A):

Worker's compensation each occurrence	9,000,000 x 1,000,000
Commercial general liability each occurrence	9,000,000 x 1,000,000
Commercial automobile liability each occurrence	9,000,000 x 1,000,000
Professional Liability (D&O and E&O) each occurrence	9,000,000 x 1,000,000

All reinsurance treaties cover extra contractual obligations (ECO) and excess of original policy limit (XPL) claims on a 100% basis within the reinsurer's limit, in addition to the loss.

Example (1) *Protecting the Reinsured- Company's Retention (Sideways Reinsurance Protection).*
Two Policy Warranty.

Tim Jones, who works for Longhaul Freight Company, is driving a truck, which is involved in an accident, caused by the Miller Construction Inc. road crew's failure to put up proper warning barriers. Besides Jones, there were two other employees of the Longhaul Freight Company in the truck. All three file worker's compensation claims for injuries. The workers compensation policy for Longhaul Freight Company is with Neptune Insurance Company, which assigns it claim # WC0713 and reserves it for $1,500,000. Two of the injured employees decide to bring a third party suit directly against Miller Construction, whose general liability policy is also with Neptune Insurance Company which assigns it claim # GL0218 and reserves it for $1,000,000.

Neptune Insurance Company has separate each occurrence reinsurance treaties for worker's compensation and general liability, retaining the first 1,000,000 for worker's compensation and 1,000,000 for general liability. Consequently, Neptune Insurance Company has two (2) retention's related to the same common loss occurrence. It has a 1,000,000 retention for the worker's compensation claims (all three combined) and another 1,000,000 retention for the general liability claim.

Casualty clash-reinsurance attaches after one retention, so in this example the second retention would be covered by the casualty clash-reinsurance.

	Claim Reserved	Neptune's Retention	Clash-Reinsurance Covers
Claim # WC0713	$1,500,000	1,000,000	1,000,000
Claim # GL0218	$1,000,000	1,000,000	

Example (2) *Protecting Against Claims, Exceeding The Reinsured- Company's Vertical Reinsurance Program. Two Policy Warranty.*

A building being worked on collapses on April 12, 2001 and debris hits two (2) adjacent buildings and injures 21 people. Both the owner of the building, Mason Real Estate, and the construction company, Ashley Construction, have general liability policies from Neptune Insurance Company, each with a policy limit of 10,000,000.

Two general liability claims develop as a result of the accident, one claim (#GL0726) is brought against Mason Real Estate for $9,000,000; another claim (#GL0751) is brought against Ashley Construction for $3,500,000. Both combined total $12,500,000 and are due to the same common casualty loss occurrence (the 4/12/01 accident). Both claims have as their insurer Neptune Insurance Company and combined they exceed Neptune's vertical reinsurance program, which is $10,000,000 each occurrence in regard to general liability claims. Casualty clash-reinsurance would respond excess of 10,000,000 each common occurrence, so it will cover 2,500,000 excess of 10,000,000.

Covers	Claim Reserved for 12/12/01 Occurrence	Clash-Reinsurance
Claim # GL0726	$9,000,000	
Claim # GL0751	$3,500,000	
	$12,500,000 Neptune's reinsurance covers up to $10,000,000 each occurrence	$2,500,000

Example (3) *Protecting Against Claims Exceeding the Reinsured- Company's (Vertical Reinsurance) Program*

For Claims Involving an Extra Contractual Obligation (ECO) Award, Excess of Original Policy Limit (XPL) Award or Runaway Loss Adjustment Expense (Indemnity is Not Covered). One Policy Can Be Involved.

(a) <u>Extra Contractual Obligation Claim/Reinsured- Company is Sued by its Policyholder</u>

Neptune Insurance Company is involved in a general liability claim from its insured St. Claire & Associates. The claim has a total value of $3,000,000, but after careful review Neptune informs St. Claire & Associates they are not going to cover the claim and will not defend it. St. Claire & Associates sues Neptune for bad faith for denying coverage and a jury eventually awards St. Claire & Associates $16,000,000 (the entire award is for punitive damages). This is an extra contractual obligation award covered by casualty clash-reinsurance excess of the underlying reinsurance coverage.

Punitive Damage Award	Underlying Reinsurance	Casualty Clash-Reinsurance Covers
$16,000,000	Maximum coverage provided by the underling reinsurer is 9,000,000 x 1,000,000, therefore the casualty clash-reinsurance will cover 5m x10m	$5,000,000

(b) Example of Excess of Original Policy Limit Claim

Smith & Smith CPA's is a certified public accounting firm which has an errors and omissions insurance policy with Neptune Insurance Company for a limit of 10,000,000. A claim is brought against Smith & Smith CPA's for their alleged errors when they performed an audit of the Millwood Bank. Shareholder Williams of Millwood Bank says he relied on the audit, included in the private placement when he invested in the shares of Millwood Bank, and he now has losses totaling $15,000,000. He sues Smith & Smith CPA's for $15,000,000. Smith & Smith CPA's urges Neptune Insurance Company to try to settle the claim for the full policy limit of 10,000,000 and make this offer to shareholder Williams, but Neptune decides not to settle and defends the claim. Eventually a jury awards the entire $15,000,000 to shareholder Williams. Hence, Smith & Smith CPA's have an award against them greater than their insurance policy limit of 10,00,000. If Neptune had made a full policy limit offer (10,000,000) to Smith & Smith CPA's there was the possibility that shareholder Williams would have accepted it and they would not be in the predicament they are now in. This is an award in excess of the original policy limit and Smith & Smith CPA's will demand Neptune pay the entire $15,000,000 and if it does not, it will sue Neptune Insurance Company. After a lengthy evaluation of the entire matter and in consultation with its underling reinsurers and its casualty clash-reinsurer, Neptune decides it has no choice but to pay the $15,000,000.

Excess of Original Reinsurance Policy Limit Claim	***Underlying Reinsurance Coverage***	***Casualty Clash-Covers***
$15,000,000	Maximum underlying reinsurance will pay $10,000,000.	$5,000,000

(c) Example of a Runaway Loss Adjustment Claim

G&A Railroad Company has a commercial general liability insurance policy with a policy limit of $10 million from Neptune Insurance Company. Ash Memorial Hospital says on 2/16/06 a pipe ruptured in a terminal which stored oil located near the hospital and is owned by G&A Railroad. It says its underground water supply was contaminated, creating numerous claims. 32 patients have filed 32 individual lawsuits against Ash Memorial Hospital, which in turn has sued G&A Railroad. The demand for all the claims exceed $20 million and it is not considerate a class-action suit; all the claims were individually filed. Neptune Insurance Company is defending the claims; casualty clash-reinsurance would cover the loss adjustment expenses 10,000,000 excess of 10,000,000.

	All claims combined related to defending G&A Railroad Claim Reserved	Clash-Reinsurance Covers
Various Claims Numbers	$20,000,000 Neptune's reinsurance covers up to $10,000,000 each occurrence	$10,000,000

Example (4) **Protecting Against Claims Exceeding The Reinsured- Company's Vertical Reinsurance Program When an Reinsured- Company's Workers Compensation (Part A) Policies Issued With Statutory (Unlimited) Limits.** One Policy Can Be Involved; Two or More Claimants or Maximum Any one Life Warranty is in the Underlying Reinsurance.

Beige Plastics, Inc. has a worker compensation and employment liability insurance policy with Neptune Insurance Company. A serious explosion occurs on 4/4/01 injuring 10 workers. The total amount of all claims reserve is $18,000,000. Casualty clash-reinsurance, would cover 8,000,000 excess of the underlying reinsurance of 10,000,000.

	All claims combined related to the 4/4/01 accident Claim Reserved	Clash-Reinsurance Covers
Various Claims Numbers	$18,000,000 Neptune's reinsurance covers up to $10,000,000 each occurrence	$8,000,000

Example (5) **Protecting Against Claims, Exceeding the Reinsured- Company's Vertical Reinsurance Program When an Reinsured- Company's Limits From one policy is Stacked by State Statute for Automobile Limits From Uninsured Motorist (UM) and Underinsured Motorist (UIM).**

Neptune Insurance Company insures Coast to Coast Truckers, Inc. with a commercial automobile policy with a limit of liability of 1,000,000 for UM/UIM. Coast to Coast Truckers, Inc., has a fleet of twenty (20) vehicles and is in states where stacking is allowed. Their policy would have potential total UM/UIM limits of $20 million. A Coast to Coast Truckers, Inc. vehicle collides with a bus and they are found negligent and liable for a total settlement of $14 million. Underlying reinsurance and retention respond up to $10 million, clash responds for $4 million.

PLEASE NOTE

In the preceding examples, an extra contractual obligation (ECO) claim and excess of original policy limits (XPL) claim are covered in the underlying reinsurance treaties 100% up to the reinsurer's limit and in addition to the loss. Other treaties may have other arrangements, which would affect how a casualty clash-reinsurance responds.

EXAMPLES OF CASUALTY INSURANCE LIKELY TO BE INVOLVED IN PURE CLASH CLAIMS (TWO OR MORE POLICIES CLASHING TOGETHER).

(1) General liability and general liability
(2) Automobile liability and automobile liability
(3) Worker's compensation and worker's compensation
(4) General liability and automobile liability
(5) General liability and worker's compensation
(6) Automobile liability and worker's compensation

Almost any type of casualty insurance can be involved in clash claims; we only provided a few examples.

PURE CASUALTY CLASH-REINSURANCE

The original concept of casualty clash-reinsurance is to provide reinsurance for those rare claims, which come about when two or more of the company's policies "come together" in the same common casualty loss occurrence.

Figure 1-1

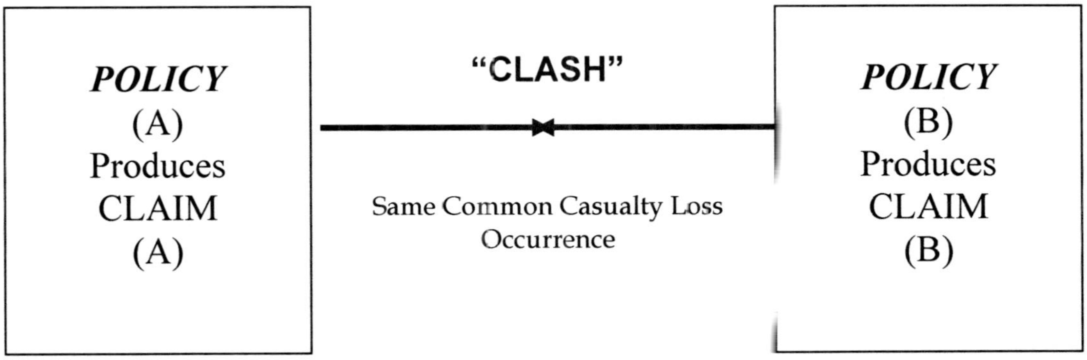

PURPOSE OF CASUALTY CLASH-REINSURANCE

(1) Provides reinsurance protection for the Reinsured- Company's retention (sideways reinsurance) as illustrated in Figure 1-1 (previous page).

(2) Provides additional reinsurance protection for the Reinsured- Company's vertical reinsurance program illustrated Figure 1-2.

Figure 1-2

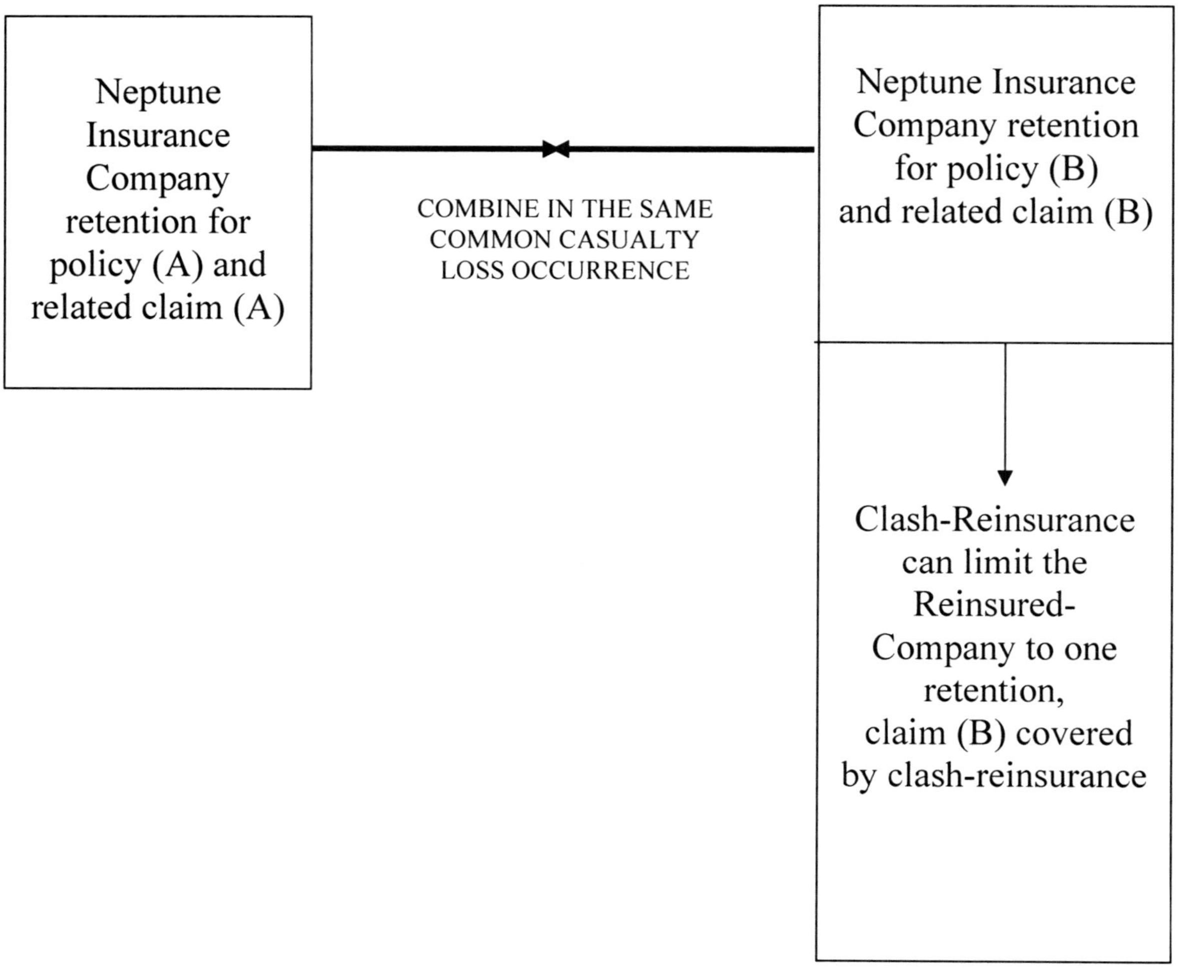

Section 16

QUOTA SHARE TREATY REINSURANCE

ASPECTS OF A QUOTA SHARE TREATY

The Reinsured- Company cedes to the reinsurer a fixed percentage of its premium (less a *ceding commission* which covers those expenses incurred by the insurer to acquire the original premium) and the same fixed percentage of its losses paid, loss reserves, incurred but not reported (IBNR) and unearned premium reserve.

A FURTHER LOOK AT THE PREMIUM CEDED TO THE REINSURER

When a policy is written the Reinsured- Company receives the original premium less commissions paid to a broker or agent. Later, the Reinsured- Company will have to pay premium taxes, board and bureau fees, and its own administrative costs. Let's say these expenses add up to 30%. These expenses must be deducted from the premium ceded to the reinsurer because the reinsurer must accept the same deductions as the Reinsured- Company. So if it receives 70 cents on a dollar, the reinsurer receives 70 cents on a dollar. Collectively, these expenses deducted from premiums ceded to the reinsurer are called a *ceding commission.* Additionally, the reinsurer may allow the Reinsured- Company a *bonus or overriding commission.* If the expenses add up to 30% and if there was an overriding commission of 5% then a total of 35% *(ceding commission)* would be deducted. That 5% in effect is pure profit to the insurer, *which is used to reduce the expenses it retains after reinsurance.*

Example (1)

80/20 Quota Share Treaty – 80% Goes to the Reinsurer and 20% is retained by the Insurer

Reinsured- Company Actual Expense	30.00%
Bonus or Override	5.00%
Ceding Commission (reinsurer is allowing a 35% deduction from premiums ceded to them).	35.00%

The Reinsured- Company cedes to the reinsurer 80% of its original gross net premium *less the 35% ceding commission*, and 80% of its losses paid, 80% of its loss reserves, 80% of its incurred but not reported (IBNR) and 80% of its unearned premium reserve.

Original Gross Written Premium	20,000,000
80% to reinsurer	16,000,000
Less ceding commission (35%)	5,600,000
Net ceded to reinsurer	10,400,000

Gross Losses Paid	1,000,000
80% ceded to reinsurer	800,000

Gross Losses Paid	3,000,000
80% ceded to reinsurer	2,400,000

Gross Unearned Premium Reserve	8,000,000
80% ceded to reinsurer	6,400,000

Gross Incurred But Not Reported (IBNR)	2,000,000
80% ceded to reinsurer	1,600,000

Example (1)

Internal Workings of a Quota Share

80/20 QUOTA SHARE TREATY

Premium and Expense Flow

Reinsured Company		Reinsurer		Reinsured- Company after Reinsurance	
100% Original Gross Written Premium	100 % Gross Actual Expenses	80% Original Gross Written Premium	80% Gross Actual Expenses	Retains 20% of Original Gross Written Premium	Retains 20% of Gross Actual Expense
	30% of the Gross Written Premium		Allows bonus or override commission 5% Total ceding commission 35%		Receives a 5% bonus or override commission which is used to reduce its expenses.

Loss Flow

Reinsured-Company	Reinsurer	Reinsured-Company after Reinsurance
100% Gross Loss	Responsible for 80% of gross loss	Responsible for 20% of gross loss

Example (1) Continued
Internal Working's of a Quota Share

80/20 QUOTA SHARE TREATY
80% GOES TO THE REINSURER, 20% RETAINED BY THE REINSURED COMPANY

Underwriting Year 2009

	100%	Ceded to Reinsurer 80%	Reinsured Company Retains 20%
Gross Written Premium (GWP)	20,000,000	16,000,000	4,000,000
Percentage of Expenses	30%	30%	30%
Gross Expenses	6,000,000	4,800,000	1,200,000
		Override allowed by reinsurer, 5% of 16,000,000. Reinsurers expenses go up 800,000	Override allowed by reinsurer, 5% of 16,000,000. Reinsured company expenses goes down 800,000
Total Expenses net	6,000,000	5,600,000	400,000
Net	$14,000,000	$10,400,000	$3,600,000

Expense Ratio

GWP to Expenses	30%	35%	10.0% expense ratio 400,000 / 4,000,000

Example (1) Continued

Internal Working's of a Quota Share

HOW A QUOTA SHARE TREATY CAN REDUCE A REINSURED- COMPANY EXPENSE RATIO

<u>80/20 QUOTA SHARE TREATY</u>

If a reinsurer is willing to reimburse an insurer for expenses in *"excess"* of the expenses it incurred to acquire the business, it's a *"bonus"* which then can be used to *lower the expenses it retains.*

Reinsured- Company Actual Expense	30.00%
Ceding Commission	<u>35.00%</u>
(reinsurer is allowing 35% deducted from premiums ceded to them)	
Bonus or Override	5.00%

In our example, the 80/20 Quota Share drastically reduced the Reinsured- Company's expense ratio from 30% to 10% because 80% of the premium and related expenses are ceded to the reinsurer. This leaves 20% of the premium and related expenses (still 30%) but the reinsurer contributes back to the Reinsured- Company a *bonus or override* of 5% on the business it accepted (carried away). Since the Reinsured- Company is left with a small premium base, the 5% or $800,000, has a big impact.

QUOTA SHARE VS. EXCESS OF LOSS

Quota Share

- *Sharing Arrangement*
  Reinsurer pays claims along with insurer from first dollar, based upon and agreed percentage (i.e. 80/20). There is no reinsurance rate needed to determine the reinsurance premium.
- The ceding Reinsured- Company experience will be almost identical to the reinsurers. There is a close relationship between the ceding Reinsured- Company and its reinsurer. A quota share reinsurer may want to be involved in how business is underwritten.
- Small insurance companies with limited surplus may need a quota share to issue higher limit policy and to protect their surplus.
- More premiums are paid to the reinsurer which reduces investment income opportunities for the insurer
- The Reinsured- Company receives a ceding commission, which is usually above the actual expenses incurred to acquire the business, and that bonus (override commission) is used to reduce its expense ratio.
- If you weren't certain about the profitability of the business to be written, want to be conservative, or want to move to the sidelines in a soft market (average policy premiums declining) you could use a quota share.

Excess of Loss

- *Excess Arrangement*
  Claims are paid by the reinsurer on an excess basis, which means the reinsurer is responsible for the larger claims. There is a reinsurance rate which determines the reinsurance premium.
- The reinsurers experience is not directly related to the ceding reinsured- company. Their relationship is further apart with an excess of loss reinsurance treaty. An excess of loss reinsurer is less likely to be involved in the underwriting.
- Major insurance companies usually buy excess of loss reinsurance because they are able to handle large retentions.
- Less premiums are paid to the reinsurer, therefore more cash available to the Reinsured- Company for investment income.
- Usually no ceding commission for the Reinsured- Company, therefore no benefit to their expense ratio.
- Reinsurer pays claims excess of a certain attachment point:
  (For the treaty 1,500,000 x 500,000 the attachment point is 500,000.)
- If you were very certain the business was going to be profitable, you would want to prudently retain as much as possible, which would lead you to Excess of Loss, assuming you had the proper surplus.

Example (2)

80/20 QUOTA SHARE
Maximum Policy 5,000,000

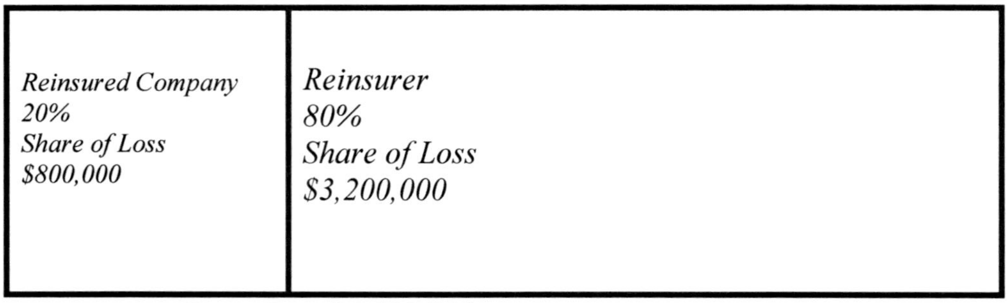

Gross Loss $4,000,000

The Reinsured- Company and Reinsurer are sharing the claims from first dollar, therefore reinsurance cost will be greater.

EXCESS OF LOSS
Maximum Policy 5,000,000

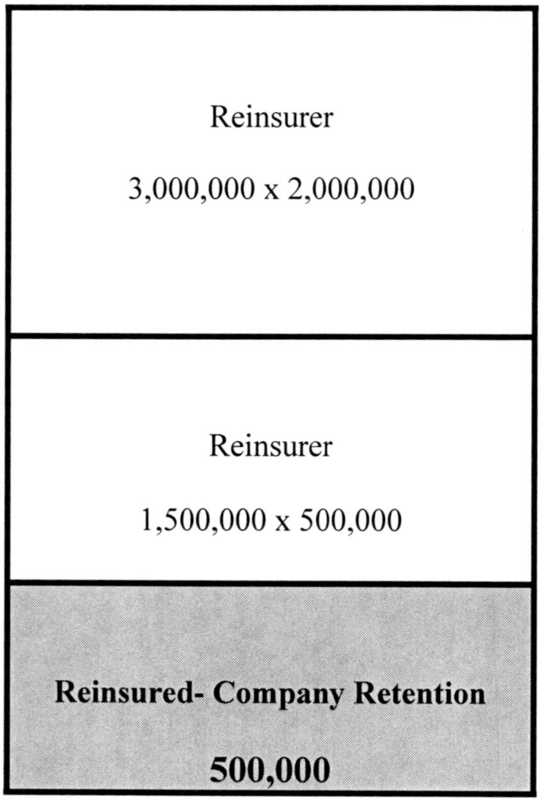

Example (2) Continued

HOW LOSSES ARE HANDLED
EXCESS OF LOSS
VS.
80/20 QUOTA SHARE

TWO TREATIES
1,500,000 XS 500,000
3,000,000 XS 2,000,000

	EXCESS OF LOSS REINSURED- COMPANY RETENTION 500,000				80/20 QUOTA SHARE REINSURED - COMPANY RETENTION 20%	
Example	**Ground Up Loss**	**Reinsured Company Pays First 500,000**	**Reinsurer Pays Excess of 500,000 1,500,000 x 500,000**	**Reinsurer Pays Excess of 2,000,000 3,000,000 x 2,000,000**	**Reinsured Company Pays 20%**	**Reinsurer Pays 80%**
#1	25,000	25,000	0	0	5,000	20,000
#2	50,000	50,000	0	0	10,000	40,000
#3	100,000	100,000	0	0	20,000	80,000
#4	250,000	250,000	0	0	50,000	200,000
#5	500,000	500,000	0	0	100,000	400,000
#6	750,000	750,000	250,000	0	150,000	600,000
#7	1,000,000	1,000,000	500,000	0	200,000	800,000
#8	2,000,000	2,000,000	1,500,000	0	400,000	1,600,000
#9	3,000,000	3,000,000	1,500,000	1,000,000	600,000	2,400,000
#10	4,000,000	4,000,000	1,500,000	2,000,000	800,000	3,200,000
#11	5,000,000	5,000,000	1,500,000	3,000,000	1,000,000	4,000,000

CEDING COMMISSION

Quota Share treaties can have a fixed ceding commission such as 30% or 32.5% or a sliding scale commission or a more precise term would be a sliding scale ceding commission. All this means is the ceding commission "slides" up or down depending on the reinsurer's loss experience with the treaty. In this way, the Reinsured- Company is automatically rewarded by the reinsurer for its good experience with a higher ceding commission and penalized for poor experience. If the reinsurer's loss ratio is low, the ceding commission slides up allowing the Reinsured- Company a higher ceding commission. If the reinsurer's loss ratio is high, the ceding commission slides down. All treaties with this type of arrangement will have a minimum and maximum ceding commission. *The reinsurer will propose a formula based on the expenses for the business being ceded and the expected loss ratio.*

Example (1):
80/20 Quota Share Treaty – Each Year Stands Alone

SLIDING SCALE CEDING COMMISSION

Sliding Scale Ceding Commission Schedule	
Minimum	25.0%
Provisional	30.0%
Maximum	40.0%

Formula

Provisional sliding scale ceding commission is 30.0% and decreases 0.5% for each 1.0% increase in the reinsurers' loss ratio above 60.0%. Minimum sliding scale ceding commission 25.0%for a loss ratio 70.0% or higher.

Provisional sliding scale ceding commission 30.0% and increases 0.5% for each 1.0% reduction in the loss ratio below 60.0%. Maximum sliding scale ceding commission 40.0% for a reinsurers loss ratio 40.0% or lower.

Sliding Scale Ceding Commission
The ceding commission can *slide* between the minimum 25.0% and a maximum 40.0% based on the formula.

Loss Ratio
The loss ratio affecting the slide of the ceding commission is between 70.0% and 40.0%

Decreases ← → Increases

Loss Ratio

40	41	42	43	44	45	46	47	48	49	50	51	52	53	54	55	56	57	58	59	60	61	62	63	64	65	66	67	68	69	70

Increases ← Provisional → Decreases

Sliding Scale Ceding Commission

40.0	39.5	39.0	38.5	38.0	37.5	37.0	36.5	36.0	35.5	35.0	34.5	34.0	33.5	33.0	32.5	32.0	31.5	31.0	30.5	30.0	29.5	29.0	28.5	28.0	27.5	27.0	26.5	26.0	25.5	25.0

Provisional 30.0% increases 0.5% for each 1.0% reduction in the loss ratio below 60.0%

Provisional 30.0% decreases 0.5% for each 1.0% increase in the loss ratio above 60.0%

Example (1) Con't:
80/20 Quota Share Treaty – Each Year Stands Alone

SLIDING SCALE CEDING COMMISSION

Year	*Earned Premium*	*Incurred Losses*	*Loss Ratio*	*Provisional Sliding Scale Commission*	*Ultimate Sliding Scale Commission*
(1)	21,041,994	9,468,898	45.0%	30.0%	37.5%
(2)	36,653,796	11,729,215	32.0%	30.0%	40.0%
(3)	42,071,311	22,297,794	53.0%	30.0%	33.5%

Example (2):
80/20 Quota Share Treaty Cumulative Basis, Each Year is added to the Previous Year

SLIDING SCALE CEDING COMMISSION

Sliding Scale Ceding Commission Schedule	
Minimum	25.0%
Provisional	30.0%
Maximum	40.0%

Formula

Provisional sliding scale ceding commission is 30.0% and decreases 1.0% for each 1.0% increase in the reinsurers' loss ratio above 60.0%. Minimum sliding scale ceding commission 25.0% for a loss ratio 70.0% or higher.

Provisional sliding scale ceding commission 30.0% and increases 0.5% for each 1.0% reduction in the loss ratio below 60.0%. Maximum sliding scale ceding commission 40.0% for a reinsurer's loss ratio 45.0% or lower.

Sliding Scale Ceding Commission
The ceding commission can *slide* between the minimum 25.0% and a maximum 40.0% based on the formula.

Decreases ← → Increases

Loss Ratio

40	41	42	43	44	45	46	47	48	49	50	51	52	53	54	55	56	57	58	59	60	61	62	63	64	65	66	67	68	69	70

Increases ← Provisional → Decreases

Sliding Scale Ceding Commission

40.0	39.5	39.0	38.5	38.0	37.5	37.0	36.5	36.0	35.5	35.0	34.5	34.0	33.5	33.0	32.5	32.0	31.5	31.0	30.5	30.0	29.5	29.0	28.5	28.0	27.5	27.0	26.5	26.0	25.5	25.0

Provisional 30.0% increases 0.5% for each 1.0% reduction in the loss ratio below 60.0%

Provisional 30.0% decreases 0.5% for each 1.0% increase in the loss ratio above 60.0%

Example (2) Con't:
80/20 Quota Share Treaty Cumulative Basis, Each Year is Added to the Previous Year

SLIDING SCALE CEDING COMMISSION

Year	Earned Premium	Incurred Losses	Cumulative Loss Ratio	Provisional Sliding Scale Commission	Ultimate Sliding Scale Commission
(1)	19,386,712	8,530,153	44.0%	30.0%	38.0%
(2)	20,981,603	9,905,589			
Years (1) & (2) Combined	40,968,315	18,435,742	45.0%	30.0%	37.5%

Example (3):

AN UNFAVORABLE LOSS RATIO FOR THE REINSURER MEANS LESS CEDING *<u>COMMISSION TO THE REINSURED-COMPANY</u>*

Loss Ratio	Sliding Scale Ceding Commission
70	25
69	26
68	27
67	28
66	29
65	30
64	31
63	32
62	33
61	34
60	35
59	36
58	
57	
56	
55	
54	

USING A QUOTA SHARE TREATY TO REDUCE THE REINSURED COMPANY'S EXPENSE RATIO ON ITS STATUATORY ANNUAL STATEMENT

A Quota Share Treaty can reduce a Reinsured- Company's expense ratio on the statutory annual statement. Here is how it can be done. If a ceding insurer can receive a ceding commission greater than its actual expense, then its expense ratio will be reduced. Let's say the insurer's actual expenses are 35% but it is able to get a ceding commission of 38%. In effect, the reinsurer is reimbursing the insurer for an amount over and above its actual expenses.

Actual Expenses *(Percent of Premium)*	35%
Ceding Commission	38%
Net Gain *(Bonus or Override)*	3%

Treaty 90/10 Quota Share

Original Gross Net Written Premium:	20,000,000
Ceded to Reinsurers (at 90%):	18,000,000
Less ceding commission for insurer (38% of 18,000,000):	6,840,000
Net to reinsurer:	11,160,000

Reinsured Company's Annual Statement

Original Gross Net Written Premium:	20,000,000
Net Written After Reinsurance:	2,000,000
Net Expenses:	160,000
Expense Ratio:	8%
(Expenses to Net Written 160,000/2,000,000)	

Summary:

	Before Reinsurance	Reinsured	Net After Reinsurance
Gross Written Premium	20,000,000	18,000,000	2,000,000
Gross Expense	7,000,000	6,840,000	160,000
Expense Ratio	35%	38%	8%

Notes:

(1) Original Gross Net Written Premium means the original premium received by the insurer less return and cancellation premium.

(2) In the example above, the reinsurer reimburses the insured for $540,000 (3% of 18,000,000) it did not incur in expenses. This amount is then used by the insured to *reduce its expenses,* therefore its *expense ratio is reduced.*

WHAT HAPPENS IF A CEDING COMMISSION DOES NOT COVER THE REINSURED- COMPANY'S ACTUAL EXPENSE?

The Reinsured- Company will be penalized with a higher expense ratio.

80/20 Quota Share Treaty

100% Original Gross Net Written Premium	Reinsured- Company 100% Actual Expense	20% Original Gross Net Written Premium Retained By Reinsured- Company	Reinsured- Company Retained Expenses	Reinsured-Company Ultimate Expense Ratio After Reinsurance
	32.5%			
10,000,000	3,250,000	2,000,000	850,000	42.5%
			3,250,000 less ceded to reinsurer 2,400,000	Unacceptably High
				850,000 divided by 2,000,000

(Expenses Retained) (Premium Retained)

80% Ceded To Reinsurer
A 30% Ceding Commission reimbursing the Reinsured- Company for their expenses inadequate.

$8,000,000 x 30.0% = $2,400,000

Actual break-even expense ration is 32.5% or $2,600,000. The short-fall is 2.5% or $200,000.

EXAMPLES OF REINSURANCE PROGRAMS FOR REINSURED- COMPANY (A)

Reinsured- Company (A)
Surplus $50,000,000
Maximum Policy Limit 10,000,000

(I) Combing a Quota Share With Excess of Loss

Plan (1)

(a) 80/20 Quota Share first 1,000,000. Reinsured- Company retains 20% up to first 1,000,000 or 200,000

(b) Excess of Loss above the first 1,000,000
Layers: 4,000,000 x 1,000,000
5,000,000 x 5,000,000

Plan (2)

(a) 80/20 Quota Share first 5,000,000. Reinsured- Company retains 20% up to first 5,000,000 or 1,000,000

(b) Excess of Loss above the first 5,000,000
Layer: 5,000,000 x 5,000,000

(II) Quota Share the entire 10,000,000
80/20 Quota Share entire 10,000,000. Reinsured- Company retains 20% up to 10,000,000 or 2,000,000

(III) Excess of Loss the entire 10,000,000
Reinsured- Company retains first 500,000
Layers: 1,500,000 x 500,000 retention
3,000,000 x 2,000,000
5,000,000 x 5,000,000

Alternatively Reinsured- Company retains first 1,000,000
Layers: 1,000,000 x 1,000,000 retention
4,000,000 x 1,000,000

AN IDEA FOR A SOFT INSURANCE MARKET

One way to deal with uncertainties of the insurance market place is to Quota Share your business with a reinsurer.

80/20 Quota Share (80% for the reinsurer, 20% retained by the Reinsured- Company), you are passing 4/5th of the soft market to the reinsurer, in effect you are moving to the sidelines.

With 90/10 Quota Share you are passing 9/10th to the reinsurer.

- One of the features of a Quota Share is the reinsurer usually will reimburse the ceding company in "excess" of the expenses it incurred to acquire the business. It's a bonus which then can be used to lower the ceding company's expenses it retains.

Reinsured- Company's Actual Expense	*20.0%*	*$2,000,000*
Reinsurer Reimburses Reinsured- Company	*25.0%*	*$2,500,000*
Bonus of Override for the Reinsured- Company's	*5.0%*	*$500,000*

- Under a Quota Share you probably would not need to buy facultative reinsurance.

- The disadvantage of a Quota Share is your investment income opportunities are basically gone, additionally, if you need current dollars to pay old claims, those dollars won't be available.

AN AREA OF POSSIBLE CONFUSION

If a Reinsured- Company has a 95/5 quota share treaty it should be covered by the Reinsurer 100% (in respect to its 95% share). If the maximum policy limit to be covered is $1,000,000, then the share for the Reinsurer is $950,000. In other words, the Reinsurer accepts 100% of 95%.

Example
Mason Insurance Company 95/5 quota share treaty.

(1) The cover note and contract signed by the Reinsurer should show coverage as: 100% of 95%

(2) Mason cedes to the Reinsurer 95% of the premiums less a ceding commission. The Reinsurer is responsible for 95% of the loss coming within the scope of the treaty.

Section 17

DEDUCTIONS FROM PREMIUM

We present this information because there will be times the Reinsured- Company and reinsurer must agree on which expenses are allowed to be deducted from a premium.

Directly Related to Original Premium

- Acquisition costs to acquire business such as commissions to agents and brokers.
- Return premiums or cancellation premiums.

Governmental Expenses

- State premium taxes
- Fire brigade charges
- State assigned risk charges
- State guaranty funds
- State workers compensation residual market charges
- State WC second injury fund assessments

Association Expenses

- Boards and bureau fees

Service Provider Expenses

- Auditing fees for CPAs
- Actuarial fees
- Captive management fees (if a captive is involved)
- Letter of credit fees for bank

Other Expenses

- Home office expenses
- Fees to association for marketing or an endorsement of the insurer.
- Override commission
- Loss control expenses
- Engineering costs or inspection costs if insured is visited
- Premium credit for insured
- Dividend returned to insured
- Policy issuing fees (if a front company is involved)

Reinsurance Costs

- Treaty and facultative reinsurance premiums

Losses

- Losses paid
- Losses reserved
- Allocated loss adjustment expenses paid
- Allocated loss adjustment expenses reserved

Section 18

FACULTATIVE REINSURANCE AND TERMS

This area of reinsurance has its own separate underwriters and its own terms.

Facultative Reinsurance Term:	**Equivalent Treaty Reinsurance Term:**
Part of Facultative underwriters use the term "part of" which is abbreviated as (P/O) and its equivalent in treaty reinsurance is quota share. 5,000,000 part of 25,000,000 excess of 10,000,000 (Often written as 5M P/O 25M x 10M) The facultative reinsurer is taking a 20% quota share participation (5,000,000) in the 25M x 10M layer.	Quota share Facultative 5M P/O 25M x 10M, the equivalent term in treaty reinsurance is an 80/20 quota share on a specific risk excess of 10M.
Contributing Excess or Contributing Excess of Loss Reinsurance is from the first dollar of the policy being reinsured. i.e., 1 million part of 5 million in lead umbrella excess primary (1M P/O 5M x Primary). Contributing excess reinsurance is for the policy immediately above the primary or the first policy above the primary. The reinsurer therefore is contributing to the excess policy limit.	Excess of Loss The equivalent term of contributing excess in treaty reinsurance is excess of loss.
Buffer Layer Facultative Underwriters refer to the layer immediately above the working layer as the buffer layer. **Example:** Working layer 250,000 x 250,000 Buffer layer 500,000 x 500,000 Catastrophe layer 1,000,000 x 1,000,000	Middle Layer Treaty reinsurers may also refer to the layer just above the working layer as a buffer layer.

PREMIUM PER MILLION

Facultative underwriters usually talk in terms of *premium per million.*

If *100 million of reinsurance limits* has total premiums of *$600,000,* what is the *premium per million*?

TO ARRIVE AT THE PREMIUM PER MILLION

Step (1) How many "*one millions*" do we have which make up the *100 million limit.*

Reinsurance Limits	
100,000,000 ÷ 1,000,000 = *100*	*Divide 100 million by 1,000,000*

Step (2)

Reinsurance Premium	
$600,000 ÷ *100* = $6,000 (Per million)	*Divide $600,000 by 100*

SAMPLE FORM FOR SUBMISSION

FACULTATIVE REINSURANCE SUBMISSION

(I) Background

Reinsured- Company & Location:

Effective:

Reinsured- Company States of Operation:

Current Carrier:

Description of Insured's Operations:

(II) Insurance Information

Line of Insurance:

Policy Form (i.e. occurrence, claims made):

RETROACTIVE DATE (IF CLAIMS MADE FORM):

DEFENSE COSTS (WITHIN THE LIMIT OR OUTSIDE THE LIMIT):
Deductible:
Self Insured Retention:

Policy Limit:

Insurance Premium Quote:

Claims Past (5) Years:

(III) Reinsurance Information

Reinsured- Company:

Facultative Reinsurance Needed:

Facultative Reinsurance Term:

Ceding Commission:

Suggested Gross Reinsurance Premium:
Ceding Commission:
Net Reinsurance Premium:

Reinsurance Intermediary Brokerage:

If Reinsurance Quote is Accepted Reinsured Shall Furnish:

1. Policy number (immediately)
2. Policy (as soon as possible)
3. Application (as soon as possible)

(IV) NOTES

UNIFORM FACULTATIVE
CERTIFICATE OF REINSURANCE

In order to complete a facultative reinsurance placement, it often requires several reinsurers. Each will issue its own certificate of reinsurance which will have a reinsuring agreement and conditions enumerated in the certificate (almost always found in small print behind the certificate). A uniform facultative certificate of reinsurance, like the one we present in the following pages, is an attempt to get all reinsurers to participate on the same terms and conditions.

SAMPLE

UNIFORM FACULTATIVE
CERTIFICATE OF REINSURANCE
BETWEEN

Mason Insurance Company
Carson City, NV
(Ceding Insurer hereinafter referred to as the "Company")

AND
SUBSCRIBING REINSURER
(Hereinafter referred to as the "Reinsurer")

Effective: April 1, 2011

Reference #:

UNIFORM FACULTATIVE
CERTIFICATE OF REINSURANCE

INSURANCE INFORMATION

DECLARATIONS

ITEM		
(1)	**INSURED AND HOME OFFICE ADDRESS**	GREENWICH PIPELINE INDUSTRIAL COMPANY 555 Walker Boulevard Greenwich, CT 06830
(2)	**CEDING INSURER (Hereinafter referred to as the "Company"**	Mason Insurance Company

CEDING COMPANY POLICY NUMBER #809611
(Reinsured Company Policy Attached)

Type of Insurance:	Umbrella Liability
Type of Policy:	Occurrence
Retroactive Date:	Not Applicable

POLICY EFFECTIVE AND TERM
April 1, 2011 – April 1, 2012 (12 months)

POLICY LIMIT
5,000,000 Each occurrence
5,000,000 In the aggregate where applicable

UNDERLYING PRIMARY POLICIES/SIR OR DEDUCTIBLES

Underlying Insurance Policies	
Commercial General Liability	1,000,000 Limit
Auto Liability	1,000,000 Limit
Employers Liability	500,000 Limit
Self Insured Retentions	
None	
Deductibles	
Commercial General Liability	25,000 each claim
Auto Liability	10,000 each claim
Employers Liability	None

(3)	**CEDING COMPANY NET RETENTION**	250,000 Each occurrence 250,000 Aggregate where applicable

(4)	**SUBSCRIBING REINSURER'S PARTICIPATION**	2,500,000 each occurrence/2,500,000 aggregate where applicable P/O 5,000,000 each occurrence/5,000,000 aggregate where applicable excess underlying 1,000,000 each occurrence, in respect to employers liability 500,000/1,000,000 aggregate where applicable, in respect to employers liability 500,000
(5)	**100% REINSURANCE LAYER**	5,000,000 each occurrence/5,000,000 aggregate where applicable excess of 1,000,000 each occurrence, in respect to employers liability 500,000/1,000,000 aggregate where applicable, in respect to employers liability 500,000
(6)	**LOSS ADJUSTMENT EXPENSES**	See Reinsuring Agreements and Conditions (D)
(7)	**REINSURED COMPANY**	Mason Insurance Company Carson City, NV
		EFFECTIVE AND TERM 12:01 a.m. Eastern Standard Time, April 1, 2011 to April 1, 2012
		TYPE OF REINSURANCE Contributing excess of loss
(8)	**CLAIMS REPORTING TO REINSURER**	See Reinsuring Agreements and Conditions (C)
(9)	**SUBSCRIBING REINSURER'S PREMIUMS**	Payable annually at inception, within 30 days per schedule of premium payments.
(10)	**CEDING COMMISSION**	20%
(11)	**REINSURANCE INTERMEDIARY**	ABC Reinsurance Intermediary, Inc. 10 ABC Street Plainville, CT
(12)	**REINSURANCE INTERMEDIARY BROKERAGE**	5.0 % of premium ceded to facultative reinsurer

SUBSCRIBING REINSURER

IN WITNESS WHEREOF, the Reinsurer has caused this Certificate to be executed and attested and it shall become valid and binding when signed by a duly authorized representative.

Signed In:

City	State or Country
Month, Day	Year

Subscribing Reinsurer

Signature/Title

SCHEDULE OF REINSURANCE PREMIUM PAYMENTS

At 100% Share

Layer	*Annual Reinsurance Premium*
5,000,000 each occurrence/5,000,000 aggregate where applicable excess of 1,000,000 each occurrence, in respect to employers liability 500,000/1,000,000 aggregate where applicable, in respect to employers liability 500,000	$172,500

At Reinsurer Share

Layer	*Annual Reinsurance Premium*
2,500,000 each occurrence/2,500,000 aggregate where applicable P/O 5,000,000 each occurrence/5,000,000 aggregate where applicable excess underlying 1,000,000 each occurrence, in respect to employers liability 500,000/1,000,000 aggregate where applicable, in respect to employers liability 500,000	$86,250

REINSURED COMPANY POLICY
Item (2) of Insurance Information Declarations

Attached to and made part herein of this Uniform Facultative Certificate of Reinsurance is the Reinsured- Company's policy and endorsements.

This sample certificate would require a jacket of detailing. Terms and conditions of the facultative reinsurance. We do not present one here.

Section 19

COMMERCIAL INSURANCE – COMMON CHARACTERISTICS/TYPES

CONCEPT OF INDEMNITY

All insurance policies are contracts and more specifically contracts of indemnity. All this means is the insurer will reimburse the policyholder for its loss in an effort to make the policyholder whole again. However, the policyholder is not entitled to make a profit from the reimbursement.

CONCEPT OF INSURANCE PREMIUM

When an insured buys an insurance policy they are paying a relatively small amount of known premium to cover losses from events, accidents, or occurrences which could be much greater.

PROPERTY INSURANCE POLICIES

These are "first party" policies which means the policyholder gets reimbursed from its insurer for the loss it suffers. Property insurance policies were the first to be developed.

THE DEVELOPMENT OF LIABILITY INSURANCE POLICIES CAN LEADS TO A GREATER UNDERSTANDING OF ALL LIABILITY POLICIES

Once you understand how liability policies come about you will be able to make sense of the dozens and dozens of different and unique liability policies now available.

The concept of liability and compensating injured individuals originated in England during the Industrial Revolution between 1820 and 1880. Machines were becoming more and more prevalent. As a result, individuals were getting hurt and wanted to be compensated. The idea that an individual injured by the wrongful act of another is entitled to compensation evolved from common law. Eventually insurance companies developed a liability policy to protect against these types of accidents. These first policies can be referred to as "general" liability policies. It is from this all other liability policies have developed.

A physician professional liability policy is a general liability policy refitted to the specific needs of the physician; their specific liability is from patients claiming faulty medical treatment. An errors and omissions liability policy purchased by an accounting firm is for their unique liabilities, which are inaccuracies during their auditing process a third party relied upon which caused damages to them. A directors and officers liability policy is a liability policy for the directors and officers of a corporation for their specific liability exposure.

The point we are making is all liability policies stemmed from the original "general liability policy" and they all have a common thread running through them.

The buyer of this type of insurance is buying protection (as enumerated in the policy) from legal actions brought from others alleging damages caused by the policyholder's negligence. The policy provides a duty to defend the policyholder, and to pay amounts on behalf of the policyholder if found legally obligated to pay the other party.

HOW COMMERCIAL INSURANCE IS SOLD IN THE UNITED STATES

Commercial insurance is more complicated than personal lines insurance such as homeowners and auto. Therefore, it is usually sold by retail insurance agents throughout the United States. There are approximately 50,000 of these retail agents. Many of these agents are small and may have a contract to sell insurance for three or four insurers. In order to give them access to many more insurers, they may upstream their business to wholesale agents. These agents may represent many more insurers. The wholesaler therefore acquires business from a large group of independent retail insurance agents and will pass on this business to the many insurers it represents. They most likely will have their own retail insurance agency.

Program Manager or can be referred to as Program Administrator, Managing General Underwriter (MGU), Managing General Agency (MGA. These organizations enter into a contractual agreement with an insurer to allow them to write insurance on their behalf... as if they were the insurance company. The Program Manager produces the business, does the marketing, underwrites, issues policies, accounting & administration. They may or may not do claims handling, some states may prohibit claims handling. The Program Manager receives a percentage of the premium. The insurer may require them to take risk in their own underwriting. This could be accomplished in several ways. 1) The Program Manager participates in a captive insurance company that reinsurers the insurance company. 2) The commission received by the Program Manager could vary based on their underwriting results. Some states now require a Managing General Agency (MGA) state license.

COMMON PURPOSE OF ALL LIABILITY POLICIES

Another way of looking at liability policies is they all have the same common purpose which is to protect the policyholder from third party lawsuits. Each type of specialized liability policy will have its unique insuring agreement and set of exclusions. We are not saying all liability policies are alike; we are saying they all have the same common purpose.

Third Party Insurance

Liability insurance is sometimes referred to as third party.

- The *first party* is the policyholder
- The *second party* is the insurer
- The *third party* is the person or business bringing the legal action against the policyholder

TYPES OF COMMERCIAL INSURANCE

Surety Insurance	Abbreviation	Most Common Type of Policy Form
Performance Bond		Losses Discovered SAA
Bid Bond	-	Losses Discovered SAA
Contract Bond	-	Losses Discovered SAA
Payment Bond	-	Losses Discovered SAA
Public Official Bond	-	Losses Discovered SAA
Judicial Bond	-	
Fiduciary Bond	-	Losses Discovered SAA
License and Permit Bond	-	Losses Discovered SAA
Custom Bond / Miscellaneous Bond	-	Losses Discovered SAA
Completion Bond	-	Losses Discovered SAA

Fidelity Insurance	**Abbreviation**	**Most Common Type of Policy Form**
Financial Institution Bond Standard Form No. 24	FIB 24	Losses Discovered SAA

Crime Insurance	**Abbreviation**	**Most Common Type of Policy Form**
Burglary and Robbery Theft	- -	Losses Discovered, Losses Sustained ISO

Commercial Marine Liability Insurance	**Abbreviation**	**Most Common Type of Policy Form**
Protection and Indemnity	P&I	Occurrence London

Commercial Marine Property Insurance	**Abbreviation**	**Most Common Type of Policy Form**
Hull	-	Occurrence U.S. & London
Cargo	CGO	Occurrence U.S. & London
Physical Damage (Property Damage) on Offshore Platforms	PD	Occurrence U.S. & London Occurrence or Claims Made

Commercial Liability Insurance	**Abbreviation**	**Most Common Type of Policy Form**
Commercial General Liability	CGL	Occurrence ISO
Commercial Auto Liability	CA	Occurrence ISO
Directors & Officers Liability	D&O	Claims made Manuscript
Errors & Omissions Liability	E&O	Claims made Manuscript
Public Officials Liability	PO	Claims made Manuscript
Law Enforcement Liability	LE	Claims made Manuscript
Hospital Professional Liability	HPL	Claims made Manuscript
Physicians Professional Liability	PPL	Claims made Manuscript
Umbrella Liability	UMB	Occurrence Manuscript

Workers Compensation and Employers Liability	WC&EL	Occurrence NCCI
Fire	-	Occurrence ISO
Business Interpretation/Business Income	BI	Occurrence ISO
Inland Marine	IM	Occurrence ISO
Boiler and Machinery	B&M	Occurrence ISO
Livestock	-	Occurrence ISO
Construction/Builder's Risk	-	Occurrence ISO
Farm owners and Agriculture	-	Occurrence ISO
Difference in Conditions	DIC	Occurrence Manuscript
Political Risk	-	Occurrence London
War Risk	WR	Occurrence London

Notes:

(1) This list of commercial insurance consists only of the most widely used policies.

(2) Businesses engaged in oil & gas exploration and production, refining, pipelines, chemicals, mining, pharmaceuticals, and hazardous waste would most likely have CGL and umbrella liability policies issued on claims made basis.

(3) If there is a policy form available from ISO, NCCI or SAA, there may also be advisory rates available from these organizations.

A SAMPLE LISTING OF THE MANY SPECIFIC AND UNIQUE LIABILITY POLICIES

Investment Advisor Professional Liability
Lawyers Professional Liability
School District Accredited Asbestos Inspection & Management Planners Professional Liability
Data Processing Policy
Discrimination Errors & Omissions Liability
Petroleum Storage Tank Contractors Commercial General Liability
Employment Practices Liability
Asbestos Abatement Consultants Professional Liability
Claims-Made Liquor Liability
General Partners Liability & Partnership Reimbursement Policy
Claims-Made Completed Operations and Product Liability
D&O Liability and Company Reimbursement Coverage
Educators Legal Liability
Employee Benefits/ERISA Liability
Arbitrators and Mediators Professional Liability
Union Liability Insurance
Automobile Racing Liability
Business Errors and Omissions Liability
Fiduciary Liability
Architects and Engineers Professional Liability
Public Officials Legal Liability
Amusement Park Liability
Commercial Excess Liability
Environmental Engineers and Consultants Liability
Consultants Environmental Liability
Professional Liability Insurance Policy for Specified Medical Professions
Investment Company Asset Protection Liability
Pollution Clean-Up Policy
Medical Testing Laboratories Professional Liability
Real Estate Agents Errors & Omissions Liability
Bio-tech and Agri-Tech Trials and Products Liability
Specified Products and Completed Operations Liability
General Liability Program for Asbestos Removal Contractors
Independent Directors Liability
Specialty Errors & Omissions Liability
Pollution Legal Liability
School Leaders Errors and Omissions Liability
Travel Agents – Tour Operators Professional Liability
Investment Adviser Professional Liability
Lawyers Professional Liability
Discrimination Errors & Omissions Liability
Business Errors & Omissions Liability
Independent Directors Liability Policy
Union Liability Insurance
Public Legal Liability
Contractors Pollution Liability
Bankers Professional Liability
Coverage Plus Excess Liability
Railroad Protective Liability Form
Educators Liability
Real Estate Agents Errors and Omissions Liability
Medical Testing Laboratories Professional Liability
Police Professional Liability

Section 20

POLICY FORM: OCCURRENCE and CLAIMS MADE

OCCURRENCE POLICY FORM

For most occurrence forms, the bodily injury or property damage the policyholder is accused of causing (legally liable) must take place during the policy period and there is an unlimited time to bring the claim. Some states have a statute of limitation for certain types of claims. Once the insured is notified of a claim the insured is required to notify the insurer as soon as practicable.

CLAIMS MADE POLICIES / SIX (6) VARIATIONS

(1) Claims made policy with retroactive date at inception, no prior acts coverage.

Insurer will pay claims meeting this one condition

a) The claim must be reported to the insurer during the policy period. The accident or event leading to the claim must take place after the inception date listed on the policy or during the policy period.

(2) Claims made policy with retroactive date prior to inception, limited prior acts coverage.

Insurer will pay claims meeting these two (2) conditions

a) The claim must be reported to the insurer during the policy period.
b) The accident or event leading to the claim must take place after the retroactive date or during the policy period.

(3) Claims made policy with no retroactive date, unlimited prior acts coverage.

Insurer will pay claims meeting this one condition

a) The claim must be reported to the insurer during the policy period. The accident or event leading to the claim could take place at any time in the past or during the policy period.

(4) Claims Made Policy with Extended Reporting Period (Tail Coverage, can be 60 days, 90 days, 1 year, 3 years or unlimited)

The extended reporting period only extends the time in which a claim can be reported to the insurer, it does not change anything else.

The extended reporting period does not change:

- The original policy period
- The original policy limits
- The retroactive date
- Or any other policy term

Insurer will pay claims meeting these two conditions

a) The claim must be reported to the insurer during the policy period or during the extended reporting period.
b) The accident or event leading to the claim must take place after the retroactive date or during the policy period. The policyholder is not covered for an event or accident which occurred during the extended reporting period.

(5) Incident Reported (Used in Professional Policies like Medical Malpractice)
This type of claims made policy expands the definition of claims reported to include incidents which are not claims but maybe become so in the future.

(6) An ISO form will provide a new set of limits for claims reported during the extended reporting period. This has come about because there is the possibility the original limits would be exhausted and therefore the additional premium for the extended reporting period does not gain the insured anything.

TAIL COVERAGE AND NOSE COVERAGE FOR CLAIMS MADE POLICY

- The "extended reporting period" on a claims made policy is often referred to as tail coverage. This coverage could be 60 days, 90 days, 1 year, 3 years, or unlimited. It is almost always at addition premium. It is called tail coverage because it would be activated at the end of the policy. Example (4) gives a greater explanation of tail coverage.
- "Prior acts coverage" is sometimes referred to as nose coverage. It is called this because it is at the beginning of the policy. Examples (2) and (3) show prior acts coverage or nose coverage

LOSSES DISCOVERED

This form is used in surety and fidelity bonds. The insured will pay claims that are discovered by the policyholder during the bond period and reported at that time or within six months of the expiration date of the bond.

Example (1) **Claims Made Policy with Retroactive Dates at Inception, No Prior Acts Covered**

Claims must be reported during policy period

Retroactive Date 1/1/09

Policy Period 1/1/09 – 12/31/09

Accident or event leading to claim must take place during the policy period because the retroactive date is at inception or 1/1/09.

Example (2) **Claims Made Policy with Retroactive Dates at Inception, Limited Prior Acts Covered**

Retroactive Date 1/1/07

Claims must be reported during policy period

Policy Period 1/1/09 – 12/31/09

The accident or event leading to the claim must take place after the retroactive date 1/1/07.

Example (3) **Claims Made Policy with No Retroactive Dates, Unlimited Prior Acts Covered**

Retroactive Date None

Claims must be reported during policy period

Policy Period 1/1/09 – 12/31/09

The accident or event leading to the claim could have taken place any time in the past or during the policy period.

Example (4) **Claims Made Policy with Extended Reporting Period**

Retroactive Date 1/1/07

Claim must be reported during the policy period or within the extended reporting period

Policy Period 1/1/09 – 12/31/09

1/1/10 – 12/31/10 12 months

The accident or event leading to the claim must taken place after the retroactive date 1/1/07 or during the policy period

(Tail coverage 12 months)

If an accident or event leading to a claim takes place during the extended reporting period it is *not* covered.

Section 21

MULTI-YEAR COMMERCIAL POLICIES

These are times when a policy will be issued for more than a one year term.

These are the advantages from the Insured's viewpoint:

- Constant premium for 2, 3 or 5 years.
- The insured and insurer do not have to go through the renewal process each year.
- The insured will know who its insurer will be in the future.
- If the insurance market hardens, the policyholder's premium is held constant.

These are the disadvantages from the Insured's viewpoint:

- If the insurance market softens, the insured has missed an opportunity to lower its premium at the annual renewal.
- Some multi-year policies have provisions to increase premiums under certain circumstances such as increased exposures due to mergers and acquisitions, increased revenues above a certain percentage, or losses above a certain amount.

Policy characteristics:

The policy limit can apply to the entire multi-year policy term. In other words, one policy limit for the whole term of 2, 3, or 5 years, or the policy can be structured to have separate limits applicable to each anniversary period.

Example (1)
One Policy Limit for the Entire Policy Term
Policy #: 73169
Policy Term: (36 months) 1/1/09 to 12/31/11
Policy Limit: 50,000,000 (one policy limit for the entire (36) months)
If the policy limit is used up within the first (24) months, the insurer is under no obligation to provide additional limits. If the insured knew its limits were exhausted, it could try to buy fresh limits.

Example (2)
Separate Policy Limits for Each Period within the Policy Term
Policy #: 74108
Policy Term: (36 months) 1/1/09 to 12/31/11

Policy Limits apply to each period

Period	Separate Limits
1/1/09 – 12/31/09	25,000,000
1/1/10 – 12/31/10	25,000,000
1/1/11 – 12/31/11	25,000,000

The limit from one period cannot be borrowed for another period. In other words, the insurer's total liability for each period is 25,000,000.

Section 22

PROPERTY INSURANCE

STANDARD FIRE POLICY

Brief History

Insuring against fire was developed in England after the great London fire of 1666 destroyed 13,000 homes and devastated the city. A year later, a builder by the name of Nicholas Barbon started to rebuild houses and saw a need for the new owner to protect their investment. He made insurance against fire practical and available to the owners of the houses he was building.

Fire Marks & Fire Brigades

Insurance companies like the "Hand to Hand" had their own fire brigade and could not afford to let their brigade put out just "any" fire. They needed to mark the place they insured. In those days, roads and streets were often given several names and houses were not numbered. This would cause confusion. So to be sure they would put out the correct fire, marks were placed on the buildings being insured. The policy number was stamped on the mark, which linked the mark, the house and the policy. Years later the practice declined because policies lapsed, companies changed and people moved. Another problem was houses often had two marks; one for the building and another for contents.

Later, it became more practical for insurance companies to pool their resources and share in the cost of putting out fires in London. In 1833, this happened with the creation of "The London Fire Engine Establishment". The insurance companies collectively contributed to its establishment and upkeep.

Basic Coverage

Originally, the standard fire policy only covered fires, but it has been expanded to now include lightning, windstorms, hail, explosions, smoke, civil commotion and vandalism. The policy may be written on a named peril or an all-risk form. The all-risk form is broader in its coverages, but it does not cover all the risks that could actually happen. In other words, a named peril form may cover 12 types of peril and an all-risk may cover 20 types of peril.

A peril is fire, lightning, windstorms, hail, explosions, smoke, civil commotion, vandalism, sprinkler leakage, sinkhole collapse, volcanic action, falling objects, weight of ice or snow, collapse from a specific and specified cause.

Special Features	Debris Removal. This is coverage for the cost of removing debris after a fire or other covered event (windstorms, etc.). The policy will exclude the cost of removing debris caused by pollution.
Policy Form	Most insurance companies use the Insurance Services Organization (ISO) policy or a modification of it.

PROPERTY INSURANCE AND REINSURANCE TERMS USED BY UNDERWRITERS

Actual Cash Value	The value of the property after deprecation.
All Risk	A policy that has broad coverage and covers losses from all perils, except those excluded.
Amount Subject	The agreed upon value of a property.
Bailee	A company which has temporary custody of property belonging to another. For instance, a trucking company transporting cargo belonging to another party would be a bailee. Bailee coverage is provided by inland marine insurance policies.
Blanket Coverage	One policy limit is for all property locations, therefore each location does not have to be listed.
Care, Custody, and Control	Property that is temporary in the possession of another party; they have a duty of care, custody and control over that property.
Maximum Possible Loss (MPL)	The highest estimate of property loss which might occur on a particular property or a group of properties, if all loss prevention methods fail, such as firewalls or sprinklers.
Maximum Probable Loss	The largest property loss that is likely to occur.
Named Perils	A policy that only covers losses which are due to the specific named perils.
Payback: (more commonly used in the 1980's and prior)	This term is used by reinsurers as a quick method to determine the adequacy of the reinsurance premium relative to the reinsurance limit.

Reinsurance Premium	Reinsurance Limit	Payback
$50,000	1,000,000	20 years

This tells a reinsurer it would take 20 years at $50,000 per year to be paid back for a 1,000,000 limit loss. The reinsurer is not actually looking to be paid back; it is just a method to compare the premium to the limit, and a 20 year payback is certainly better than an 80 or 100 year payback.

Probable Maximum Loss (PML) — The most likely estimate of a property loss under normal loss conditions.

Rate on Line (ROL) — This is the premium divided by the limit.

Premium	Limit	Rate Line
50,000	1,000,000	5.0%

50,000 ÷1,000,000

This is the inverse of payback and is more commonly used.

Replacement Cost — Insurer will pay for the replacement cost of the property if destroyed by a covered peril. The insurer may not provide unlimited replacement cost but may have an overall total limit.

Schedule of Values — Each property location has an individual limit which is listed.

Sum Insured — This term is the same as total insured value.

Total Insured Value — For purposes of the policy and underwriting, a value will be assigned for a property. For instance, a 20 story building that is 10 years old cannot be assigned an exact value, so an assigned value is determined by the property underwriter.

BUSINESS INTERRUPTION
(May also be known as Use and Occupancy or Business Income)

Brief History

This type of insurance had its origination in England sometime in the mid to late 1700's. Property was being looked at not only for its value, but also as a source of income. Under English Common Law, an individual who had a lease on a property and was paying rent under that lease was obligated to keep paying rent even if the property was ruined by fire. Insurance was eventually formulated to cover the anticipated income.

In England in the 1800's, there were at least two cases brought by owners of property against the insurer. In both cases, the owners of the property sustained property losses and both wanted to collect in the property loss and the loss of income that the property generated. Both times the British Court decided against the policyholder.

These cases established that the property insurance policy did not cover the loss of income when the property was destroyed or impaired. Separate insurance to cover the loss sustained from the loss of income has originated.

In 1821, the Beacon Fire Insurance Company issued policies to cover the loss of rent during the "rebuilding of premises." Early insurance was called Profits Insurance and that essentially is what business interruption insurance is today.

BUSINESS INTERRUPTION (CON'T)

Brief and Easy Description	Covers the net profits and those extra expenses that are over and above the normal expenses to keep the business going during the period of interruption. The policy does not cover the business interruption, but the profits that would have been generated if it wasn't for the interruption. The policy also covers the extra expenses needed to get the business going again.
Extra Expense Coverage	a) This is not business interruption insurance, but an aspect of coverage within business interruption. These are the "extra expenses" incurred by the business after a loss to bring it back to its original state of operation. b) Extra Expense may also be provided on a monoline basis; in other words business interruption is not provided, only Extra Expense Coverage.
Time Element	Business interruption is sometimes referred to as time element because it is the length of time of the interruption which causes the earnings to be impaired that will determine in part the amount the insurance will pay. In effect, the passage of time is an element in the insurance.
Why Business Interruption is Sometimes called Use and Occupancy?	This is a term that was started in the United States in the late 1800's. It is a term borrowed from property policies.
Basic Coverage	The coverage is designed to reimburse a business (policyholder) for the loss of income (net profits) and to pay some of the extra expenses needed to restore the business so once again it can generate income.
Policy Form	Most insurance companies use the Insurance Services Organization (ISO) policy or a modification of it. ISO refers to business interruption as business income coverage.

PROPERTY INSURANCE

BOILER & MACHINERY INSURANCE

(Also Known As Mechanical Breakdown Insurance, Equipment Breakdown Insurance, System Breakdown)

Brief History

The story of how boiler and machinery insurance came about starts with the history of steam being used as a source of power.

England, 1712 - steam was put into use as a source of power. In 1720, steam boilers began to be used and between 1769 and 1775, the steam engine was developed. The steam boiler was also widely used in the United States in the 1830's and onwards.

Even though steam was being used, very little was known about its pressure properties.

During the period of 1720 and 1830, relatively few boilers exploded because the steam pressure was relatively low.

In the 1830's, improvements were made in the boilers, which allow for greater pressure, which could increase their power. But still little was known about steam and pressure, so more and more boilers started to explode. In the United States in the 1850's and 1860's, boiler explosions became almost weekly events.

It was the frequency of boiler explosions that led to attempts to reduce these accidents. In 1841 in England, a group was formed called the Voluntary Society of Boiler Users. The object was to carry out systematic inspections of boilers to reduce accidents. It is believed that "Boiler Insurance" came into use in England in 1858 with a company called Steam Boiler and Steam Power.

BOILER & MACHINERY INSURANCE (CON'T)

In the United States, the first boiler insurance policy issued on February 14, 1867 by the Hartford Steam Boiler and Inspection Company. This company was formed by a group of businessmen who owned and used boilers in the plants and were interested in avoiding accidents by the use of inspections and providing insurance to one another if the accident they were trying to avoid took place anyway.

In the 1920's, boiler insurance evolved into a more comprehensive type of insurance and would cover more then boiler explosions. It would continue to evolve, and today it covers all types of boiler and machinery accidents, not just explosions.

In Europe, boiler and machinery insurance is known as machinery breakdown insurance. Perhaps that is what it should be called.

Brief Description

Insurance on machines.

Covers the machine's property value when the machine malfunctions due to an accident and is damaged, such as a part breaking loose and causing damage to other areas of the machine.

Basic Coverage

Covers the failure of boilers, machines, motors and other equipment from claims such as these caused by bursting, breakdown, cracks, mechanical failure, disintegration, explosions, motor burnout, cracked blocks and freezing.

Almost any mechanical or electrical device or machines can be covered such as air conditioning, refrigerators, generators, steam engines, compressors, internal combustion engines, motors, generators, transformers, circuit breakers and others too numerous to list.

BOILER & MACHINERY INSURANCE (CON'T)

General Categories of Coverage

- Pressure and Refrigeration objects (machines)
- Mechanical objects (machines)
- Electrical objects (machines)
- Turbine objects (machines)

Policies use the word object. Here, we are defining them as machines so the reader can more easily understand this type of insurance.

Why Do You Need Boiler and Machinery Insurance?

Because the standard property insurance policy does not cover breakdown of machines due to accidents.

Policy Form

Most insurance companies use the Insurance Services Organization (ISO) policy or a modification of it.

Some General Causes of Accidents

- Errors in design
- Mistakes in operation of the machine
- Improper maintenance or poor maintenance
- Overuse of the machine
- Lack of water in the steam boiler
- Lack of understanding in the use of the machine
- Explosion due to pressure
- Excessive vibration
- Storm damage, frost, ice
- Excessive centrifugal forces
- Age of machine
- Testing phase of new machine

Note

The Boiler and Machinery policy form may also include Business Interruption coverage.

PROPERTY INSURANCE

BUILDER'S RISK INSURANCE

Brief History: After World War I, there was increased construction activity in Europe. Builders sought ways to insure risks for large-scale construction projects.

In 1929, an all-risk policy was issued for the construction of the Lamberth Bridge in England, and this opened up the market and popularity of builder's risk insurance.

Builder's Risk policies became prevalent as the years went by because of:

- Increased construction due to economic development.
- High-risk construction in cities.
- Road construction intensified.

Basic Coverage: This is insurance which covers a new building or project while it is being constructed. It provides the same property coverages as in the standard property policy with several additional features.

The policy covers the property under construction as well as the equipment and materials at the site waiting to be installed in or on the property under construction.

It does not cover the contractor's equipment used in the construction process.

Why is a Special Policy Needed for Property Under Construction? Property under construction is more vulnerable to certain types of losses, such as windstorms, fire, theft, and vandalism.

Some of the Coverage's an All-Risk Policy Form Covers: Fire, lightning, windstorms, hail, explosions, smoke, civil commotion, vandalism, sprinkler leakage, sinkhole collapse, volcanic action, falling objects, weight of ice or snow, collapse from a specific and specified cause.

BUILDER'S RISK INSURANCE (CON'T)

What A Builder's Risk Insurance Policy "Isn't":	It is not insurance coverage for a contractor or architects in the building process. It is not coverage for the contractor's equipment.
Who Usually Buys Builder's Risk Insurance?	The owner of the building or project under construction or the general contractor may buy the policy. They may do that because they know what is required.
Policy Form:	Most insurance companies use the Insurance Services Organization (ISO) policy or a modification of it.

PROPERTY INSURANCE

DIFFERENCE IN CONDITIONS INSURANCE (DIC)

Brief History:	The concept of using an insurance policy to fill a "difference in conditions" for an insured holding another policy goes back to the founding of modern marine insurance around 1680 in England, although it did not have a formal name. In the 1960's, modern DIC insurance became better known and more formalized. Today DIC insurance is thought of as a property insurance because that is where you see it most.
What is the Difference In Conditions Insurance:	It is a property insurance policy, which provides coverages absent from the standard property policy. That missing coverage supplied by the DIC policy is the unusual or uncommon risk such as earthquake and flood. To look at in a practical way, an insured has three plants in California with property insurance which excludes earthquake. The insured could buy a difference in conditions insurance policy to cover earthquake and other perils not covered in their standard insurance program. The DIC policy will exclude those perils covered in the standard policies, which usually are fire and the extended coverages. The goal of the DIC policy is to fill in the gaps but not to provide duplicate, umbrella or excess insurance limits; however a DIC policy could provide high limits for the GAP coverages it alone is providing.
Type of Coverage Usually Provided By DIC Property Insurance:	Earthquake, landslide, mudslide, and other earth movement. Collapse, Floodwater damage (due to heavy rainstorm, water main breaks). Freeze damage, snow load, subsidence, pollution cleanup, debris removal.
Policy Form:	Manuscripted.

PROPERTY INSURANCE

COMMERCIAL LIVESTOCK INSURANCE

Brief History:	A very old form of insurance; the exact date of its creation and origin are not known. It may have begun in Continental Europe in one of these countries: France, Germany, Switzerland, Sweden, Denmark, or Italy. These countries have predominately small farms with relatively few animals, therefore there is a strong need to protect the animals against accidental loss. The insurance may have begun with small local mutuals. Lloyds of London is one of the main writers of livestock insurance also referred to as bloodstock insurance.
Basic Coverage:	Livestock insurance is a form of property insurance covering the death of animal(s) by accident or disease. It usually excludes death by transportation, fire, lightening, breeding or flood. If the insurer has paid a claim, it is entitled to receive the proceeds from the sale of the carcass. The policyholder usually is required to contact the insurer within (24) hours in regard to illness or accident for the animal(s) insured.
Animals covered:	Generally confined to cattle and horses. It can also include sheep and pigs. Pedigreed animals are insurable at high premiums.
Policy Form:	Most insurance companies in the United States use the Insurance Services Offices (ISO) policy or a modification of it.

PROPERTY INSURANCE

POLITICAL RISK INSURANCE

Basic Coverage:

The policyholder is usually a corporation doing business overseas with an investment such as a plant or other facility they own or in a partnership. Political risk insurance can protect that investment in a foreign country in these three main areas:

(1) Currency Inconvertibility
Protects policyholder against the inability to convert local currency received in the form of earnings in the overseas investment into U.S. dollars, and to transfer those dollars out of the local country.

(2) Expropriation
Protects policyholder against confiscation, nationalization, or appropriation by the foreign government.

(3) Political Violence
Protects policyholder against a loss of assets due to civil war, revolution or other political violence.

Overseas Private Investment Corporation (OPIC)
Washington, D.C.
See www.OPIC.gov.

Charted by the U.S. Congress in 1969 this is an agency of the United States Government. This organization assists U.S. investors doing business overseas.

(1) Provides political risk insurance for a premium.

(2) Provides loans and loan guarantees for projects.

(3) Can provide financing to private investment funds that provide equity to overseas businesses.

(4) Advocates American business in overseas areas.

Political Risk Insurance Offered By OPIC Per Their 1999 Annual Report:

Currency Inconvertibility
Deterioration in an investors ability to convert profits, debt service and other remittances from local currency into U.S. Dollars and to transfer those dollars out of the host country.

Expropriation
Loss of an investment due to expropriation or

confiscation by a foreign government.

Political Violence
Loss of assets or income due to war, revolution, insurrection, or politically motivated civil suit, terrorism or sabotage.

OPIC does not insure against currency devaluation nor does it guarantee that investors will earn a profit.

Insurance From Private Carrier: Because political risk insurance is high hazard, very few commercial insurance companies offer it.

PROPERTY INSURANCE

INLAND MARINE INSURANCE

Brief History: Inland marine insurance is an outgrowth of marine insurance. This form of insurance evolved in the United States around 1910 and became prevalent in the 1920's. Merchandise (property) sent by sea to the U.S. was covered by ocean marine cargo insurance but coverage stopped when the merchandise reached its port of destination. The U.S. was expanding rapidly in the 1920's with railroads and roads improving, therefore greater amounts of merchandise could be sent inland across the country. Inland marine insurance evolved from the need to cover this merchandise while it was in transit inland by land or rail as it went through the country.

The term marine in inland marine insurance has nothing to do with marine. The easiest way to understand inland marine insurance is to disregard the reference to marine.

Ocean marine cargo insurance protects merchandise or cargo (property) while it is in transit on board the ship. Inland marine protects property when it is in transit inland on rail, land or air. It is simply insurance to cover goods while they are in transit by railroad, commercial land carriers such as trucking companies, airplane or other non-marine method. Goods, merchandise or property that would most likely require an inland marine insurance policy would be medical instruments, television sets, computers, etc.

Basic Coverage:

<u>Property Coverage</u>
Coverage is for damage or an outright loss to property while it is in transit by rail, land or air.

<u>Liability Coverage</u>
Inland marine policies may provide liability coverage to the Bailee in respect to bills of landing, shipping receipts.

Who Principally Are The Purchasers of Inland Marine Insurance:

(a) Transportation Companies:
These companies are considered Bailees, which is a legal term in contract law and has become a standard insurance term. A Bailee is a company which has temporary custody of property belonging to another.

Companies in the business of transporting property such as a trucking company, an airfreight company, overnight delivery company, or rail company, do not own the property transported. It only has been temporarily transferred to their care, custody and control while it is being delivered to destination. Inland Marine Insurance provides coverage to them for this property belonging to others. Standard property policies do not cover this exposure of care, custody and control of property belonging to others.

(b) Owners of unique property being transported would buy their own inland marine policy (i.e., a museum transporting its art collection by truck to be displayed in another city or a medical technology company transporting medical instruments by air). These organizations would buy their own Inland Marine Insurance because they do not want to solely rely on the transporting company's Inland Marine Policy.

Policy Form:

There are many different Inland Marine Policy forms but many insurers use the Insurance Services Offices (ISO) policy or a modification of it. The policy form most prevalent is all the risk, which covers losses from fire and allied lines, flood, burglary, holdup, theft, and transportation risks such as collisions with another vehicle.

Floater Policies:

These are specialized types of Inland Marine Insurance covering the property that you might say is floating in transit such as jewelry, furs, and stamp and coin collections.

Warehouse Operators Legal Liability:

This is contingent or defense coverage.

A warehouse is liable for:

(a) Property cannot leave the warehouse due to the warehouse's negligence coverage.

(b) Fire in the warehouse was caused by negligence, they did not have fire alarms.

(c) Water damage due to leaky roof and goods get spoiled.

Insuring Tunnels, Bridges, Dams and Other Unique Properties With An Inland Marine Policy:

It has evolved over decades that inland marine policy forms are often used to insure tunnels, bridges and other forms of unique property. This has come about because there was a time when only those underwriters would venture into this field.

Section 23

WORKERS' COMPENSATION AND EMPLOYER'S LIABILITY

Brief History	Workers' Compensation insurance was developed in England from 1880 to 1906. Under the common law of England, an injured citizen could collect damages from the negligent party that caused the injury. However, under the doctrine of common employment, an employee could not collect from their employer. In 1880, the Employers Liability Act was passed which made the employer in England liable for some types of injuries. Some of the larger employers did not want to assume that potential financial risk and purchased insurance for it. Those employers who did not buy insurance became known as "self insurers," a term that still exists today. Eventually England passed The Workman's Compensation Act of 1897 and 1906 which made employers more and more responsible and liable for workers' injuries.
Basic Coverage	The policy is designed to compensate injured employees in the course of their employment with the policyholder (employer). The policy has two basic coverages: 1. Workers compensation 2. Employer's liability
Workers' Compensation	The injured employee cannot sue the employer, but in return the employer provides workers' compensation benefits which include medical benefits. These benefits are mandated by each individual state; the insurer's policy pays these benefits, without regard to who is at fault. Death Benefits are in place of the worker's wages. They are paid to the worker's family upon the worker's death.
Employer's Liability Section of Policy	The possibility always exists that regardless of the intent of workers' compensation law, an injured employee may sue their employer. Basically, the only reason for doing so is to claim the employer was negligent by knowingly and intentionally operating an unsafe workplace. The policy provides for the defense of the employer.
Workers' compensation laws are specific to each of the 50 states	Each state has specific laws in regards to workers compensation benefits and how employers can qualify to be self-insured and other matters.
Policy Form	The policy issued by insurance companies almost always is the standard one designed by the National Council on Compensation (NCCI).

National Council on Compensation (NCCI)	Provides the policy form and the rate basis most insurance companies use. There are various state bureaus providing the same services.
Self Insurance Retention (SIR)	Some states permit an employer or a fund consisting of many employers, which usually are homogeneous, to self-insure and buy insurance only above their self insurance retention.
Workers' Compensation Benefits	Mandated by each state.
Types of Workers' Compensation Benefits	Weekly funds paid to the injured worker to make up for their loss of salary. Medical payments to pay for the injured worker's doctor, hospital, and rehabilitation bills. Death benefits are paid to the family of the worker killed on the job.
Rating of the Workers' Compensation and Employers' Liability Policy	Most insurance companies use the NCCI rates as a guide in the rates they charge. These are called manual rates which come from a "book" referred to in the insurance industry as a "manual."
Experience Rating	If an employer generates premium above a certain amount, the employer is eligible to be rated on its own experience. What this means is a factor called an "experience modification" is derived and used to increase or decrease the manual rate. Experience Modification Unity: 1.00 Greater than 1.00 increases the manual rate (debit). Less than 1.00 decreases the manual rate (credit).

WORKERS' COMPENSATION AND EMPLOYER'S LIABILITY (CON'T)

Workers' Compensation Policy Limits	The Workers' Compensation policy is issued without specific policy limits because the amounts that can be paid out by the insurer are according to the benefit schedules promulgated by each state. Furthermore, each state does not limit the amount that can be paid for an injured worker's medical care. Therefore, we say the Workers' Compensation policy limit is statutory which means according to the law. The employer's liability portion of the policy does have specific limits and they generally are: Per accident: 500,000 Per disease: 500,000 Aggregate disease: 500,000 We point out it will be extremely rare that the employer's liability portion of the policy will be utilized.
Federal Laws Governing Compensation	States regulate Workers' Compensation in their own state. However, there are classes of employees that are not governed by state regulation, but by federal regulation. These classes of workers do not collect state benefits, but federal benefits. The standard NCCI workers compensation and employers liability policy does not provide coverage for a number of federal laws unless specifically endorsed
Long Shore Harbors Workers Compensation Act (LSHWCA) Enacted in 1927	This is a federal workers' compensation act passed in 1927 for long shore and harbor workers.
Outer Continental Shelf Lands Act	A federal workers' compensation act, it broadens the classes of the employees covered by USL&H to employees working on offshore rigs and platforms which are in the outer continental shelf.
Federal Coal Mine Health and Safety Act of 1969	A federal workers' compensation act that stipulates benefits for coal miners with pneumoconiosis (black lung). Provides coverage over and above state benefits it they are not adequate.

WORKERS' COMPENSATION AND EMPLOYER'S LIABILITY (CON'T)

Migrant and Seasonal Agricultural Worker Protection Act (MSAWPA)	This is not a federal compensation act, but a federal act that allows a railroad worker to sue their employer for injuries due to the employer's negligence.
Merchant Marine Act of 1920 (commonly referred to as the Jones Act)	This is not a federal compensation act, but a federal act that allows a seaman aboard a ship or vessel to sue his employer for injuries caused by the employer's negligence.
Death on the High Seas Act of 1920	This is not a federal compensation act, but an act that allows the estate of seamen and others killed on vessels more than three miles from the United States to sue the wrongful party (vessel owner or others).
Black Lung Benefits Act of 1977	A tonnage tax is levied and collected from all coal producers which goes into the federal trust fund used to pay benefits to those miners or their survivors that suffered from black lung disease.
Defense Base Act Enacted	A federal workers' compensation act, it broadens the classes of the employees covered by USL&H to civilian employees working on U.S. defense bases overseas. These workers are usually employees of contractors.
Federal Employees Compensation Act (FECA)	Covers civilian employees of the U.S. government, basically within the United States.
War Hazards Compensation Act	Pertains to certain types of civilian employees employed overseas by the U.S. government or contractors doing business for the U.S. government.
Civilian Employees of Non-appropriated Fund Instrumentalities Act	This act covers civilian employees working in U.S. military bases post exchanges.

WORKERS' COMPENSATION AND EMPLOYER'S LIABILITY (CON'T)

General Information on Insurance Companies Rating of Workers Compensation Policies

Two Basic Methods to Determine the Premium
Guaranteed-Cost
Loss Sensitive Rating

Guaranteed-Cost
The insured (employer) is charged a fixed rate that is not subject to adjustment due to losses that occur during the policy term. In a guaranteed cost policy, the only variable affecting the premium is the final audited payroll.

Loss Sensitive Rating
The insured (employer) is charged a premium which is based on the loss experience during the policy term. Low loss activity means low premiums; high loss activity means high premiums.

Loss Sensitive Rating Plans

- Retrospective rating plan (the most popular)
- Retention rating plan
- Sliding scale dividend rating plan
- Paid loss retro's rating plan
- Large deductible rating plan

General Information
Within the Guaranteed-Cost Plan and the Loss Sensitive Plans are many variables that effect the premium.

Experience Rating is a factor within the two (2) general rating plans, guaranteed-cost and loss sensitive.

Each state has strict laws governing rating of the Workers' Compensation policy in its state.

If premiums exceed a certain amount and the company has been in business for (2) or more years, they qualify to be experience rated. This means the guaranteed cost fixed premium is effected by the employer's own experience.

Experience rating will affect the loss sensitive plan's minimum and deposit premiums.

WORKERS' COMPENSATION AND EMPLOYER'S LIABILITY (CON'T)

Factors in the rating of a specific insured (employer):

... exposure base, which is the employers total payroll.
... classification of the employer's employees according to codes, the code classifies the occupation according to potential for a workers compensation injury.
... amount of payroll by code classification.
... size of premium, if it exceeds a certain amount, the employer qualifies for experience rating.
... state in which employer is located, state laws govern rating.
... deductible or self insurance.
... safety plan.
... dividend.

Methods States Permit an Employer to Meet its Workers' Compensation Requirements

Monopolistic State Funds
Some states require an employer to buy its workers' compensation from the state fund.

Competitive State Funds
Some states have funds which sell workers' compensation insurance just like private insurers; you could buy your workers' compensation from the state fund or elsewhere.

Self Insurance
Some states permit an employer to self insure if they meet certain requirements. An employer usually files with the state an application, payroll information, financial statement, loss experience for the past several years, safety program, explanation of the company's operation.

Group Self Insurance
Some states permit an employer to join a group or fund and to receive a workers compensation policy from that organization.

WORKERS' COMPENSATION AND EMPLOYER'S LIABILITY (CON'T)

Coverage For Workers Injured By Disease

The Workers' Compensation Part of the Policy

If a disease is contracted by a worker during employment and is directly related to their job, it is covered under the workers' compensation part of the policy.

(1) Indemnity benefits are mandated by the individual state.
(2) Medical benefits are mandated by the sate, buy all of them require the policy to provide unlimited medical expenses.

The Employer's Liability Part of the Policy

If an employee contracts a disease which is not directly related to their job but believes the employer has some responsibility due to its negligence, then the employee could bring a suit against the employer. The employer's Employer's Liability part of the policy will cover this employee suit.

Limits of Liability For Employer's Liability Section of Policy

This section has three (3) Parts:

(1) a limit for bodily injury per accident
(2) a limit for bodily injury by disease for any single employee
(3) a limit for bodily injury by disease for the entire Employers Liability part of the policy

Residual Markets

This term is used when referring to state run workers' compensation funds and state assigned risk plans for employers having difficulty securing workers' compensation coverage in the commercial market.

Managed Care for Medical Expenses

The medical coverage provided by the workers' compensation and employer's liability policy is unlimited, therefore for catastrophe injuries the medical costs could be huge. Some claimants will require a lifetime of care; costs could be hundreds of thousands of dollars or even millions. More and more workers' compensation insurers are using managed care networks to provide medical care to injured workers, especially for catastrophic losses but lesser losses as well.

Second Injury Fund

Most states have second injury laws and run a second injury fund. The purpose of the second injury fund is to pay benefits to an employee in the event of injury on the job, in cases where the employee has a pre-existing injury or disability.

Section 24

LIABILITY INSURANCE

COMMERCIAL GENERAL LIABILITY (CGL) POLICY

Brief History	Conceived in England from 1820 to 1880. Developed from the concept of compensating individuals hurt while using machines, which were becoming prevalent during the Industrial Revolution era. The idea of compensation evolved from common law, which entitled an individual to be compensated for injuries sustained by the wrongful act of another.
Basic Coverage	Covers the policyholder who has a legal action brought against it for causing either bodily injury (BI), property damage (PD), or personal injury (PI) to another.
Section (I) Coverages	**<u>Coverage (A)</u>** Bodily Injury (BI) The policy will cover legal actions brought against the policyholder for bodily injuries it caused to another person. Property Damage (PD) The policy will also cover the policyholder against legal actions of others who claim the policyholder did damage to their property. The property being referred to is not the policyholder's property, but the property of another person damaged by the policyholder. **<u>Coverage (B)</u>** Personal Injury (PI) This section of the policy is covering legal actions against the policyholder from others who are claiming the policyholder injured their character by libel, slander, false arrest, defamation, or malicious prosecution. Personal injury (PI) as defined in the policy has nothing to do with "physical" injury. **<u>Coverage (C)</u>** Medical Payments This section of the policy is covering medical expenses ("regardless of fault" to a third party) caused by an accident on the insured's premises or because of the insured's operations. The insured itself is not covered for medical expenses.

LIABILITY INSURANCE

COMMERCIAL GENERAL LIABILITY (CGL) POLICY

Supplementary Payments For
Section (I) Coverage (A) and (B)

The policy in this section is providing expenses to defend claims in addition to the Limits of Insurance (Section III) which covers damages. That includes attorney fees, investigation fees, prejudgment and post judgment interest.

Section (II) Who Is Insured

In a typical CGL policy, there are three (3) classes of insureds.

(1) **Named Insured:** The declaration page will require an insured to be named in a commercial policy. This could be an individual, corporation, company, partnership, association, joint venture or other commercial organization. The named insured is the one the policy is issued and is entitled to receive protection from the insurer. More than one named insured may be included on the policy. Named insureds have certain policy rights and when more than one named insured is named the first listed named insured is granted authority in these areas:

(a) Can request changes in policy or cancel
(b) Received cancellation and non-renewal notices
(c) Is responsible for payment of the premium
(d) Is the payee for return premium, if any
(e) Responsible for maintenance of records

When there is more than one named insured, the primary named insured will be listed in the declaration page and the other named insured will be attached to the policy.

(2) **Other Automatic Insureds:** These are persons granted insured status automatically. They may be employees or directors and officers of the company.

(3) **Additional Insureds:** These are persons granted insured status by endorsement.

LIABILITY INSURANCE

COMMERCIAL GENERAL LIABILITY (CGL) POLICY

Section (III) Limits of Insurance

The policy has six (6) limits specified in the declaration page:

(1) General Aggregate Limit
(2) Products-Completed Operations Aggregate Limit
(3) Personal and Advertising Limit
(4) Each Occurrence Limit
(5) Fire Damage Limit
(6) Medical Expense Limit

(1) **The General Aggregate Limit**

The policy will pay claims up to the aggregate limit for Section (I) Coverages (A), (B) and (C) except for claims which fall under the category of products and completed operations because this has its own aggregate limit.

(2) **Products – Completed Operations**

The commercial general liability policy contains coverage for products and completed operations.

Products Liability covers bodily injury (BI) and property damage (PD) claims brought against the policyholder for harm caused to others by their products.

Completed Operations Liability covers bodily injury (BI) and property damage (PD) claims brought against the policyholder for harm caused to others by its completed operations. The policy has an aggregate limit it will pay for all products and completed operations claims.

(3) **Personal and Advertising Injury Limit**

This is the most the policy will pay for all third party damages due to personal injury and advertising injury stemming from any one person or organization. Personal injury is defined in Section (I) Coverage (B). This limit is subject to the General Aggregate Limit and also qualifies as an Each Occurrence Limit.

LIABILITY INSURANCE

COMMERCIAL GENERAL LIABILITY (CGL) POLICY

(4) **Each Occurrence Limit**
This is the most the policy will pay for any one occurrence loss. It is subject to the General Aggregate Limit and the Products-Completed Operations Aggregate Limit.

(5) **Fire Damage Limit – Any One Fire**
This is the most the policy will pay for property damages (Section (I) Coverage A) to a third party when an insured rented or temporarily occupied a premises in which there has been property damage from any one fire in which the insured is negligent. This limit is subject to General Aggregate Limit and the Each Occurrence Limit.

(6) **Medical Expense Limit – Any One Person**
The policy provides for a small amount of medical payments ($5,000, some policies are now $10,000) on a no-fault basis to any one person. This is done for compassionate reasons and to possibly avoid future lawsuits. This limit is subject to General Aggregate Limit and the Each Occurrence Limit.

Section (IV) Commercial General Liability Conditions

The section of the policies enumerates the general conditions of insurance, such as:
(1) Bankruptcy
(2) Duties in the event of occurrence, offense claims or suits
(3) Legal action against insurer
(4) Other insurance
(5) Premium audit
(6) Representation
(7) Separation of insureds
(8) Transfer of rights or recovery against others to us.
(9) When insurer does not renew
(10) Other

LIABILITY INSURANCE

COMMERCIAL GENERAL LIABILITY (CGL) POLICY

Section (V) Definitions	This section defines advertising injury, bodily injury, coverage territory, insured contract, occurrence, personal injury, property damage, products-completed operations, product and other definitions not listed here.
Policy Form	Most insurance companies use the Insurance Services Offices (ISO) policy or a modification of it. Most policies are issued on an occurrence basis. Claims made is usually used for insureds in the oil, chemical and other businesses perceived to be difficult insurance risks and ones with an exposure to pollution.

Note: In 1986, Insurance Service Office officials changed the name of the policy from "Comprehensive" General Liability to Commercial General Liability.

LIABILITY INSURANCE

COMMERCIAL UMBRELLA LIABILITY INSURANCE

Brief History

Lloyds of London is generally credited with the origination of the umbrella policy in the 20th century. Its original name was blanket catastrophe liability insurance.

Umbrella liability insurance came to the United States in the 1940's.

Description

The umbrella liability policy "sits" above a company's primary liability insurance policies or self insured retentions (SIR) providing this type of coverage:

(1) Excess Limits
(2) Aggregate Limits (Drop Down Coverage)
(3) Broader/Gap Coverage

Excess Limits
On a per occurrence or per accident basis. This has the effect of creating higher limits.

Aggregate Limits/Drop Down Over Exhausted Primary Aggregates
The umbrella liability policy will drop down and provide limits when an underlying policy has an aggregate limitation that becomes exhausted. For instance, the CGL policy has an aggregate for products-completed operations; if that becomes, exhausted the umbrella policy will drop down and provide limits in regard to products-completed operations claims. Also the CGL policy has a General Aggregate limitation which may become exhausted; if that happens, the umbrella policy will provide limits. The Workers' Compensation and Employers Liability policy has an aggregate for employer's liability in respect to disease; if this became exhausted, the umbrella policy would respond by providing limits. The Each Occurrence Limit in the CGL could also be used up because of multiple claimants in the same occurrence; the umbrella policy would respond to new per occurrence limits.

LIABILITY INSURANCE

COMMERCIAL UMBRELLA LIABILITY INSURANCE

Broader/Gap Coverage	Theoretically, the umbrella liability policy should provide broader coverage than the underlying primary policies and fill in missing coverages. Many umbrella policies provide reduced coverage because the underlying policies have become broader and therefore there are less gaps.
What Are The Most Likely Underlying Policies The Umbrella "Sits" Over	• Commercial General Liability Policy (CGL) • Auto Liability Policy • Employer's Liability Section of the Workers' Compensation and Employer's Liability Policy • Aircraft Liability Policy
Duty To Defend Insured	If the umbrella policy drops down when the primary policy is exhausted the duty to defend becomes the umbrella policy obligation. Also if the umbrella policy provides broader coverage it has the duty to defend when there isn't any primary policy providing coverage in that area.
Policy Form	Most companies have their own form. Many contain the same wording, but each must be reviewed for differences. ISO introduced an Umbrella form in 2001.

LIABILITY INSURANCE

The Commercial Umbrella Liability policy provides excess limits over primary liability insurance policies.

UMBRELLA LIABILITY LIMITS

	10,000,000 Per Occurrence Limit xs	10,000,000 Per Accident Limit xs	10,000,000 Per Occurrence Limit xs	10,000,000 Per Occurrence Limit xs
Primary Insurance Policies with Per Occurrence or Per Accident Limits	CGL Per Occurrence Limit 5,000,000	Automobile Liability Per Accident Limit 2,000,000	Employers Liability Per Occurrence Limit 2,000,000	Aircraft Liability Per Occurrence Limit 25,000,000

The umbrella liability policy provides "aggregate limits" over primary policies, which have within them separate limits on an aggregate basis. The umbrella can also restore the per occurrence limit if that becomes exhausted.

UMBRELLA LIABILITY LIMITS

	10,000,000 In the Aggregate Xs	10,000,000 In the Aggregate xs	10,000,000 In the Aggregate xs	5,000,000 Per Occurrence xs
Primary Insurance Policies with Coverage Limits On an Aggregated Basis	CGL General Aggregate 5,000,000	CGL Products and Completed Operations Aggregate 5,000,000	Employer's Liability For Disease Aggregate 2,000,000	Each Occurrence Limit 5,000,000 If this limit becomes exhausted, the umbrella will provide a per occurrence limit.

LIABILITY INSURANCE

DIRECTORS & OFFICERS INSURANCE

Brief History	This policy can trace its history back to the 1930's developed at Lloyds of London, but did not become popular until the 1970's.
Basic Coverage	Covers the directors or officers of a corporation when they are named as individuals in third party lawsuits. It is intended to protect the individual's personal assets. Entity Coverage: The original directors and officers policies were not intended to cover the corporation itself when it is named in a third party lawsuit. However, more and more directors & officers (D&O) policies provide entity coverage by endorsement or within the policy. Additionally, employment practices liability coverage has been added to some D&O policies.
Special Features	There is no standard D&O policy but most will have three (3) types of deductibles. 1. Each director and officer will have a deductible 2. There is an aggregate deductible for all directors and officers combined. 3. There is a corporate reimbursement deductible. The corporation can, within its bylaws, protect an individual directors or officer when they are named in certain types of lawsuits. In this case, the corporation is able to reimburse the individual director or officer. This reimbursement by the corporation also acts as a deductible in the D&O policy.
Policy Form	Manuscripted; most policies are claims made.

LIABILITY INSURANCE

DIRECTORS & OFFICERS INSURANCE (CON'T)

Basic Duties of a Director and Officer	▪ Duty of diligence ▪ Duty of loyalty ▪ Duty of obedience ▪ Fiduciary duty

Who Brings D&O Suits?	Most likely source of claim
Shareholders of the Corporation	▪ Derivative suits alleging director or officer breached basic duty. This could stem from a merger, acquisition or many other situations.
Government Agencies	▪ Discrimination in employment ▪ Employee Retirement Income Security Act of 1974 (ERISA) ▪ Violation of security laws ▪ Environmental ▪ Anti-trust
Employees	▪ Wrongful discharge, discrimination
Customers	▪ Abrupt removal of credit which causes damage to their business, for instance, when a bank terminates its line of credit ▪ Contracts
Creditors	▪ Personal guarantee issues
Fraud	▪ Fraud is almost always excluded from directors & officers insurance policies

LIABILITY INSURANCE

ERRORS & OMISSIONS

Brief History	Probably originated with London underwriters in the 1940's.
Basic Coverage	Covers the policyholder, who is usually a professional, against legal actions from third parties alleging they suffered a monetary loss because of an error or omission. Professionals who buy error and omissions liability policies include architects, engineers, lawyers, travel agents, insurance brokers, real estate brokers and many others.
Policy Form	Manuscripted; most insurance companies use a claims made policy form.

LIABILITY INSURANCE

PUBLIC OFFICIALS

Brief History of Suits Against Public Officials	There has been a sharp increase in suits against public officials because of the Supreme Court decision in 1978 that said a municipality was subject to suits under 42 USC Section 1983 Civil Rights Act of 1871. Suits against public officials are usually brought in Federal Court when sovereign immunity is not available for defense.
Basic Coverage	Provides liability coverage for errors and omissions made for public officials at municipalities and other governmental agencies and entities.
Policy Form	Manuscripted

Types of Claims Against Public Officials

Job Discrimination

- Hiring, promotion, or termination because of race, sex, religion, age, handicap

Zoning

- Refusing to issue building permits or certificates of occupancy
- Rezoning area
- Ordinates limiting or restricting the use of property

Police

- False arrest

Police (con't)

- False imprisonment
- Malicious prosecution
- Unlawful search and seizure

Who Brings Public Official Suits

- Private citizens
- Public Action Groups
- Employees or former employees
- Prisoners
- Students
- Unions
- Commercial companies
- Other

LIABILITY INSURANCE

PUBLIC OFFICIALS

Who Is Sued?

- Local Cities and townships
- Counties
- Colleges and universities
- School districts
- Fire departments
- Police departments
- Members of the Board
- Groups of public officials or an individual official

LIABILITY AND PROPERTY INSURANCE

COMMERCIAL AUTO INSURANCE (BUSINESS AUTO)

Coverage	Liability coverage for bodily injury (BI) and property (PD). This is the same type of coverage that is in the comprehensive general liability policy.
Other coverages (first party)	Physical damage coverage refers to property insurance for the insured's own auto. This covers such events as fire or theft. When offering physical damage coverage, insurance companies use the terms comprehensive and collision. Collision (physical damage coverage) covers the insured's auto when it collides with another auto or object.
Hired Auto Physical Damage and Liability	What if you rent or lease another auto? Hired auto coverage provides excess coverage for you if you rent or lease an auto. The coverage is over and above any other insurance that may be in place on the hired autos.
Non-owned Auto (liability only)	What happens if you use an auto that belongs to one of your employees? Non-owned auto coverage provides coverage to you. You must review the specific policy for coverage.
Medical Payments Coverage	Covers the medical and funeral expenses of the of those involved in an accident on a no-fault basis.
Personal Injury Protection (PIP)	Some states with no-fault laws require insurance companies to provide benefits to injured persons. In return, the injured persons have limited rights to sue.
No-fault laws	The goal of no-fault insurance is to lower auto insurance premium for the policy holder by reducing the number of expensive litigations involved in auto accidents. The policyholder collects from their own insurance company regardless of who is at fault. Each state needs to be reviewed for (1) are they a no fault state (2) if so, what is it in regard to. Some states' policyholders are permitted to choose between standard coverage and no-fault coverage. Some states have repeated their no-fault laws.
Uninsured Motorist Laws Underinsured Motorist Coverage	Almost all states have a uninsured motorist law and about half of all states require auto policies sold in that state to require the policyholder to carry this coverage.

	The coverage provided by the policy is for the negligence caused by a motorist with no auto liability insurance or inadequate auto liability insurance, for instance, very low limits. The policy will also cover hit and run accidents.
Bobtail Coverage (liability only)	Specific to the trucking industry. When a trucking company uses an "independent owner operator" with its own auto to haul freight for it, this bobtail coverage covers the trucking company while the independent owner/operator is hauling the freight for the trucking company. This coverage only applies while the freight is being hauled, not for the return trip when they are without cargo.
Motor Carrier Act of 1980 (with later revisions)	Requires the trucking company to carry a minimum of 1,000,000 in liability limits - 5,000,000 if the freight being hauled is classified as hazardous.
ISO Broadened Pollution coverage	ISO endorsement CA 9948 broadened coverage for pollution. It covers BI and PD from cargo. It also includes clean-up costs.
Is the driver of the auto covered or is the auto?	Most commercial policies cover the auto being driven by any driver designated to do so.

LIABILITY INSURANCE

PHYSICIANS PROFESSIONAL LIABILITY (MEDICAL MALPRACTICE)

Basic Coverage	The policyholder is the physician with the policy covering allegations of malpractice in the performance of a physician's services. Malpractice is considered the failure of the physician to exercise the proper level of skill, diligence and attention to duties. A heart specialist or orthopedic specialist or other medical specialist will be held to a higher standard in their specialty than a general practitioner.
Policy Form	Manuscripted; most insurance companies use a claims made policy form. Policy limits can be structured in multiple ways because many physicians are part of a group or part of a physician practice management corporation: (A) Limit for physician only (B) Limit for corporation only (C) Shared limit among physicians (D) Shared limit between physicians and corporation
Other Medical Personnel That Can Be Covered Within A Physicians Professional Liability Policy; Each Policy Will Have a Definition of Covered Employees That Should Be Reviewed	Nurse RN Nurse practitioner Nurse anesthesiologist Nurse midwife Physician assistant Lab personnel Surgical assistant Paraprofessional X-ray technician Other medical personnel
Defense Costs	Extremely important in medical malpractice; some policies cover defense costs within the policy limit, some are in addition to the limit.

LIABILITY INSURANCE

PHYSICIANS PROFESSIONAL LIABILITY (MEDICAL MALPRACTICE)

Short History Of Medical Malpractice Lawsuits In The United States

The first recorded malpractice case in medicine was in England in 1374. J. Mort, a surgeon, was sued for negligence; the plaintiff lost the case. In the United States, the first malpractice case was reported in 1794. A husband sued a doctor for the physician's negligence in performing an operation on his wife, who died; the plaintiff got a verdict in his favor.

<u>1920'S – 1950'S</u>
This was a time the family physician handled almost all the medical problems for a family, including delivering their children and doing less complicated surgery. It was a time a doctor made house calls and very few thought about suing.

<u>1960's – 1970's</u>
In this era, the United States society became more sophisticated and so did medicine. Family physicians referred patients to specialists possessing a higher level of training and better equipment. More medical care was performed at the hospital and the overall medical cost to the patient and its medical insurer increased sharply. The larger society expected more, patients expected more and they became less inhibited about suing their physician. In the 1970's, medical malpractice claims skyrocketed culminating in the crisis of 1975 when numerous commercial insurers withdrew from the market. Some faced insolvency; suddenly physicians couldn't buy medical malpractice insurance. Those still selling it commanded sharply higher premiums.

With the leadership of the various state medical societies and associations, physicians banded together to form their own physician-owned insurance companies. Today, even with consolidation, there still are about 40 physician-owned insurers operating in 29 states. Almost all are members of the Physician Insurers Association of America (PIAA).

LIABILITY INSURANCE

PHYSICIANS PROFESSIONAL LIABILITY (MEDICAL MALPRACTICE)

1980 – 2011

Medical malpractice is still a very difficult line of insurance; multi-million dollar awards are no longer unusual.

The Business of Healthcare in the United States and the Rise of Health-Maintenance-Organizations (HMO's) and Physician Groups:

The structure of medicine up to the 1980's was very simple and straightforward. Independent physicians were dominant with hospitals employing a relatively small number of them; independent physicians applied for privileges at the hospital to treat their patients. In the 1980's and 1990's, health-maintenance- organizations (HMO's) became much more popular and changed the medical landscape. The emphasis was to control medical costs. Eventually the term "managed care" came to be used to describe the controlling of medical costs.

Health-Maintenance-Organizations (HMO's)

The first organization of this type may have started in the 1960's. At first these organizations had their own buildings and medical facilities in which patients would visit but they evolved in the 1980's and 1990's whereby a patient could visit a physician in their office at their local area. This was accomplished by the HMO signing contracts with physicians and physician groups all over the United States to provide medical services. Some HMO's own hospitals, outpatient surgery centers, and urgent 24 hour clinics and employ a large number of physicians.

LIABILITY INSURANCE

PHYSICIANS PROFESSIONAL LIABILITY (MEDICAL MALPRACTICE)

Physician Groups

In order to be competitive and profitable, physicians came together in group practices and partnerships. Consolidation offered an opportunity to negotiate better rates and contracts from health-maintenance-organizations (HMO's), reduce overhead costs through centralization of administration, provide purchasing power for medical equipment and supplies. Some of these groups consist of 3 or 4 physicians, others are much larger with hundreds of physicians. There still are a lot of independent practitioners, but more and more are becoming part of a group. There are single specialty groups and multi-specialty groups.

Physicians Practice Management Companies (PPM)

Physicians practice management companies are professionally run corporations in the business of group medicine. They have grown rapidly by purchasing existing medical groups. Sometimes the physicians in the purchased group will end up as an employee or continue to practice at some level of independence. The PPM will provide a host of business services.

Services Provided By PPM:

- Negotiate contracts with numerous health-maintenance-organizations
- Maintain an information system and database
- All office administration and accounting, which includes completing the medical forms needed to receive reimbursement from insurance companies, Medicare, health-maintenance-organizations, and patients.
- Buying medical supplies and equipment in volume thereby saving costs

LIABILITY INSURANCE

PHYSICIANS PROFESSIONAL LIABILITY (MEDICAL MALPRACTICE)

Universe of Physicians In The United States

Total estimate of All Physicians: 860,000

Where Physicians Are Employed

- Independent physicians
- Small physician group
- Large physician group
- Health-maintenance-organization (HMO)
- Small physician practice management (PPM)
- Large physician practice management (PPM)
- Hospital based health systems
- Independent practice association (IPA)
- Management service organization (MSO)

Independent Practice Association (IPA)
An affiliation of independent physicians that negotiates contracts with employers, insurers, HMO's and others.

Capitation
The HMO pays a stipulated amount to a physician or physician group to cover the cost of medical service to a single person.

Management Service Organization (MSO)
An organization providing services to its members, like administration, management, and contract negotiating. MSO's might be formed by a group of hospitals or physician groups.

LIABILITY INSURANCE

HOSPITAL PROFESSIONAL LIABILITY (HOSPITAL MEDICAL MALPRACTICE)

Brief History	An outgrowth of the concept of physicians' malpractice.
Basic Coverage	The policyholder is the hospital and the policy covers allegations of malpractice by the hospital. The hospital has a duty to provide skillful care with a competent staff and proper equipment.
Policy Form	Manuscripted; most insurance companies use a claims made policy form.
New Developments	Hospitals have been merging and managed care has reduced the length of a patients in-hospital stay. Larger hospitals are using self-insurer retention (SIR) and buying excess insurance above the SIR. There also has been a trend when buying excess insurance to purchase an umbrella liability policy instead of a straight excess hospital professional liability policy. The umbrella would cover commercial general liability, hospital professional liability, auto liability, and employer's liability.

MARINE INSURANCE

HULL (PROPERTY) AND LIABILITY INSURANCE

Brief History	May be considered the oldest form of insurance. It was practiced over 700 years ago. Modern marine insurance came about by necessity in England in the late 1600's as merchants needed to insure their cargo coming to the New World. This is the beginning of the term underwriters and Lloyds of London.
Types of Marine insurance	Hull (Property or physical damage) is insurance for the ship itself. Liability (protection and indemnity P&I) is the same concept of coverage as a general liability policy except it is specific to the owner or operator of a ship or vessel. P&I covers (just like a general liability policy) the third party claims of bodily injury and property damage, plus more. To put it another way, P&I covers the ship owner from bodily injuries brought by third parties aboard the ship as well as bodily injuries and property damage the ship itself might cause to a third party. Seamen aboard the ship (if injured) do not necessarily collect workers' compensation but may bring actions against the ship owner. In effect, the seamen are third parties, just like any other third party and represent the most likely source of bodily injury claims against the ship owner.

MARINE INSURANCE

PROTECTION AND INDEMNITY (P&I) LIABILITY INSURANCE

- Covers liability claims brought by any member of the crew against the policyholder which is the ship owner or operator.
- Covers liability claims brought by passengers and guests.
- Covers liability claims brought by shore workers while they are on the vessel.
- Covers liability claims such as the loss of cargo.
- Covers liability claims such as the ship running into another ship, dock, buoy, offshore oil rig or other structure.
- Covers pollution liability claims.
- Covers the removal of wreckage if the ship owner or operator is legally obligated to remove that wreck. Removal of wreckage is simply the removing of a sunken ship that may be hazardous to other ships.
- Covers certain types of fines and penalties that may be levied on the policyholder.

There are other coverages specific to a ship owner or operators that are covered:

- Repatriation of a crew member.
- Claims in regard to cargo needing refrigeration.
- Claims in regard to passenger's baggage.
- Claims in regard to cargo improperly stowed.
- Claims in regard to the issuance of bills of lading.
- Claims in regard to freight on cargo.
- Claims for expenses in the resisting of mutiny aboard the ship.
- Claims in regard to quarantining of the ship.
- There are numerous other coverages.

MARINE INSURANCE

PROTECTION AND INDEMNITY CLUBS (P&I)

Brief History	Protection and Indemnity clubs started in England during the era when ships were sent to the thirteen colonies owned by England. Underwriters and Lloyds would not cover all the potential hazards, so the P&I clubs covered the part that they didn't cover.
Background	There are seventeen P&I clubs and all are connected by membership in the International Association of Clubs. The clubs issue P&I policies to their members.
Who Can Join the Club	Most members are vessel owners, but some are charter operators.
Unlimited Liability	A unique feature of the P&I policies issued by the P&I clubs is that they are issued for unlimited liability, except in regard to pollution which is limited to $500 million. The clubs are debating whether to continue the tradition of unlimited liability.
What are P&I Clubs?	They are mutual insurance organizations owned by the members which provide those same P&I insurance policies.

MARINE INSURANCE

OCEAN MARINE CARGO INSURANCE

Covers the goods or merchandise on board a vessel that is in transit. There are two basic types of cargo policies:

- Single Voyage Policy - this covers one trip and is used by the customer making infrequent shipments.
- Open Cargo Policy - this covers all shipments made by the customer within the policy period.

Section 25

WRAP UP INSURANCE PROGRAM

Wrap Up is not a policy but refers to a *series of policies*, which are centrally controlled and cover a large construction project.

These polices could consist of builders' risk, general liability, umbrella liability, workers' compensation, marine (if needed). It may sometimes include architects and engineers.

Instead of each contractor and subcontractor procuring its own insurance, it is all purchased and controlled by one source *which is often the owner of the construction project.* The owner or his broker will then collect the applicable premiums from all the parties involved in the construction.

The main reasons for using a wrap up are:

- Discount on premiums
- Centralized loss control and claims handling
- Possibility of manuscripting policies to get more specific coverage
- Better overall control of the insurance being purchased
- Greater limits

Section 26

FIDELITY BONDS

Brief History

Fidelity may have started in the 1840's with the Guaranty Society in London.

Basic Coverage

Fidelity bonds are bought by an employer covering dishonest acts of employees from mailroom employees to the president of the company. The bond will pay the employer suffering a loss due to their dishonest acts. Coverage includes misappropriation of funds, embezzlement, fraud and larceny.

In the United States, fidelity bond premiums now exceed \$1 billion. Prime buyers of fidelity bonds are financial institutions because the FDIC and state banking regulators require them to have a fidelity bond.

Policy Form

Most insurance companies use the Surety Association of America (SAA) bond form or a modification of them.

Most Popular Fidelity Forms

The Financial Institution Bond, Standard Form No. 24, was initiated in 1986 by the Surety Association of America and replaced the Bankers Blanket Bond, Standard Form No. 24, originally introduced in 1941. The Financial Institution Bond Standard Form No. 24 has six (6) insuring agreements:

(a) Fidelity
(b) On Premises
(c) In Transit
(d) Forgery or Alteration
(e) Securities
(f) Counterfeit Currency

FIDELITY BONDS

Triggering of Coverage for a Claim Under the Bond

Fidelity bonds are issued on a losses discovered basis when the loss is discovered and reported to the insurance company (surety company). That notification and subsequent proof of loss triggers the coverage for the reported loss. The reason fidelity bonds are issued on a losses discovered basis is an employee who has been stealing will try their utmost to keep that activity secret and will cover up their paper trail. Therefore, it is often impossible to tell when the theft started; what is known is when it was discovered.

Section 27

SURETY BONDS

Brief History

Developed in England, the Guaranty Society of London was formed in 1840 for the purpose of guaranteeing the fidelity of a person holding a financial position of trust. In 1853, the state of New York passed the first act in the United States authorizing the formation of surety companies. The first company was formed in 1875.

Basic Coverage

Surety bonds are not insurance policies but bonds issued by the insurer referred to by those in this business as the surety company or "the surety."

The surety bond is a financial guarantee given to a third party. Most surety bonds originate from the construction industry. Work is being performed for governmental and non-governmental projects and the construction firms will be required to post a surety bond with the owner-obligee. If the work is not completed, the surety bond will respond. Federal, state, city, and local governmental agencies will require the surety company to be on their approved list.

There are three parties named in a bond:

Principal
This is the party that must perform as enumerated in the contract with the bond guaranteeing the performance of the contract. The bond is obtained by the principal but it is for the benefit of the owner of the project - obligee. The bond is issued by the surety company and delivered to the principal. The principal signs the bond and sends it to the obligee who holds it until the agreed upon obligation is completed. If the principal is not able to perform, the surety company will pay the owner - obligee the actual amount of the loss up to the limit of the bond or can chose to complete the contract.

Obligee
This is the party the surety bond will pay if the principal can not perform.

Surety Company, Usually Referred to as The Surety
The company issuing the surety bond.

SURETY BONDS

Penal Amount

There is a penalty if the principal does not complete its performed duties, hence the term penal amount has been used in the surety industry and it is equivalent to an insurance policy limit.

Types of Bonds for the Construction Industry

Contract Bonds Also Referred to as Contract Surety or Construction Bonds
Bonds are needed in the construction industry because owners of the projects being constructed want guarantees the project will be completed.

Performance Bond
This guarantees a contractor has fulfilled its obligations under the construction contract. The bond is issued to the contractor–principal that is responsible for completing the project. If the project isn't complete, the bond makes payment to the owner–obligee of the project for the uncompleted work.

Payment Bond
The bond is guaranteeing the contractor-principal will make all the payments to suppliers and subcontractors on the bonded project.

Combination of Performance and Payment Bond
This bond combines the performance and payment under one bond form.

Private contract bonds are issued for significant non-governmental projects.

Public contract bonds are issued for city, state, federal and other governmental entities.

Bid Bond
Most construction projects will require contractors to bid for the contract and will require a bid bond be presented by the contractor-principal when it enters its bid on the project. The bond guarantees the bidder, if successful, will enter into a contract for the amount bid and provide the required performance and payment bonds. A bid letting is a public forum to open sealed bids and read the bids aloud.

SURETY BONDS (CONT'D)

Completion Bond

This type of bond is guaranteeing that the project will be completed to the satisfaction of a party other than the owner. For instance, a private road is to be re-paved and sewer lines repaired. The owner of the private road, Mason Street Association, is having the work done by Ashley Construction. The town of St. Matthews, NH required that Ashley Construction post a completion bond with it.

Treasury List

This is the Federal Government's way of assuring itself that for federal projects the contractor-principal can perform its duties to complete the project and if it cannot, they will have the proceeds of the bond. The treasury list itself is a list of approved surety companies whose bonds are acceptable security. To find treasury sureties go to www.fms.treas.gov.

Collateral

The surety company may require collateral or a personal indemnity agreement from the principal before it will issue a bond. Another form of protection to the surety company is the escrow account or custodian account, which is used to control the project's financial disbursements. This insures that those disbursements are for the project.

Other Types of Bonds

Public Officials Bond

A public official, such as tax collector, treasurer, and supervisor may have to have a bond in regard to their handling public funds. The bond is protecting the public.

Judicial Bond

This is a financial guarantee bond and relates to court decisions in which monies may be awarded. The bond is guaranteeing the party requiring the bond can meet its obligation if there is an adverse judgment and there is a monetary award. If the party can't meet the obligation, the judicial bond pays.

SURETY BONDS (CONT'D)

Fiduciary Bond
Guarantees that someone acting in a fiduciary capacity will act in accordance with the laws governing its transactions.

License and Permit Bond
Guarantees the party requiring the bond will comply with local, state, or federal agency regulations governing the activity to be engaged in.

Custom Bonds
Guarantees the payment of duties by the party requiring the bond who is an importer or exporter in regard to U.S. Custom Service Regulation.

Miscellaneous Bonds
Under miscellaneous bonds are the numerous other specialty bonds that are available.

Co-Surety — This is when more than one surety company participates and shares in a bond.

Salvage — If the surety company has sustained a loss because it was required to make a payment under a bond then it is entitled to receive reimbursement from any subrogation or salvage recoveries in regard to the loss under that bond.

Attorney In Fact — A surety company without a local office may appoint an individual or company to be its representative in the area and grant them the legal power to execute bonds and other documents on their behalf.

Surety Association of America — Formed in 1908 in an attempt to standardize forms and provide rate guidelines.

Surety Forms — Bond requirements of the obligee can be very different, therefore there are hundreds of different bond forms. It is the obligee that dictates the type of bond form needed.

SURETY BONDS (CONT'D)

The 3 C's	Surety underwriters will evaluate companies-principals and individuals-principals requiring a bond in three main areas of character, capital and capacity. For example, let's look at Wilson Construction Company: <u>Character</u> What is Wilson's reputation for completing projects and making all payments? <u>Capital</u> Does Wilson possess the proper amount of capital to take on the project? <u>Capacity</u> Does Wilson have the ability to perform the work? Do they have the proper equipment, labor force, supervisors, knowledge and expertise for the project?
Triggering of Coverage for a Claim Under the Bond	Surety bonds are issued on a losses discovered basis. When the loss is discovered and reported to the surety company, that notification and subsequent proof of loss triggers the coverage for the reported loss.

A TYPICAL CONSTRUCTION PROJECT

Obligee:	Fairlakes Township, N.J.
Project:	Build a new library Total Project Cost - $2,600,000 Put architectural plans out to contractors to bid on.
Bid Bond:	All contractors – principals required to post bid bond with the Fairlakes Township – obligee.
Contract Awarded To:	Ace Construction Corporation, which bid $1,789,000 to perform the construction portion of the project.
Performance and Payment Bond:	Ace will be required to post with Fairlakes Township - obligee a performance and payment bond.
Neptune Surety Corporation Warrensville, TN:	Ace, prior to bidding, would obtain a commitment from Neptune Surety Corporation to be issued a combination performance and payment bond. Neptune would issue the bond for this specific project to Ace – principal. Ace would sign and hand deliver to Fairlakes Township - obligee. The bond would list the particulars for the construction job.

Section 28

FEDERAL INSURANCE PLANS

The United States Congress and the past Presidents have recognized the importance of insurance and have enacted laws designed to make insurance available when the private commercial market has been reluctant to do so. The plans set up by the federal government are designed to assist the state governments to set up insurance plans in their state. Often, the federal government acts as a reinsurer.

FAIR ACCESS TO INSURANCE REQUIREMENTS (FAIR PLANS)
This originated in 1968 with the passage of the Urban Property Protection Reinsurance Act of 1968, which made certain types of property insurance available in urban areas. Additional modifying legislation would come later. Each state may have its own specific FAIR plan unique to its state.

NATIONAL FLOOD INSURANCE PROGRAM
This originated with the National Flood Act of 1968 and with other legislation at later times, such as the Flood Disaster Protection Act of 1974, to make flood insurance available to those property owners with homes or business in flood-prone areas.

FEDERAL CRIME INSURANCE PROGRAM
This started in 1971 with the passage of the Housing and Urban Development Act and makes crime insurance available, such as burglary and theft, to inner city areas.

FEDERAL CROP INSURANCE CORPORATIONS (FCIC)
The Federal Crop Insurance Act became law in 1970. It is designed to make certain types of crop insurance available to farmers.

OVERSEAS PRIVATE INVESTMENT CORPORATION (OPIC)
This was established in 1971 under the name Overseas Private Investment Corporation (OPIC). This organization can trace its roots all the way back to the Marshall Plan of 1948. Its purpose is to encourage corporations to make investments in developing countries by protecting its assets in those countries by buying insurance from OPIC for certain types of political risks. OPIC is an agency of the United States government and its obligations are ultimately backed up by the full faith and credit of the U.S. government.

Types of Insurance Available From O.P.I.C.

- Currency Inconvertibility
- Expropriation
- Political Violence

TERRORISM INSURANCE PROGRAM

The genesis for this program was the terrorist act upon the United States on September 11, 2001. This created an inability for businesses to obtain property and casualty insurance at reasonable and predictable prices for acts of terrorism.

The Terrorism Risk Insurance Act of 2002 was signed into law on November 26, 2002 as a temporary program terminating on December 31, 2005 unless extended, which it was. The Act established a program within the United States Department of the Treasury. All property and casualty insurers are required to participate and provide coverage for certified acts of terrorism. The Federal government shares, with the insurance industry, the risk of loss from future certified acts of terrorism. The Act is triggered when the Secretary of Treasury certifies a loss meeting the definition of "an act of terrorism." Insurers will receive reimbursement from the Federal government for a portion of their paid loss after a total industry wide certified act of terrorism exceeds $5,000,000. Collectively, all property and casualty insurer losses caused by certified acts of terrorism and reimbursable by the Federal Government are capped by the Act at $100 billion per year. In other words, the Government's reimbursement shall not exceed $100 billion per year.

The Terrorism Risk Insurance Act of 2005
Signed into law December 22, 2005, this extended the original Act for two years.

The Terrorism Risk Insurance Program Reauthorization Act of 2007
Signed into law December 26, 2007 this extends the Terrorism Risk Insurance Act of 2002 and 2005 through December 31, 2014. The key additional provisions of the Reauthorization Act are summarized in the U.S. Department of the Treasury Interim Guidance Concerning the Terrorism Risk Insurance Reauthorization Act of 2007:

- Extends the Terrorism Program through December 31, 2014.

- Revise the definition of "Act of Terrorism" to remove the requirement that the act of terrorism be committed by an individual acting on behalf of any foreign person or foreign interest in order to be certified as an "act of terrorism" for purposes of the Act.

- Define "Insurer Deductible" for all Additional Program Years as the value of an insurer's direct earned premium for commercial property and casualty insurance for the immediately preceding calendar year multiplied by 20 percent.

- Set the Federal share of compensation for insured losses (subject to a $100 million Program Trigger) for all Additional Program Years at 85 percent of that portion of the amount of insured losses that exceeds the applicable insurer deductible.

- Require Treasury to submit a report to Congress and issue final regulations for determining the <u>pro rata</u> share of insured losses to be paid under the Program when aggregate insured losses exceed the annual liability cap of $100,000,000,000.

- Require the Secretary of the Treasury to notify Congress not later than 15 days after the date of an act of terrorism as to whether aggregate insured losses are estimated to exceed $100,000,000,000.

- Require for policies issued after the date of enactment, that insurers provide clear and conspicuous disclosure to the policyholder of the existence of the $100,000,000,000 cap at the time of offer, purchase, and renewal of a policy (in addition to current disclosure requirements).

- Revise the recoupment provisions of the Act. For purposes of recouping the Federal share of compensation under the Act, the ''insurance marketplace aggregate retention amount'' for all Additional Program Years is the lesser of $27.5 billion and the aggregate amount, for all insurers, of insured losses during each Program Year. With regard to mandatory recoupment of the Federal share of compensation through policyholder surcharges, collection is required within a certain schedule specified in the Reauthorization Act. The limitation that surcharges not exceed 3 percent of the premium charged for property and casualty insurance coverage under the policy is eliminated (but remains in the case of discretionary recoupment).

- Require Treasury to issue recoupment regulations within 180 days of enactment, and publish an estimate of aggregate insured losses within 90 days after an act of terrorism.

- Require the President's Working Group on Financial Markets to perform an ongoing analysis regarding the long-term availability and affordability of terrorism risk insurance and submit reports in 2010 and 2013.

- Require the Comptroller General to examine and report on the availability and affordability of insurance coverage for nuclear, biological, chemical, and radiological terrorist events; the future outlook for such coverage; and the capacity of insurers and State workers compensation funds to manage the risk associated with nuclear, biological, chemical, and radiological terrorist events.

- Require the Comptroller General to study and report on the question of whether there are specific markets in the United States where there are unique capacity constraints on the amount of terrorism risk insurance available.

- Treasury will be issuing regulations to administer and implement TRIA, as amended by the Reauthorization Act. This notice is issued to assist insurers in complying with certain new statutory requirements pending the issuance of such regulations. This notice contains interim guidance concerning compliance with the mandatory availability or "make available" requirements in section 103(c) of the Act, and the disclosure notice requirements in section 103(b) of the Act. Other requirements in current regulations remain in effect.

Section 29

SELF-INSURED RETENTION VS DEDUCTIBLE

SELF INSURED RETENTION (SIR)

You might say this is the area of no insurance; all the risk within the self-insured retention is retained by the insured. Within the self-insured retention the insured handles its own claims. The insurer's policy is above the SIR. For instance, if a 1,000,000 policy's limits are above the SIR, it is for a full 1,000,000.

Key Points

1. Insured handles its own claims within the SIR
2. The insurer policy is for the full policy limit above the SIR

Self-Insured retention (SIR) - 100,000
Policy Limit - 1,000,000. This 1,000,000 does not contain the SIR of 100,000.

DEDUCTIBLE

The insurance is on a primary basis with the deductible inside the policy. The insurer has the responsibility to handle the claims.

Example: A 1,000,000 policy limit with a 100,000 deductible: The insurer settles the claims and then deducts 100,000. Does that mean the policyholder has only 900,000 of true coverage? The answer is yes - and no. Here's why:

Claim Settled	Deductible	Policyholder's Coverage
1,000,000	100,000	900,000
1,100,000 or more	100,000	1,000,000

Key Points

1. Insurer handles claims even inside the deductible, which is deducted after the claim has been settled.
2. The insurer's deductible is inside the policy limit.
3. Policy limit - 1,000,000 (the deductible is within the 1,000,000).

Section 30

STRUCTURED SETTLEMENT

One way for an insurer to settle a claim is to write a check for the entire claim amount. Another way is to structure a settlement so the claimant receives funds over a long period of time, often throughout their lifetime. This is usually done because the claimant's injuries will require lifetime care.

Simple Definition: Structured Claim Settlement

The settlement of a claim by agreeing to make guaranteed installment payments over a length of time, after an initial cash settlement.

Example of a claim settled by a structured settlement

Claimant receives one-third (1/3) immediate cash for the payment of legal fees, medical cost incurred up to that point and other necessary expenses. Two-thirds (2/3) of the settlement will be paid over the claimant's lifetime for medical expenses and a guaranteed monthly installment to compensate for being only partially able to work.

Factors considered for a structured settlement

- State statutes, judicial rulings and insurance department regulations governing structured settlements
- Age of claimant, life expectancy, lost earnings, inflation, the size of the settlement, claimant's family situation
- Type of injuries
- How much continuous medical care will be needed over the claimant lifetime.
- Type of medical care
- How much are the estimated expenses for physical and occupational rehabilitation
- Custodial care expenses while at home such as home care taker
- Special equipment for the home and transportation needs such as a specially equipped van

A method to provide guarantee monthly installments

Life insurance companies sell life annuities, which can provide those guaranteed monthly installments over a claimant's life time. One initial payment is made to the life insurer for the annuity. The life insurer is able to offer installment payments over a claimant's lifetime for one initial cash payment because that cash can be invested and held over a long period which creates sufficient income to make monthly payments over a claimant's lifetime *greater* than the initial cash. The money held by the life insurer has a value (time value of money), and in order to determine how much initial cash must be paid up front, you need to determine the "present value" of the agreed upon guaranteed monthly payments. In another words, how much money do you need in the beginning to pay out a fixed sum over a long period of time (those guaranteed monthly payments)?

<u>Example</u>:

- Claimant settles for $8,000 per month, which is $96,000 per year.
- Claimant Life Expectancy 30 years
- Total Expected Payout $2,880,000

The life insurer would compute an interest rate they expect to receive on the initial cash they receive. They would then present value the $2,880,000 and arrive at a discounted amount of initial cash paid to them immediately (let's say $1,500,000).

Section 31

CAPTIVE INSURANCE COMPANIES

Keep in mind when people say captive, they really mean "captive insurer." A captive is an insurer, just like other insurance companies, except it is formed and controlled by the insured for the purpose of insuring its own risk. Captive insurance companies can also be formed by a group of insureds to collectively insure their own risk.

The total number of captives worldwide is estimated to be over 5,000. Over 3,000 are offshore and over 1,250 are domiciled in various states. Over 2,000 U.S. corporations have captives.

States such as Vermont, Colorado, Hawaii and Arizona and twenty other states have enacted laws to facilitate the formation of captives. Vermont is the leading state for onshore captives and Bermuda is the leading location for offshore captives.

SINGLE INTEREST CAPTIVE INSURANCE COMPANY (MAY BE CALLED PURE CAPTIVE)

This type of captive only insures the parent company which owns the captive; another way of saying this is the captive only insures a "single" company…which is its owner. Example, ABC Industrial, Inc. forms a captive insurer and calls it ABC Insurance Ltd. It only insures ABC Industrial, Inc.

A captive insurer owned by the insured with direct access to reinsurers adds a new dimension to its insurance programs and increases its flexibility. Like a coach having a player come off the bench to play at a moments notice, the captive sits quietly waiting to come in if insurance rates are raised to unrealistic levels. It can also be part of the negotiating strategy to assist in bringing those rates down or if terms and conditions become burdensome.

There are numerous combinations of events and circumstances the captive can play to give the "insurance coach" flexibility. The captive is there to be integrated into the commercial insurance program of the insured to make that program better.

Reasons for SINGLE INTEREST Captive Formation

- To give the corporation a valuable insurance tool to assist in controlling and stabilizing their insurance program, directing the focus to controlling risk and insurance cost.

- Potential savings on the corporation's premiums by recapturing some of their own premium and investment income derived from holding that premium.

- Defensive mechanism against the commercial insurance market's arbitrary and capricious rate increases. In a hard market there may be an unavailability of certain insurance at a reasonable cost or the insurer may want to exclude the coverage's you need.

- Incentive to do general and specific loss prevention to reduce accidents. This may include the reengineering of machines and redesigning workstations.

- The captive's retention can be adjusted depending on whether it is a hard or soft market.

- Create or supplement the commercial insurance market's capacity. For instance, if the captive participates in the lower layer, it could increase capacity above.

- The captive will pay the parent company's legitimate claims.

- Ability to manuscript policies and provide coverages needed by the insured not available from the commercial insurers such coverage's may be pollution liability, pollution clean up, political risk.

- Access reinsurers, most now have alternative risk departments set up specifically to reinsure captives.

- Assist in insurance negotiations on price and coverage.

- If the captive's underwriting results and investment income are good, eventually the captive can become a major asset for the corporation.

- Possible tax benefits (changing and complex topic).

APPLICATIONS OF CAPTIVE INTERACTING WITH INSURANCE PROGRAM

Hypothetical Example (1):

Neptune Insurance Company is a recognized expert and specialty writer of boilers. Let's say they want to charge $1,000,000 as an annual insurance premium. Analysis of losses shows only two losses in the past ten years totaling $1,300,000. Premiums for those ten years are found to be $7,000,000.

You don't want to eliminate Neptune, but the captive could retain a portion of the coverage and reduce Neptune's participation or induce Neptune into providing a better deal by simply suggesting the captive may be thinking of taking a large portion of the risk, hence reducing Neptune's premium.

Hypothetical Example (2):

A Fortune 500 company purchases 200 million in insurance limits for its general liability exposure; however the pollution coverage is very restrictive. The company wants to expand the coverage and add some other unique coverage. Its commercial insurers are not able to respond and are adamant about keeping the policy as it is. The Fortune 500 Company could form a captive insurer, manuscript its own policy putting in the coverages it wants, and then go into the reinsurance marketplace to obtain coverage over its retention. In cases like this, you will find you can approach not only the reinsurers but also insurers can participate as well even though technically it is reinsurance; therefore you are able to access the reinsurance and insurance market. They can participate side by side, which means you created more capacity for your program. If you do this, it is also a good idea to ask the reinsurer and especially the insurers to only put down their *net line*. If you don't, they may all try to beat a path to the same few reinsurers for reinsurance support behind them. This may create confusion in the marketplace. Also, if there is too much reinsurance behind a reinsurer or insurer participating on your program, they will be subject to the whims of their reinsurer.

You may also find some exclusions and conditions in your policy were mandated by reinsurers. Communicating with them through the captive, these exclusions might be removed and unwanted conditions mitigated.

GROUP CAPTIVE INSURANCE COMPANY
ASSOCIATION CAPTIVE INSURANCE COMPANY

These captives insure a group of insureds, which are its owners. The captive is formed by the insureds because they share a common insurance purpose, for instance they are in the same industry.

An association which represents one specific industry group is an ideal candidate to form a captive to insure their members.

Hypothetical Example (3):
The association of retail drug stores consists of 1,000 members. 400 members make a capital contribution and form Drug Stores Captive Insurance Company for the purpose of insuring drug stores that are members of the association.

An advantage of this type of captive is the management of the captive would be dedicated to the members' insurance needs. The premium the captive charges its members would reflect the member's experience. The captive could retain risk and in a hard market or a very difficult line of insurance this may be the best way to provide insurance. The captive also has access to the reinsurance market place.

An association captive brings together members that would otherwise not meet and could lead to a number of *value added* opportunities.

THE DISADVANTAGES OF FORMING A CAPTIVE INSURER

- Capital and start up costs are needed to form the captive.

- The formation and running a captive will be time consuming.

- Adverse claims development, especially in the early years, could lead to the captive failing or for a need of additional infusion of capital.

- Single interest captive insurance companies face changing tax laws, IRS regulations and tax court decisions.

- In a soft insurance market commercial insurers, because of severe competition, may charge a premium below expected expenses and losses; therefore insurance may be purchased from commercial insurers for less than the captive needs to charge to break even.

- If the captive is being set up to write insurance it must have a license in each state or it will require a fronting insurer which adds costs due to fronting fees and administration. If the captive is going to be a non-admitted reinsurer it will need to furnish a letter of credit or other security to the front insurer.

LINES OF INSURANCE A CAPTIVE INSURANCE COMPANY CAN OFFER

No inherent restrictions, a Certificate of Authority from the governing authority could be granted for general liability, product liability, medical liability, professional liability, property, and many other lines of insurance.

SINGLE CELL CAPTIVE / RENT A CAPTIVE / SPONSORED CAPTIVE

This started exclusively as an offshore captive structure but the concept is starting to become accepted onshore with a few states such as Vermont and Rhode Island passing legislation's allowing a form of this arrangement.

Here is a general overview (In Vermont it is called Sponsored Captive):
A captive is formed and managed for the purpose of allowing other organizations to utilize the captive for a fee. Those renting the captive are given their own ***cell*** within the captive. The advantages of using this method there is little or no capital infusion, no startup costs and time in forming a captive, and no administration cost of maintaining a captive. Rent A Captive (single cell) is tailored to the smaller organizations which cannot afford their own captive.

WHY ARE CAPTIVE INSURERS ESTABLISHED OFFSHORE?

ADVANTAGES OF BEING OFFSHORE

- Less insurance regulation, a friendly environment in which to operate, confidentially laws and the ease in which a captive insurer can be formed; there are minimal capital requirements. Domiciles such as Bermuda do have laws governing insurance, but you are not subject to 50 state insurance departments. Bermuda is the leading location for offshore captives with about 1400. They collectively write $23 billion in premiums.

- Bermuda and other offshore domiciles generally have no corporate income taxes or other taxes on corporations.

DISADVANTAGES OF BEING OFFSHORE

- If the captive is writing insurance, it will always need a front company, and therefore will not have an opportunity to acquire state licenses, which could be very valuable, especially if the captive wants to broaden itself into standard insurer.

- The captive will be under constraints not to market in the United States.

- Premiums paid to the offshore captive will probably be subject to Federal Excise Tax (FET). This is now a fairly complex subject. Your CPA firm will need to guide you on this topic.

- Public entity captives do not pay corporate income taxes, so there is little advantage for them to be offshore.

- Some states have enacted enabling laws allowing captive insurance companies to be formed quicker and easier and may provide some favorable tax treatment. Vermont is the leading onshore domicile. Other states with laws favorable to captives are Colorado, Hawaii, Delaware, Kansas, Rhode Island, Florida, Georgia, West Virginia, Virginia, Tennessee, and New York.

CAPTIVE AND TAXES

Tax questions basically revolve around single interest captives and whether the parent corporation can deduct as expenses the insurance premiums paid to its own captive. This is a complex subject with changing IRS regulations and court decisions; we will not deal with it here. You can start by talking to your certified public accounting firm.

HOW TO GET STARTED IN FORMING A CAPTIVE INSURER

- Do a *feasibility study* to determine if a captive is feasible. Will it be cost effective? Will your management commit the capital, time and effort? Do they understand they will be forming an insurance company with a separate board of directors? What do you want the captive to do; what are its aims? What types of insurance policies will it issue, or will it do reinsurance? Is there a problem with availability of insurance? If not, why is the captive being formed?

- If it is a group captive, survey the potential members to build a data bank in regard to commitment of capital to the captive, location of members, description of their operations, gross sales, premiums and rates they are currently paying to commercial insurance companies, the related losses paid and reserved, types of polices, policy limits, deductibles, terms and conditions, exclusions, and loss control. Are they having a problem obtaining insurance?

- It needs to be decided whether the captive will be managed by a captive manager or using a dedicated staff which would have to be set up and the domicile chosen.

- Choosing service providers:
  - ...A law firm will be needed to incorporate the captive, acquire a Certificate of Authority from the domicile, and develop its bylaws. A local law firm may be needed to navigate through the specific domicile regulations.
  - ...If a captive manager is chosen to administer the captive it will also be involved in marketing, compliance with the Insurance Department regulations or other governing authorities, which includes filing statutory financial statements, underwrite the risks insured, claims administration, purchase reinsurance, accounting and administration.
  - ...Actuarial firm needed for insurance rates, review of loss reserves.
  - ...Certified public accounting firm to audit the financials and provide tax counseling in regard to income taxes, Federal Excise Tax (FET), dividends, and capital gains taxes.

- Investment advisor will be needed and investment philosophy.

- Reinsurance broker to provide the best reinsurance and to find the proper fronting company if it is needed.

- Select a bank to deposit funds, arrange letters of credit, bank wires and other services.

- Choosing the captive insurer's domicile...onshore or offshore and location. The application process may include the feasibility study, business plan, strategic plan, biographical of the principals and pro forma balance sheets.

Section 32

RISK RETENTION GROUPS (RRG)

Liability Risk Retention Act of 1986
15 USC 3901-3906 Amends Product Liability
Risk Retention Act of 1981

BACKGROUND

1970's

In 1979 in reaction to a severe shortage for product liability in insurance, the United States Department of Commerce asked Congress to enact legislation to facilitate the group purchase of product liability insurance for those engaged in the manufacturing, distributing, and selling of products. This became the Product Liability Risk Retention Act of 1981. Its goal was to provide an alternative market to standard commercial insurance to those groups having trouble acquiring product liability insurance.

1980's

The very soft insurance market of 1980 to 1985 ended abruptly, dramatically creating the unprecedented hard market of 1986. Almost overnight insurance and reinsurance markets shrank, primarily in the area of *liability insurance.* Certain classes of insureds were hit especially hard such as municipalities, day care centers, public housing authorities, truckers, taxi cabs operators, bus companies, physicians, hospitals and many more. In reaction to this crisis the United States Congress expanded the 1981 Product Liability Risk Retention Act passing the Liability Risk Retention Act of 1986 enabling groups of homogeneous buyers of *liability* insurance to join together to form their own liability insurance company. The act requires the phrase "Risk Retention Group" be included in the name. The act also permitted the formation of "Risk Purchasing Groups".

CRITERIA FOR THE FORMATION OF A RISK RETENTION GROUP

- The risk retention group must qualify under the Liability Risk Retention Act of 1986.

- The group must be homogeneous; members must be in a common or similar business.

- The risk retention group must acquire an insurance license in one state. In order to do this the risk retention group must submit a business plan which will include a feasibility study, financial plan, lines of insurance, surplus, policy form, policy limits, rates, reinsurance and other relevant information. After this license has been granted, the risk retention group will need to inform and register with each state it will issue a policy.

- The risk retention group can issue only commercial liability policies. No personal lines of insurance, no property insurance and no workers' compensation.

- Under the 1986 Act, risk retention groups are not permitted to domicile offshore. There are a few offshore risk retention groups, which were permitted under the 1981 Act.

- Risk retention groups are required to meet minimum capital requirements, which most likely will come from its members.

POLICY FORM
Only liability policies permitted. The act does not specify the type of form so it could be occurrence or claims made.

TYPES OF POLICIES OFFERED BY RISK RETENTION GROUPS

- Commercial General Liability
- Automobile Liability
- Physicians Professional Liability
- Hospital Professional Liability
- Environmental Liability
- Aviation Liability
- Fiduciary Liability
- Employment Practices Liability
- Products Liability
- Directors and Officers
- Errors and Omissions Liability
- Lawyers Professional Liability
- Architects and Engineering Liability

THE MANAGING OF RISK RETENTION GROUPS
Most risk retention groups have hired firms to manage their operations; some manage their own operations.

BENEFITS OF FORMING A RISK RETENTION GROUP
The chief benefit is (if you have homogenous group which needs commercial liability insurance) you are able to write insurance in all (50) states by obtaining a license in only one state. RRG's are exempt from ***some*** State laws, rules, and regulations, including licensure, policy forms, rates and any law which will prevent the accomplishment of the purpose of the Act. It is not exempt from State laws such as unfair claim practices, discrimination, no fault laws, agent licensing and other such state laws.

STRESS BETWEEN STATES AND RISK RETENTION GROUP
Even though the Liability Risk Retention Act of 1986 permitted risk retention groups to enter states easily, many insurance regulators have been reluctant to embrace that idea for the following reasons: Many risk retention groups have very limited surplus; in the early years no rating, no meaningful track record and were simply viewed as a means of circumventing regulation. Several risk retention groups have gone into liquidation. On the other hand, there are well managed successful risk retention groups. Most of the stress seems to revolve around the risk retention group financial responsibilities.

STATE PREMIUM TAXES
Must be paid by the risk retention groups to each state in which it writes policies, the same as a standard insurer.

RATES AND FORMS
Basically exempt from state laws.

FEDERAL AND STATE INCOME TAXES
Risk retention groups pay all Federal and State taxes unless they have a non-profit status.

CAPITAL CONTRIBUTION
Original members most likely would be required to contribute capital to the original surplus of the risk retention group; however that is not the only way it can acquire its original capital, but it is more than likely the way it is done.

CERTIFICATE OF AUTHORITY FORM ONE STATE
In order for a risk retention group to start issuing policies it first must obtain a Certificate of Authority from one state.

REINSURANCE
The risk retention group will retain some risk and reinsure the rest. Good reinsurance will be vital to its success. A risk retention group may only reinsure liability insurance from other risk retention groups or group members with liability risks that are similar or related to those of the group assuming the risks.

COUNTER SIGNATURE LAWS

Exempt from all state counter signature laws.

PURCHASING GROUP (PG)

A purchasing group is a group of homogeneous insurance buyers collectively buying liability insurance from one insurer, almost always through a broker. The insurer must be an admitted insurer or surplus lines company in each state policies are issued.

CRITERIA FOR THE FORMATION OF A PURCHASING GROUP

- The purchasing group must qualify under the Liability Risk Retention Act of 1986.
- The purchasing group must have homogeneous members in a common or similar business.
- The purchasing group can only buy commercial liability policies, no property, and no workers' compensation.
- The insured must become a member of the purchasing group before they can buy the insurance offered by the group.
- Purchasing groups cannot retain risk.
- Each insured within the group can have a separate policy or a group master policy can be issued with individual certificates issued to the insureds.
- Most states will require an agent or broker to place business from the purchasing group with the insurer.

POLICY FORM

Only liability policies permitted. The act does not specify the type of form so it could be occurrence or claims made.

BENEFITS OF FORMING A PURCHASING GROUP

Purchasing groups are exempt from state laws relating to the creation of groups for the purchase of insurance, prohibition of group purchasing or any law that will discriminate against any group or its members. In addition, an insurer shall be exempt from state laws, which prohibits providing or offering to provide to a purchasing group or its members, advantages based on their loss and expense experience not offered to other persons with respect to rates, policy forms, coverage, or other matters (Not Exempt From Rate and Form Filling and Approval Requirements). A purchasing group shall be subject to all other applicable state laws.

- The group working with its broker and insurer can devise a manuscript policy specifically for the group which could include a divided plan for its members. If there is a tailor-made policy this could be a big advantage.
- A purchasing group has marketing advantages and purchasing power that come with a group purchases.
- If the group becomes successful, it could try to convert itself into a risk retention group.
- There are no capital requirements for the member-insureds of the group.

STATE PREMIUM TAXES

The insurer insuring the purchasing group members will be responsible for paying premium taxes not the purchasing group. The insurer will pay tax at the same rate it pays for all other premiums.

STATE GUARANTY FUNDS

Insurer issuing policies to a purchasing group must comply with all state guaranty fund laws. If the insured is a surplus lines company its policyholders are not protected by state guaranty fund laws.

SIZE OF GROUP

The 1986 act does not specify that the purchasing group must be a minimum or maximum size.

STATE LAWS

Must register in all states policy is providing coverage.

COUNTER SIGNATURE LAWS

The insurer insuring a purchasing group is not exempt from state counter signature laws.

CAPITAL CONTRIBUTION

The members of the purchasing group do not contribute capital.

RISK RETENTION GROUP VS. PURCHASING GROUP

Risk Retention Group	Purchasing Group
• An insurance company that must acquire an admitted license in one state and can issue policies in other state in which it is registered.	• A purchasing group is not an insurance company but a group of insurers which buy liability insurance from one insurer.
• Must raise capital.	• No capital raising requirements.
• Insureds must be homogeneous.	• Insureds must be homogeneous.
• Only commercial liability policies.	• Only commercial liability policies.
• Will issue individual policies.	• Purchasing groups have individual policies or a master policy with individual certificates.
• Must have "Risk Retention Group" within its overall name.	• No requirement to put purchasing group in the name.
• Exempt from state laws in regard to licensure after they gain a license in at least one state. Must register in the other states.	• Insurer which accepts business from an purchasing group must meet state requirements for being an admitted insurance company or surplus lines company.
• Except for its state of domicile, the RRG is exempt from state laws in regard to policy form and rates.	• Exempt from state laws in regard to policy form and rates.
• Can issue a manuscript policy with endorsements that suits specific needs of insured. Policies can have dividend plans specific to their insureds.	• Can issue a manuscript policy with endorsements that suits specific needs of insured. Policies can have dividend plans specific to their insureds.
• Risk retention group can retain risk.	• Purchasing group can not retain risk.
• Reinsurance vital to its success.	• Purchasing group does not have to concern itself with reinsurance.
• May accept business from agents, brokers, or directly.	• Almost all states require business flow through an insurance broker or agent.
• Exempt from state guaranty funds.	• Insurer issuing policies to purchasing group must comply with all state guaranty fund laws, unless it is a surplus lines company. Surplus lines companies can not be covered by guaranty funds.
• Risk retention group will pay state premium taxes.	• Insurer which accepts business from a purchasing group must pay premium taxes.

HOW TO START A RISK RETENTION GROUP OR PURCHASING GROUP

Survey Potential Members For
...Interest in joining group, is there a real need not being met by commercial insurers.
...Description of operations.
...What lines of insurance do members need, commercial general liability, products liability, professional liability, D&O, etc.

Criteria for Joining Group
...What is the homogenous business all potential insureds have in common?

Advantage to Member in Joining Group
...Manuscript policy provides coverage members need.
...Stable rates and premiums.
...Loss control specific to the members industry.

Compile a Database on Potential Members:
...Premiums and loss information by member, type of policy occurrence or claims made (if claims made will there be a retroactive date?), policy limits, deductible, self insured retention.
...Determine the maximum policy limit and the average policy limit.
...Is there a specimen policy now available?
...Which states will the group operate?

Insurance Rates and Premiums:
...Is there a rating schedule available?
...Will rates be promulgated by a recognized actuarial firm?
...What will rates be based on?
...Will there be a minimum premium?
...Any idea of average premium?

Marketing/Securing Business:
...How will the group acquire business? Direct solicitation, independent agents, captive agency force? If independent agents are to be used will they be paid a commission, if so what percentage?

Competition
...What other insurers, by state, are offering the same lines of insurance?
...What type of policies and rates are those insurers offering?

Legal
...What form will the group be and where will they domicile?

Financial Consideration

...Are potential members willing to contribute capital?
...Where will this capital come from?
...Will the insureds be quoted a premium and be required to make a capital contribution?
...Who will be the owners?
...Will the new group have any debt?
...Pro forma financial statements.
...Does the group plan to be annually audited by a certified CPA firm? If so which one?
...Does the company plan to have its reserves annually certified by an actuarial firm? If so which one?
...Breakout of all expenses/fees/brokerage/commissions.

Percentage of Premium

Premium taxes:
Commission & brokerage to agents:
Commission to association:
Management fee:
Legal, actuarial and audit fees:
Boards & bureaus fees:
Other:

Administration:

... Will the group employ its own dedicated management staff or will it appoint a management company?

Reinsurance:

...What will the group retain on each policy?
...Does the group want to retain as much risk and as much premium as it can?
...If the groups capital is low and limits are high, quota share reinsurance may be the only way this can be accomplished.

Section 33

RATING COMMERCIAL INSURANCE & REINSURANCE

A SIMPLE OVERVIEW

An insurer's income consists of premiums and investment income; its outgo is losses and expenses and the difference creates profits.

AN INSUERS INCOME: RATES, PREMIUM AND INVESTMENT INCOME

Insurance ratemaking actuaries promulgate rates used in the calculation of premium by analyzing the components of loss, expense and profit. During this process they will review benchmark rates provided by rating bureaus, if available. They may also review their competitor's rates on file at the state insurance department. The actuary's final rates will be further reviewed by management which will consider competition, the investment income potential; rates will also be reviewed by their legal staff to be certain they comply with insurance department regulations.

The final rates will be published in the insurers manual rate guide to be used by their underwriters to calculate premium quoted to a potential insured. Underwriters will also modify the rates charged in their underwriting process. For any given insured their premium could rise (debiting) or could be reduced (crediting). We provide a sample of this in Schedule (A). In summary, there are a number of factors influencing insurance rates. The premiums generated are invested and is a major source of income for all insurers.

LOSS COMPONENT

In the loss component, the ratemaking actuary is trying to predict the frequency of losses occurring in the future and predicting how many will be severe; combined, this is referred to as "expected future losses." In order to do this the ratemaking actuary will use statistical loss distribution curves available to measure loss severity, also used will be models and simulations to make assumptions about distribution of losses. They are looking at losses in the aggregate, however specific past claims within their model will be *trended and developed.* The ratemaking actuary is looking to come up with a pure lost cost rate. That is the rate needed to generate premiums just to cover the expected future losses, then the actuary with the input of management and within the legal environment insurance companies operate will increase that rate for expenses and profit and come up with a final rate that can be placed in the insurance manual rating guide.

Trending Factors: Roughly translate into inflation factors.

Developing Factors: Roughly translates into predicting the future value of claims. Individual case reserves are set by claims personnel but when claims are actually settled they could be above or below those reserves. Developing looks reserves in total and makes certain assumptions.

Insurance losses are looked at in regard to *frequency* and *severity:*

Frequency refers to how often losses occur, small losses occur often and provide good data for the ratemaking actuary and are the basis for formulating rates and premiums for the basic policy limit.

Severity refers to large losses which happen infrequently, are difficult to predict, and hence *do not* provide good data for the ratemaking actuary.

Determining insurance rates for the excess policy limit is always a difficult task for the actuary because the losses in those layers only occasionally happen and therefore very difficult to predict, a combination of methods may be used to arrive at the rate for the excess layers.

Statistics show losses are frequent and numerous at the lower layers and the further up you go, the less numerous and frequent. An actuary usually does not have enough loss data at the higher layers to predict losses, so they rate the lower layers and use that to predict the losses for the higher layers and promulgate a rate.

Rating bureaus provide benchmark data for the actuary to use to assist in promulgating rates for specific lines of insurance such as automobile, general liability, workers' compensation, and many more.

Expense Component

The ratemaking actuary will need to factor into its rates all fixed and variable expenses, such as office expenses, expenses related to acquire the business such as brokers commissions, premium taxes, board & bureau fees, and other expenses.

Profit Component

The insurer is receiving a premium for the promise to pay unpredictable claims sometime in the future. Profit is the reward for putting its capital at risk. A good deal of profit comes from investment income it makes on the float. An insurer receives premium less expenses; the difference is invested, and sometime later (and it could be years later) claims are paid.

Schedule (A)

THIS IS A SIMPLE EXAMPLE OF HOW AN INDIVIDUAL INSURANCE UNDERWRITER MIGHT CALCULATE PREMIUM FOR ONE INSURED

(I) Manual Rates

POLICY LIMITS	INCREASED LIMITS FACTORS	*PREMIUM*
1,000,000 (BASIC)	1.00 (BASIC)	10,000 (BASIC)
1,500,000	1.25	12,000
2,000,000	1.50	15,000
3,000,000	2.25	22,500
4,000,000	2.50	25,000
5,000,000	2.75	27,500

Increased limit factors (also referred to as *optional limit factors*) are used to increase the basic premium for the excess layers. They are factors expressed as percentages.

(II) Schedule Debits (+) or Credits (-)
The insurance underwriters can increase premium by debiting the manual premium or decrease the manual premium using credits. Often the underwriter will be allowed unlimited debits and a maximum credit of 25% or 40%.

Debits
- Poor loss experience
- Deficiencies in loss control inspection report

Credits
- Competition
- Good loss control report
- Long time insured with company
- Excellent loss experience

(III) Manual Premium Adjusted By Schedule Debit or Credit

(IV) Other Adjustments (+) or (-)

(V) Final Premium Charged Insured

THE LAW OF LARGE NUMBERS

The law of large numbers is a principle of mathematical statistics the insurance and reinsurance industry utilizes extensively. To put in the simplest terms:

In order to make accurate predictions, you need a large sample of similar units. The larger the sample, the more confident you can be of your predictions. The larger the number of similar units, the greater the accuracy when those units are simplified. Or you could say the wider the base, the more units will be in the base; the better the base is to predict future results.

ADVERSE SELECTION

This is not a mathematical or statistical principal; it is more or less an insurance truism.

If an insurer does not classify its risks correctly, they may be selected against. For instance, an insurer's rate may cause a class of insured to avoid insuring with them. Let's look at a simple example:

Insurer (A) only offers one automobile liability rate. The rate was derived from data from truckers going long haul and some doing short haul. The long haul, especially the large fleet truckers, had more time on the road, more accidents and overall their experience was not as good as the short haul truckers especially those with less than 50 trucks. However, Insurer (A) decided to have the same rate, making no distinction. Their average premium for a $1,000,000 limit policy is $7,000 per truck. Insurer (B) recognizes the difference, offering short haul (the truckers with excellent loss experience) the same policy limit for an average premium of $5,000 per truck. The better short haul trucking companies will select Insurer (B). Therefore, they adversely select against Insurer (A).

REINSURANCE RATING OF LIABILITY TREATIES

A reinsurer will *exposure* rate and *experience* rate (loss rate) a potential reinsurance treaty.

REINSURANCE EXPERIENCE RATING (LOSS RATING) USUALLY USED FOR QUOTA SHARE AND WORKING LAYER EXCESS OF LOSS TREATIES

This rating method uses the insurers own loss experience and in order for it to be meaningful the reinsurer must have a significant number of individual claims to review. The actuary will look at all prior individual claims trending and developing each to its estimated ultimate amount to arrive at a total estimated losses incurred. If it is a quota share treaty, the reinsurance underwriter and actuary will try to determine if the expected reinsurance premium is sufficient to cover estimated total losses incurred and expenses producing a profit.

If the reinsurance treaty under review is a working layer excess of loss treaty, the actuary will want to calculate the *loss cost percentage* (this is referred to in property as the burning cost). This is the total estimated annual losses incurred divided by the total estimated annual subject premium. This percentage represents the *annual pure premium* need to cover losses incurred.

i.e.	Working layer excess of loss treaty	250,000 x 250,000
	Total estimated subject premium	10,000,000
	Estimated annual total losses incurred to reinsurance layer	700,000
	Loss cost percentage	7.0%

REINSURANCE EXPOSURE RATING

In the past reinsurers mainly reviewed prior loss experience, but over the last 15 years they have come to rely more and more on exposure ratings because they found past loss experience not to be accurate or not sufficiently complete to be reliable for predicting future loss distributions.

Exposure rating reinsurance actuaries aren't looking at losses that actually occurred, but performing a theoretical calculation predicting which reinsurance layers losses will fall into based on the insurer's policy limit distribution and corresponding premiums.

Reinsurance actuaries exposure rate and evaluate where reinsurance losses will occur and then translate that into a reinsurance rate.

It will always be a guessing game as to what a loss distribution curve should look like for a particular insurer, especially at the far end of the curve (higher layer losses).

JUDGMENTAL RATING

Often excess of loss reinsurance treaties will involve exposures lacking credible or relevant statistics and where the rating approach is drawn from the experience and judgment of the reinsurance underwriter.

SOME SPECIFIC COMPONENTS WHEN RATING A REINSURANCE TREATY THE REINSURANCE UNDERWRITER WILL REVIEW:

- How often is a treaty exposed to policies issued by the Reinsured- Company?
- Insurance rates and increased limits factors (optional limit factors) used by the Reinsured- Company. What are they and how do they compare to the industry in general?
- Potential for frequency or severity loss.
- Type of risk written.
- Line of insurance business. Are the policies occurrence or claims made?
- Reinsurer's treaty limit.
- Reinsurer's attachment point.
- Reinsurer's past overall experience loss on the line of insurance/reinsurance.
- Reinsurer's past experience loss for the specific Reinsured- Company.
- Does the Reinsured- Company have some unique way of profitably underwriting the business their competitors do not. Is it a national insurer, regional, one state?
- Territories for the Reinsured- Company's business written.
- Is the business long tail casualty or professional liability which means it will be many years before you know the true results. Often in these lines of business the most difficult claims are settled last.
- How will the overall economy effect the company and the business it writes.
- There may be some difficulties such as not enough claim data to experience rate, limited number of years in business, relatively low surplus. New programs present a number of challenges because there isn't going to be any prior Reinsured- Company experience to look at.

Section 34

KEY INSURANCE RATIOS

Ratios are an integral part of the insurance industry. Within the key ratios there are a myriad of variations, such as gross or net, including or excluding loss adjustment expense, including or excluding IBNR, including or excluding reinsurance costs and reinsurance recoveries.

- Loss ratio
- Expense ratio
- Combined ratio
- Direct Written Premium to Policyholder Surplus ratio

Basic "Loss ratio" is losses incurred expressed as a percent of earned premium.

Variations

- Gross Net Earned Premium to Gross Losses Incurred-ground up (includes paid losses, paid loss expense, reserved losses, reserve loss expense and IBNR)
- Gross Net Earned Premium to Gross Losses Incurred-ground up (includes paid losses, paid loss expense, reserved losses, reserve loss expense excluding IBNR)
- Earned Premium less reinsurance costs to Losses Incurred less reinsurance recoveries and including IBNR)
- Earned Premium less reinsurance costs to Losses Incurred less reinsurance recoveries and excluding IBNR)

Basic "Expense ratio" is direct expenses expressed as a percent of direct written premium.

Variations

- Gross Direct Written Premium to Direct Expenses (expenses directly related to acquiring the premium, sometimes referred to as acquisition expenses or costs)
- Direct Written Premium less reinsurance costs to Direct Expenses

Basic "Combined Ratio" is the loss ratio and the expense ratio added together.

Basic "Direct Written Premium to Policyholder Surplus ratio" is the policyholder surplus expressed as a percent of direct written premium.

Variations

- Gross Direct Written Premium to Policyholder Surplus
- Net Direct Written Premium (less reinsurance costs) to policyholder surplus

Section 35

<u>WHY A REINSURER'S RESULTS ARE MORE VOLATILE THAN AN INSURER'S</u>

A reinsurer's results are more volatile because the reinsurer is reinsuring many companies writing the same business...so it could have large profits if things go well or suffer huge losses. The reinsurance losses, when they do occur, most likely will be larger which adds to the volatility.

Example (1)

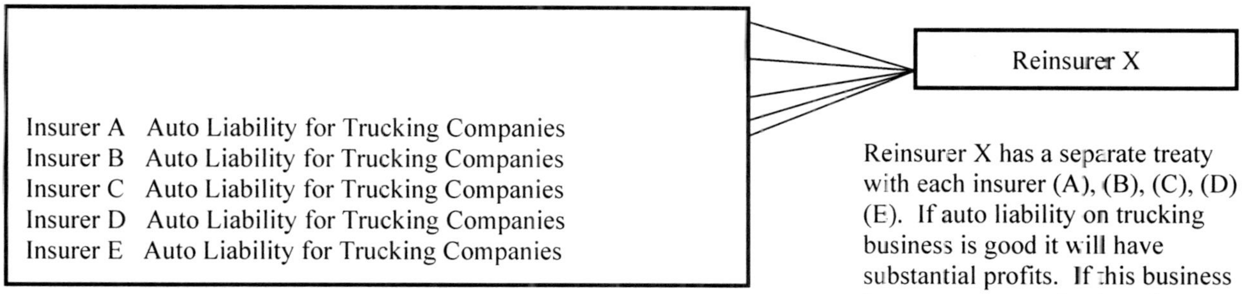

Reinsurer X has a separate treaty with each insurer (A), (B), (C), (D) & (E). If auto liability on trucking business is good it will have substantial profits. If this business has very poor results the reinsurer stands to have very heavy losses.

Example (2)

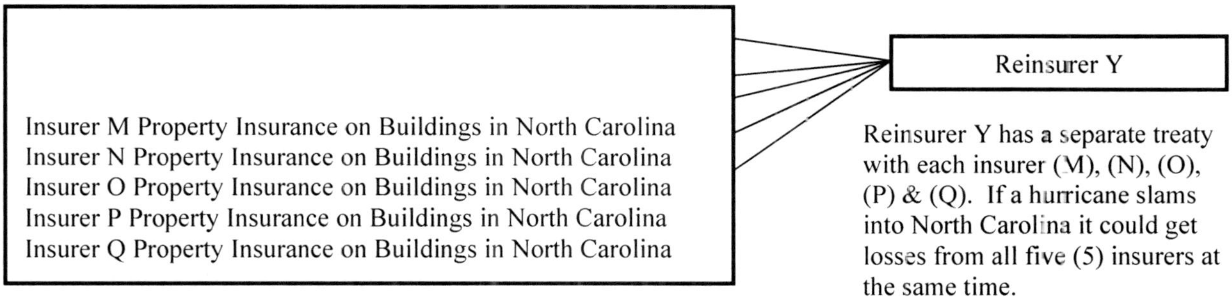

Reinsurer Y has a separate treaty with each insurer (M), (N), (O), (P) & (Q). If a hurricane slams into North Carolina it could get losses from all five (5) insurers at the same time.

PRICING PROBLEMS OF THE REINSURANCE ACTUARY

Specific Reinsurance Coverage Terms And Conditions Create a Challenge for the Actuary:

(I) Coverage terms provided by the reinsurance underwriter are often highly individualized for a specific treaty. For instance, a treaty could contain a profit commission, no claims bonus, or sliding scale ceding commission. An experience account may be included in a treaty which recognizes the time value of premiums paid to the reinsurer, or the reinsurance underwriter may have been able to negotiate a significant deposit premium payable in advance. All of these make it difficult for the reinsurance actuary to come up with a reinsurance rate for a specific treaty when he has to take these into consideration.

(II) Data Problems
One of the goals of a reinsurance actuary is to improve upon the often sparse and difficult to decipher data provided to the reinsurer. Insurers file statutory annual statements with insurance departments so there is a certain amount of uniformity in the statistics of all insurers, but behind each of these reports there are a myriad of ways insurers store and retrieve data. All the data a reinsurer needs is available but often not supplied or difficult to get. Insurers are not in the business of keeping statistics for the reinsurer; their job is to sell insurance policies.

(III) Nature of Reinsurance
In reinsurance, claims frequency is usually low and severity is high. There are often long delays in the reporting of claims to the reinsurer and since the reinsurer is involved in large claims, they may be the most complicated to settle, causing further delay.

(IV) Reinsurance Results are Highly Variable and Difficult to Predict
The reinsurer is more leveraged than the insurer. Let's look at just one instance of this:

Individual Claim (A)	Insurer Reserve	Insurer Retention	Reinsurance 600,000 x 400,000	Reinsurer Reserve	Ultimate Settlement of Claim (A)	Insurers Shortfall	Reinsurer Shortfall
	300,000	400,000		0	750,000	100,000 33.3% below its reserve	350,000 350% below its reserve

(V) No Rating Bureau for Reinsurers
Reinsurers do not have any rating bureaus to compare and benchmark rates.

(VI) Models and Simulations
Reinsurance actuaries will use claim distribution models to assist them in predicting where claims will fall for a reinsurance treaty. Such models are Parendo Distribution, Burr, log normal, and others. Simulation models allow any actuary to simulate a claim distribution, hundreds or thousands of times.

EXPOSURE RATING

The reinsurer is looking for the insurance premiums it is exposed. This is done by splitting the insurance premium into bands by using the insurers own increased limit factors.

If the reinsurance treaty is a 1,000,000 x 1,000,000, it isn't exposed to any premiums related to policy limits below 1,000,000. It is only exposed to premiums for policies issued above 1,000,000. When a Reinsured- Company issues a policy for 5,000,000 and charges a premium of $42,600 how much of that premium is the reinsurer exposed to for a 1,000,000 x 1,000,000 reinsurance treaty? The key to exposure rating is the reinsurers limits exposed premium, which is the Reinsured- Company's policy limit premium the reinsurer is exposed. The reinsurance actuary is trying to estimate at each insurance policy limit how much the reinsurer should get for its exposure.

INCREASE LIMIT FACTORS (Optional Rating Factors)

The actuary is reviewing the Reinsured- Company's limit profile and determining which limits and corresponding premium the reinsurance treaty will be exposed to for losses.

For instance, if a treaty is 500,000 x 500,000 any policy issued below 500,000 will not expose the reinsurer to a loss. If a policy is issued for 1,000,000, the reinsurer is exposed to losses excess of 500,000. The exposure rating actuary needs to calculate the amount of insurance premium between 500,000 and 1,000,000. Let's assume its $9,500; that is the limits exposed premium.

EXAMPLE OF REINSURANCE EXPOSURE RATING OF TREATIES

There may be a dozen different methods of exposure rating; we present one.

Step (1) Unadjusted Exposure Rate

The actuary will ascertain a reinsurance gross rate. This is done by determining at each insurance policy limit the reinsurers' exposure. The actuary is determining the insurance premium policy limit.

Step (2) Expected Loss Ratio

The actuary will then try to find relevant loss data that can be used to come up with an expected loss ratio. If it is absolutely not available, then a subjective assumption will need to be made.

Step (3) Final Reinsurance Exposure Rate

Note

The actuary does not look at any actual individual claims.

EXPOSURE RATING

Layer: 1,000,000 x 1,000,000

Policy Limit	Insurer Estimated Gross Written Premium For The Upcoming Year	Increased Limit Factor (ILF)	Insurance Rate For Layer 1m x 1m	Insurance Premium For Its Exposure	Reinsurer
300,000	1,000,000	.75	0	0	
400,000	1,000,000	1.00	0	0	
500,000	1,000,000	1.20	0	0	
750,000	1,000,000	1.50	0	0	
1,000,000	1,000,000	1.75	0	0	
2,000,000	1,500,000	2.1875	20.0%	300,000	These are the insurance premiums the reinsurer is exposed to.
3,000,000	2,000,000	2.45	17.9%	358,000	
4,000,000	500,000	2.7125	16.1%	80,500	
5,000,000	2,000,000	2.975	14.7%	294,000	
Total	11,000,000		9.38%	1,032,500	

1,032,500 - 11,000,000 = 9.38%

Excess Factor Calculation

ILF $\frac{2.1875 \;-\; 1.7500 \;-\; .43750}{2.1875 \;-\; 2.1875}$ = 20.0% (percentage of premium insurer receives on 2,000,000 policy)

The increase for 2,000,000 is 2.1875 and 1,000,000 is 1.75. Between one and two is the premium

ILF $\frac{2.1875 \;-\; 1.7500 \;-\; .43750}{2.45 \;-\; 2.450}$ = 17.9% (percentage of premium insurer receives on 3,000,000 policy)

Determine premium by band

Policy Limit	Increased Limit Factor		Excess Factor
2,000,000 – 1,000,000	2.1875 – 1.7500	=	20.0%
2,000,000	2.1875		
2,000,000 – 1,000,000	2.1875 – 1.7500	=	17.9%
3,000,000	2.45		
2,000,000 – 1,000,000	2.1875 – 1.7500	=	16.1%
4,000,000	2.7125		
2,000,000 – 1,000,000	2.1875 – 1.7500	=	14.7%
5,000,000	2.975		

REINSURANCE GROSS RATE ADJUSTED TO FINAL REINSURANCE EXPSOURE RATE

Unlimited Exposure Rate		9.38% (reduced to 7.50%) the entire premium component before adjustments
- Primary Insurer Expense and Profit		
Assumed Loss Ratio		80.00%
Pure Loss Component of Premium		7.50% (9.38% + 80%) Grossed up to 9.09%
Plus reinsurer's Expense and Profit:		
Home Office Expense	5.00%	
Acquisition Cost Expense	5.00%	
Profit	5.00%	
	15.00%	
		1.59%
Final Reinsurance Exposure Rate		9.09%

Note:

(1) The pure loss component (7.50%) is grossed up by the Reinsurer's Expense and Profit (17.50)
In this manner 100.00 less 17.50% = 82.50
7.50 - 82.50 = 9.09%

State another way to look at this is the reinsurer's expense and profit are 17.50% of 9.09% or 1.59%.

Treaty 1,000,000 x 1,000,000

Estimated Subject Premium For Upcoming Year	$11,000,000
Final Reinsurance Exposure Rate	9.09%
Reinsurance Premium (according to model)	$999,900

EXPOSURE RATING (CON'T)

ILF	$\frac{2.1875 - 1.7500}{2.7125}$	-	$\frac{.43750}{2.7125}$	=	16.1%	(Percentage of premium reinsurers should receive on 4,000,000 policy)
ILF	$\frac{2.1875 - 1.7500}{2.975}$	-	$\frac{.43750}{2.975}$	=	14.7%	(Percentage of premium reinsurers should receive on 5,000,000 policy)

HOW LOSS DATA CAN BE CLASSIFIED

(I) ACCIDENT YEAR

Claims are placed into the calendar year which coincides with the date of the accident. Claims with an accident date of 2009 will go into calendar year 2009.

Accident Year
Loss Data — The date of the accident will determine which calendar year the loss will be placed.

Accident Loss Amount	Accident Date	Calendar Year	Loss Amount
10,000	4/20/90	1990	10,000
25,000	9/30/90	1990	25,000
15,000	6/21/91	1991	15,000
20,000	7/12/92	1992	20,000

Premiums earned are placed into the calendar year they are recorded.

(II) POLICY YEAR

Claims will follow the effective date of the policy covering that claim. The policy will be classified into calendar years.

Policy Year
Loss Data — The effective date of the policy will determine which calendar year the loss will be placed.

Policy #	Policy Term	Loss Covered By Policy	Date of Loss	Loss Put Into Calendar Year
73180	4/15/00 – 4/15/01	9,380	6/28/00	2000
73169	11/1/00 – 11/1/01	10,620	9/15/01	2000
74122	2/16/01 – 2/16/02	6,212	1/18/01	2001

Premiums earned are placed into the calendar year they are recorded.

(III) CALENDAR YEAR

Premiums earned are placed in the calendar year in which they are recorded. Claims are placed into the calendar year they occur.

(IV) UNDERWRITING YEAR USED IN REINSURANCE

The underwriting year matches the annual term of the reinsurance treaty. For instance, a treaty has a term of 6/1/00 to 6/1/01; this is the underwriting year. Premiums for all policies which have an effective date between 6/1/00 and 6/1/01 will be placed into that underwriting year. Claims will follow the policy term.

HISTORICAL AVERAGE PREMIUM SCHEDULE

Developing a historical average premium schedule is one method to review the premium trend of an insurer. In order to compare "apples to apples," the line of insurance, class of insureds, and policy limit size should be similar.

Example:
Neptune Insurance Company

Historical Premium Schedule
Line of Insurance: Automobile Liability
Class of Insured: Trucking Companies

Year	*Policy Limit Size*	*Average Premium*
1994	1,000,000	6,039
1995	1,000,000	11,841
1996	1,000,000	13,568
1997	1,000,000	14,070
1998	1,000,000	13,811
1999	1,000,000	13,629
2000	1,000,000	13,264
2001	1,000,000	13,058
2002	1,000,000	11,041
2003	1,000,000	10,578
2004	1,000,000	10,329
2005	1,000,000	10,146
2006	1,000,000	9,657
2007	1,000,000	9,771
2008	1,000,000	9,989
2009	1,000,000	9,813

This schedule shows the average premium is up approximately 62% from 1994 to 2009; premiums peaked in 1997 and declined all the way up to 2007. This schedule alone is not sufficient to make assumptions that premiums in any given year were adequate or inadequate to meet the insured's incurred claims, expenses and profit. In effect, it does not tell you whether the business was good or bad in any given year. It does however serve a very useful purpose because it does show the company's premium trend.

Section 36

EXTRA CONTRACTUAL OBLIGATIONS (ECO) LOSS IN EXCESS OF POLICY LIMITS (XPL) PUNITIVE DAMAGES

PUNITIVE DAMAGES

Background: The historical basis of punitive damages can be traced back to thirteenth century England, which developed a judicial system of monetary penalties referred to as amercements. Several provisions of the Magna Carta are devoted to the topic of amercements. In the United States, punitive damage awards were recognized by the Supreme Court in 1818. However, up until recently, complaints seeking punitive damages were rare. In the past, even if punitive damage claims were made by the plaintiff, the court would usually remove them.

General Definition: Punitive damages are not compensation for injuries, but fine(s) imposed by a jury to punish reprehensible conduct and to deter its future occurrence.

Plaintiffs seeking punitive damages must show conscious disregard of their rights or reckless conduct by the other party.

Amount of Awards: Since punitive damages are not assessed against actual injury, there is no standard for limiting their amount. Awards depend upon the financials of the party at fault. The amount of the award is based upon the sum needed to punish or deter the wrongful conduct.

States: Each state has established its own requirements that must be present in order for a plaintiff to receive punitive damage awards; they vary widely from state to state in states permitting awards the conduct needed to collect punitive damages generally falls into four categories: (1) malice, (2) conduct exceeding gross negligence, (3) gross negligence, and (4) various statutory requirements.

ARGUMENTS AGAINST PUNITIVE DAMAGE AWARDS

The eighth Amendment to the Constitution of the United States Constitution (which is part of the Bill of Rights) says:

> "Excessive bail shall not be required, nor *excessive fines imposed*, nor cruel and unusual punishments inflicted."

For the most part, this amendment has been applied to criminal cases rather than civil, but it now has been used to challenge the constitutionality of large punitive damage awards. However, punitive damages are a part of the American civil judicial system and have been for a very long time.

INSURABILITY OF PUNITVE DAMAGES

Some states permit insurance companies to reimburse the insured for punitive damage awards made against them, other states do not. It can be argued that insurance reduces or eliminates the insureds punishment. Since punitive damages are awarded to punish or deter persons who engage in wrongful conduct, insurance coverage may undercut this deterrent.

Insurance to cover punitive damage awards is determined by (1) the language of the policy and (2) the state's public policy regarding the shifting of the punitive damage award to the insurer.

Most courts in those states permitting the insurance of punitive damages have held an insurance policy which provides coverage for *damages* and includes coverage for punitive damages, unless it is specifically excluded in the policy.

PUNITIVE DAMAGES AWARDED DIRECTLY AGAINST THE INSURANCE COMPANY

These are cases in which the insurer *itself is sued* and the plaintiff seeks punitive damages. Insurance companies generally are sued for *bad faith* and punitive damages are usually sought. It is possible to sue for *bad faith* and not seek punitive damages, however, they almost always go hand in hand.

The basis of *bad faith suits* is routed in the doctrine of contract law. It is implied on both sides of a contract that there is a covenant of "good faith and fair dealing" and that one party shall not hinder the other party from receiving benefits under the contract.

These are some instances of bad faith on the part of the insurer:

...Wrongful refusal to defend an insured

...Failure to provide an adequate defense to the insured

...Unreasonably rejecting a settlement at the full policy limit

...Breach of its duty to settle; breach of its duty to indemnify, breach of its general covenant of good faith and fair dealing.

AWARDS IN EXCESS OF POLICY LIMITS

An insurer may be liable for amounts exceeding its "original policy limit" if it is proven they acted in bad faith by failing to adequately consider the interests of the insured by *not settling the claim within the original policy limit.*

For example, an insured has a liability policy with a *limit of 50,000.* An action is brought against the insured for $100,000 by a third party. The insurer takes control of the defense and in the course of litigation, the third party offers to settle for $50,000 (assume here the case has merit and the offer is reasonable and attractive).

The insurer, however, decides not to settle. From the point of view of the insured, declining the offer of settlement (within policy limits) is to gamble with the insured's money, since any verdict over $50,000 would have to be paid out of the insured's pocket.

Since the control of the defense, including the right to settle, is with the insurer (under the terms of the policy) the issue arises "is the insurer acting in good faith with the insured?" The California District Court of Appeals (1957) was the first to recognize the covenant of "good faith and fair dealing" applied an insurer's duty to consider the interest of the insured in settling a claim(s) by a third party.

REINSURANCE

A Reinsured- Company owes its reinsurer a duty of good faith for it is obligated to make coverage determinations without regard as to whether or not a given risk is reinsured. In cases where the insurer itself is sued directly for bad faith in regard to failing to settle or defend a claim, reinsurers have taken the position that such litigation/judgments are not reinsured because they are not part of the reinsurance agreement (and are not the risks, perils or line of business reinsured). They are the actions levied directly against the insurer and are "extra-contractual."

In Employers Reinsurance Corp. vs. American Fidelity and Casualty Co. (1959), the court held in the absence of a treaty provision expressly providing coverage for "bad faith" damages, a reinsurer is not liable for the "extra-contractual" liabilities of a ceding insurer. However, bad faith actions against a Reinsured- Company for failure to settle within the policy limits may be reinsurable (even if no extra contractual provisions are in the reinsurance agreement) because the reinsurer acquired or concurred with the ceding insurers decisions. The Extra Contractual Obligations Article and the Losses in Excess of Policy Limits Article are often placed into the reinsurance agreement extending the reinsurers' liability into some of those extra-contractual areas the ceding insurer may find itself.

REINSURANCE COVERAGE FOR EXTRA CONTRACTUAL PUNITIVE DAMAGES IN STATES THAT DO NOT PERMIT PUNITIVE DAMAGES TO BE COVERED BY INSURANCE

If a reinsurance agreement includes extra contractual liability for bad faith on the part of the Reinsured- Company, such liability may not extend to punitive damages in those states which do not permit punitive damages to be covered by insurance (and in this case, reinsured).

Section 37

THE UNITED STATES LEGAL SYSTEM

Insurance and reinsurance professionals will see numerous references in trade publications and daily newspapers on court decisions. It is important to know something about the court system in the United States so that the relevance of these decisions can be understood.

OVERVIEW

The United States has a federal court system and a state court system.

FEDERAL SYSTEM

The federal system is a three-tier system:

Level One: Trial Courts	United States District Courts. Each state is divided into geographical districts. Each district has a trial court of general jurisdiction at which most disputes, both civil and criminal, are initially adjudicated. In a few exceptional situations, a court case can begin in an Appellate Court and, even more rarely, in the U.S. Supreme Court.
Level Two: Intermediate Appellate Court	United States Court of Appeals. The U.S. Court of Appeals is divided into twelve geographical regions, termed circuits. The circuit courts of appeal base their decisions on the record of the trial court below. Decisions are published on a selective basis. If a party does not appeal to the U.S. Supreme Court, the decision of the Circuit Court of Appeals stands as the final decision.
Level Three: Court of Last Resort	The Supreme Court of the United States is located in Washington, D.C. and represents the highest federal court. The court is comprised of nine justices – one chief justice and eight associate justices. Not all cases brought before the U.S. Supreme Court are heard. The Court often chooses to hear a case when there is a conflict among the U.S. Courts of Appeal on specific questions of law.
Special Courts:	United States Tax Court, United States Claims Court, United States Court of Veteran Appeals, United States Court of International Trade.
U.S. Supreme Court and the State Decisions Doctrine: Binding Authority of Published Decisions:	Lower courts are bound by the decisions of higher courts within the same jurisdiction; logically, higher courts are not bound by the decisions of the lower ones. Most courts and most decisions of a state court are not binding on a federal court. Decisions from other jurisdiction may

provide persuasive authority.

STATE COURT SYSTEM

The court systems in all 50 states are similar in that they have trial-level courts and at least one appellate court. Beyond this, however, the court structure and nomenclature vary from state to state. Some states, such as Maine and Montana, do not have an intermediate court between the trial court and the court of last resort.

LAW CIVIL LAW AND CRIMINAL

Civil law basically deals with the violations of laws in place to protect individuals. Cases are brought by injured parties. Criminal law deals with the violation of laws in place to protect the community.

DEFINITIONS

Arbitration:	A non-court method to resolve a civil dispute. An arbitrator or panel of arbitrators is appointed by the parties and the decision reached is binding. Arbitration is subject to some limited court review.
Attorney In Fact:	A company that appoints an individual with the legal authority (power of attorney) to sign documents on their behalf. Often used in surety when an attorney in fact is needed at the local level to sign the various legal instruments, such as bonds, riders, and cancellation notices. The attorney in fact will attach its power of attorney form to the documents it executes.
Bad Faith:	Unfair conduct, which could include fraud, misrepresentation, deceit or other such inappropriate acts.
Comparative Negligence:	The doctrine of law that says negligence is to be measured by percentage. For instance, if a claim is brought and it is found the insured is 10% at fault, they shall only be able to collect 90% from the other party.
Estoppels:	A party (by taking an action or by taking no action) may cause by being stopped from taking or acquiring certain positions.
Excess of Original Policy Limit:	An insurer may be required by a court award to pay a loss that exceeds its original policy limit. This usually comes about when the insurer is found to have acted in bad faith by failing to adequately consider the interest of the insured by not settling the claim within the original policy limit.

Extra Contractual Obligation:	Those obligations which are "extra contractual" meaning they are outside of the reinsurance contract. The most likely source of an extra contractual obligation is when the insurer found liable for obligations not covered by the insurance policy.
Hold Harmless:	A written agreement that sets forth that one party will hold the other party blameless (harmless) under a given set of circumstances.
Intentional Acts:	Claims arising from an insured intentional causing an accident or other harmful event are generally not covered by insurance policies.
Joint and Several Liability:	Together and separately their parties are obligated to one another. Each is responsible for the entire liability.
Joint Liability:	Liability is apportioned among the parties.
Jurisdiction:	The authority the court has to decide a specific case.
Mediation/Mediator:	The process of resolving a dispute by the parties appointing an impartial individual to assist in settlement.
Pain and Suffering:	It is recognized in tort law that the plaintiff is allowed to seek an award for its pain and suffering caused by the negligence of another party
Post Judgment Interest:	This is interest which accrues to the benefit of the plaintiff while the case is on appeal.
Pre-Judgment Interest:	This is interest awarded for the benefit of the plaintiff which accrues from the date of the event.
Punitive Damages:	These are damages awarded by jury over and above the compensation damages in a court case to punish the wrongdoer. Punitive damages can be awarded against an insurer. This is usually in regards to their bad faith in handling a claim.
Rescission:	Voiding an insurance policy or other contract back to the inception with a complete return of all premiums or considerations. In effect, it is as if the policy or contract was never in effect.
Reservation of Rights:	Usually this takes the form of a letter from the insurer to

	the policyholder or from the reinsurer to the ceding company (insurer). The reservation of rights letter is almost always sent out regarding a claim. For instance, the ceding company sends a notice of a claim to the reinsurer who reviews the claim and feels there may be no coverage under the reinsurance treaty. The reinsurer may send a reservation of rights letter to the ceding company saying they have certain reservations in regards to the claim and are reserving the right to say (at a later date) there is no coverage. They are not saying there is no coverage, but reserving their right to say that in the future. If they don't reserve their rights and remain silent, they may lose that right.
Several Liability:	Separate, not related to the other parties. Separate and distinct from the liability of another. Independent action may be brought without others.
Summary judgment:	A party in a civil proceeding can file a motion before a judge that states that there are no issues of fact and that as a matter of law, the motion is entitled to judgment. Each of the parties is individually bound.
Tort:	That area of civil law that awards damages to party injured by the violation of a duty imposed by law.
Treble Damages:	Damages awarded that are tripled in amount.

Section 38

STATE REGULATION OF INSURANCE AND REINSURANCE

(I) State Regulation of Insurers

(A) Insurance is a heavily regulated industry. Each state has its own insurance laws, regulations, insurance commissioner, and insurance department.

The National Association of Insurance Commission (NAIC) was founded in 1871 and its membership consists of all 50 states insurance regulators, territories and possessions. One of its purposes is to provide uniformity in state regulations. Although each state has its own laws and regulations, some of them are similar because of the influence of the NAIC. In 1989, the NAIC adopted an accreditation program whereby each state that met specific regulatory criteria was granted accreditation status. The purpose of this program was to make insurance regulations uniform in certain respects. At present, over (45) states have qualified for NAIC accreditation status.

(B) Individual State Requirements

- Each state legislature formulates insurance statutes and each state's insurance commissioner formulates regulations. In some cases the NAIC model laws and regulations form the basis for such enactments will be insurance laws enforced by the individual state insurance departments.

- Each state requires that before doing business in their state, an insurer apply for and obtain a license to do business. This license is sometimes referred to as a Certificate of Authority. A state will authorize a company only for those lines of insurance it offers in its licensed domicile state.

- Each state insurance department will require a licensed insurers' policy form and insurance rates.

- Each state will conduct an examination of insurers domiciled in that state and upon occasion join an examination of an insurer domiciled in another state.

- Each state will require licensed insurers to file an NAIC Annual Statement prepared on a statutory accounting basis. It is often referred to by those in the industry as the "convention blank" or sometimes the "yellow annual statement" because its front cover is a bright yellow.

- An insurer can be granted by the state a surplus lines status which means their policy can be issued in the state but only for difficult and unusual risks not available from a licensed insurer.

- Each state will require that any agent, surplus lines broker, third party administrator or managing general agent retained by the insurer be appropriately licensed. Licensing requirements vary from state to state.

(C) Insurers Status in States

• Admitted or Authorized	This is an insurer which has a license in the state to sell policies in that state.
• Domestic Insurer	This is an insurer incorporated in the state.
• Foreign Insurer	This is an insurer incorporated in another state.
• Alien Insurer	This is an insurer formed under the laws outside of the United States.
• Surplus Lines Insurer	This is an insurer which is not admitted in the state but has a surplus lines status. States will require the insurer to have a license in its home state and provide financial statements and other relevant information.
• Risk Retention Group	Can issue commercial liability policies (no workers' compensation) in all states without a state license if they qualify under the Liability Risk Retention Act of 1986. This is a federal law which does require the risk retention group to acquire a license in one state. The RRG will need to notify each state prior to issuing any policy in their state. Exempt from state laws in regard to policy forms and rates.
• Purchasing Group	Must qualify under the Liability Risk Retention Act of 1986, only commercial liability policies. The insurer must be admitted or excess and surplus lines in each state policies are issued. Exempt from state laws in regard to policy forms and rates.

(D) State Counter Signature Laws

Many states have a law requiring insurers domiciled in another state that issues policies in their state to have those policies countersigned by a licensed agent or broker in the state. For instance, an insurer licensed in Alabama but domiciled in Pennsylvania that issues a policy in Alabama must have that policy countersigned by an agent or broker in Alabama.

(II) State Regulation of Reinsurers:

Insurance departments in each state do not regulate reinsurance rates, forms or contracts. Therefore, reinsurers have much more freedom than primary insurers. Reinsurers also do not pay state premium taxes. However, reinsurers are regulated by each state with the emphasis on their financial strength.

(A) Reinsurer Status In The Various States

It is a standard part of the insurance industry to cede a certain portion of risk to reinsurers. Reinsurers, in turn, are accepting and are responsible for a certain portion of the primary insurer's unearned premium reserve, case reserves, and incurred but not reported reserves; therefore each state has regulations pertaining to reinsurers. In order for the primary insurer to take credit for reinsurance recoveries for their reserves, each state will have regulations which requires the reinsurer to be either admitted, authorized, approved, accredited or licensed. States may also permit primary insurers to take credit for reinsurance recoverables for reinsurers for unauthorized or unlicensed reinsurers. In some cases, they can provide a form of security such as a letter of credit from an approved bank covering the reinsurer's portion of reserves; the reinsurer maintains a trust account in the state for the benefit of primary insurers; the reinsurance is on a funds withheld basis or the reinsurer can provide another acceptable form of security permitted in the state.

(B) NAIC Model Credit for Reinsurance Act

This act has been adopted in whole or in part by most states. Credit for reinsurance will be allowed when domestic insurer cedes to:

(1) A licensed insurer or reinsurer in the state.

(2) The reinsurer is accredited in the state.
In order to be accredited, the reinsurer must comply with the following: files with the insurance commissioner in the state recognizing its jurisdiction, permit the state to examine its books and records, holds a license for insurance or reinsurance in at least one other state, files an annual report each year with the insurance commissioner, files its most recent audited financial statement and maintains policyholder surplus of $20,000,000 or greater.

(3) Insurer or reinsurer domiciled and licensed in at least one state with credit for reinsurance standards similar to the state.

(4) (a) A single insurer maintain a trust fund in a qualified U.S. financial institution and has a surplus of $20,000,000 or greater.

(b) A group of incorporated or unincorporated underwriters maintain a trust fund in a qualified U.S. financial institution and has a surplus of $100,000,000 or greater. Additionally, each underwriter within the group must submit to the states insurance commissioner an annual certification of solvency from its regulator of domicile and its independent public accountant.

(c) A group of incorporated insurers under common administration business outside the U.S. for at least (3) years and have:
   (1) Aggregated surplus of U.S. $10 billion or greater
   (2) Maintain a trust account with U.S. $100 million or greater
   (3) Permits the state to examine its books and records
   (4) Each member of the group submits to the states insurance commissioner an annual certification of solvency from its regulator of domicile and its independent public accountant.

(5) Credit for reinsurance can be permitted for reinsurers not meeting the above requirements in the following manner:
   (a) The ceding insurer can withhold funds covering the reserves ceded to the reinsurer.
   (b) The reinsurer can provide a letter of credit to the ceding insurer to cover reserves ceded to the reinsurer.

(III) State Regulations of Insurance Producers

(A) Agent or General Agent

An individual or corporation authorized in writing to act as the insurers agent for the purposes of soliciting business, collect premiums, send notices of cancellation and countersign the company policies. The agent must secure the appropriate license in each state they perform these duties.

(B) Broker

An individual or corporation representing the insured in securing insurance and must have a proper state license in each state it transacts its business.

(C) Excess and Surplus Lines Broker

An individual or corporation to place business with a non-admitted insurer. An appropriate license is required and the broker is usually subject to due diligence requirements regarding the availability of the requested coverage.

(D) Managing General Agent and Third Party Administrator

This is an agent of the insurance company authorized to solicit business, bind risk, issue policies, collect premiums and perform other duties on behalf of the insured. Some states now require these agents to be licensed or present detailed plans of their operations filed with the department.

(E) Non-Resident Agent

An agent holding a license to do business in a state other than the one it is domiciled. For instance, an agent domiciled in Connecticut with a non-resident license in Texas.

(IV) State Taxes

(A) State Premium Tax

Each state has a premium tax that insurers issuing policies in their state must pay base on premium volume in the state

(B) Excess and Surplus Lines Tax

Each state has an excess and surplus tax which is paid in addition to the premium by the insured when they receive a policy that is issue by an excess and surplus line insure

STATE GUARANTY FUNDS

Since insurance is regulated by the states, each state has its own guaranty fund provisions. These funds are to make claim payments to policyholders whose licensed insurer cannot meet its obligations due to insolvency. The important point to remember is the insurer must be licensed in order for the policyholder to be covered by the state's guaranty fund. Therefore, policies issued on an excess or surplus lines basis would not be covered by a state's guaranty fund.

Another important point is states may have a limitation on the amounts it will pay a policyholder. The insurance companies in each state are assessed as are the amounts needed to make the claim payments to the policyholders of the insolvent insurance companies.

If a policy is issued and it is not covered by a Guaranty Fund, almost all states will require a notice to that effect appear on each policy issued in that state.

Section 39

FRONTING/ WHAT IS IT?/ IS IT WISE TO DO?

Fronting is the term used to describe when an insurer not licensed in a state enters into an agreement with a licensed insurer, whereby the licensed insurer issues policies which are substantially reinsured by the non-licensed insurer and the licensed insurer retains little risk for the policies it is issuing.

SPECIFIC REASONS FOR FRONTING

- The insurer does not have a state license.
- A captive insurance company, which is domiciled offshore will not have state license or onshore with limited state licenses.
- It could be an insurer which has a license pending in the state.
- It also could be a reinsurer without an insurance license wanting to write direct insurance.
- Sometimes fronting will come about when an insurer has a state license but does not have an acceptable A.M. Best rating and enters into an arrangement with a licensed insurer with an adequate rating.
- Perhaps a reinsurer has an insurance license, but does not want to be perceived as an insurer, will engage in fronting.
- Under certain circumstances a single parent captive insurance company may need to be fronted.

Risk retention groups are not permitted to front nor have their policies fronted except by another risk retention group. A risk retention group can be a reinsurer except when it reinsures another risk retention group.

SURPLUS LINES INSURER

Sometimes an insurer with a non-admitted status will front assuming the actual business written can be written in the state on a surplus lines basis.

SECURITY

A licensed insurer reinsured by a non-licensed insurer or non-admitted reinsurer will want security for its unearned premium reserve, case reserves and incurred but not reported (IBNR) reserves. This security most likely will be a letter of credit or reinsurance trust account.

A letter of credit is a non-negotiable instrument issued by a bank guaranteeing the payment of a stipulated amount to a third party. A letter of credit can be revocable or irrevocable. Revocable means the issuing bank reserves the right to rescind its obligation before the expiration date. If it is irrevocable it can not be cancelled prior to the expiration date. If this type of security is used, it should always be irrevocable. Letters of credit usually have a specified expiration date; not many are issued for an unlimited term. A letter of credit issued on an Evergreen basis means it automatically renews from year to year unless a notice of cancellation or non-renewal is sent. Most banks are reluctant to issue a letter of credit on an unlimited or Evergreen basis.

CAUTIOUS APPROACH

There are numerous examples of insurers getting themselves in deep trouble by being a fronting insurer; some were placed into receivership by insurance departments. Because they retained little risk or no risk in the business written on their behalf they had no interest in the results for the policies issued in their name. That's never a good idea. There have been examples where policies were issued by Insurer A (retaining no risk) using a Managing General Agency (MGA) (retaining no risk) then reinsured with Reinsurer B (retaining only a small amount of risk) then pasting it on to a series of other reinsurers, to far away from the original business written to monitor or provide input. This is usually a recipe for extremely poor results as those writing the business have no vested interest in the final outcome. Meaning, little attention is paid to the ultimate losses that will surely come. There are insurance departments that may not permit fronting in their state or frown on the entire concept.

A r*einsurance trust account* is another form of security that can be used instead of a letter of credit. The account would be set up at a bank or investment firm in the name of the front insurer. All funds received from premium income less agreed upon fronting fees and other expenses would be deposited in the account. Losses that need to be paid would come out of this account. Once a year, or earlier if needed, the account would be reviewed for its adequacy.

If an underwriting manager is involved that organization will need funds on hand to pay claims and transact business so an *escrow account* would be established with a local bank. From time to time funds would be transferred from the reinsurance trust account to the escrow account as needed.

NO FRONTING IN SOME STATES

Some states may not permit fronting or frown upon the practice.

FRONTING FEE

Typically the fronting insurer will require a fee for fronting but not always. A professional reinsurer which also owns a licensed insurer, which agrees to front, could waive the fee if it is doing the reinsurance and it believes the underlying business will be profitable and it has favorable reinsurance terms. Most fronting companies do charge a fronting fee. It is important to ask if that fee includes or excludes the fronting insurer paying state premium taxes, board and bureau fees, or other expenses.

IMPORTANT ASPECTS OF FRONTING

- Fronting agreement should stipulate the maximum annual premium value.

- Irrevocable and Evergreen letter of credit or reinsurance trust account or other security needs to be in place.

- Escrow Account probably will be needed if there is an underwriting manager.

- Claims handling, it must be clear to all parties who is handling claims and what their responsibilities are for reporting those claims to all the parties.

EXAMPLE OF FRONTING – (5) METHODS

Mason Insurance Company is the licensed front insurer issuing policy limits of 1,000,000.

Vik Captive Insurance Company initiated the fronting agreement by approaching Mason and will retain the *first 200,000* of liability for each policy issued by Mason Insurance Company. Vik is not licensed in the state policies are to be issued.

XYZ Re is a professional reinsurer with an admitted status in the state in which policies are issued and will provide reinsurance outlined in the methods we describe.

It has been decided when Vik needs to provide security, it will be in the form of a letter of credit (LOC).

FRONTING METHODS

(1)	(2)	(3)	(4)	(5)
Mason Insurance Company Issues Policies 1,000,000 Limit	Mason Insurance Company Issues Policies 1,000,000 Limit	Mason Insurance Company Issues Policies 1,000,000 Limit	Mason Insurance Company Issues Policies 1,000,000 Limit	Mason Insurance Company Issues Policies 1,000,000 Limit
↓	↓	↓	↓	↓
Mason 100% Quota Share Reinsured by XYZ Re	Mason 100% Quota Share Reinsured for first 200,000 by Vik Captive Insurance Company	100% Quota Share 80% reinsured by XYZ Re 20% reinsured by Vik Captive Insurance Co.	Mason 100% Quota Share reinsured by Vik Captive Insurance Company for first 1,000,000	Mason 100% Quota Share for the first 200,000 by Vik Captive Insurance Company
↓	↓		↓	↓
First 200,000 retroceded to Vik Captive Insurance Company	Mason reinsured by XYZ Re Excess of Loss 800,000 x 200,000		Vik Captive Insurance Company reinsured by XYZ Re for 800,000 x 200,000	Mason Insurance Company 100% Quota Share reinsured by XYZ Re excess of 800,000
Security Requirement Mason is reinsured 100% by XYZ which is an admitted reinsurer, therefore Mason does not need a LOC. XYZ Re may require Vik to provide a LOC. If an insurer insists that only an admitted reinsurer can be behind it, this method can be used. The 100% quota share can be modified to a 95/5 or a 90/10.	***Security Requirement*** Mason is reinsured with two (2) treaties; one by Vik for the first 200,000 and the second by XYZ Re for 800,000 x 200,000. Vik provides LOC to Mason for its treaty which is 200,000.	***Security Requirement*** Mason is 100% quota share reinsured; XYZ Re has an 80% share and Vik has 20%. Vik will need to provide a LOC for its 20% participation.	***Security Requirement*** Vik is providing all the reinsurance to Mason, therefore will need to provide a LOC for the entire 1,000,000 liability. XYZ Re is reinsuring Vik but that does not effect Vik's LOC requirements.	***Security Requirement*** Mason has two (2) quota share treaties; one with Vik for the first 200,000; therefore Vik needs to provide a LOC. The second quota share is with XYZ Re for the next 800,000.

SINGLE PARENT CAPTIVE

Captive insurance company insures its Fortune 500 parent.

- no fronting
- reinsurance is utilized to provide coverage

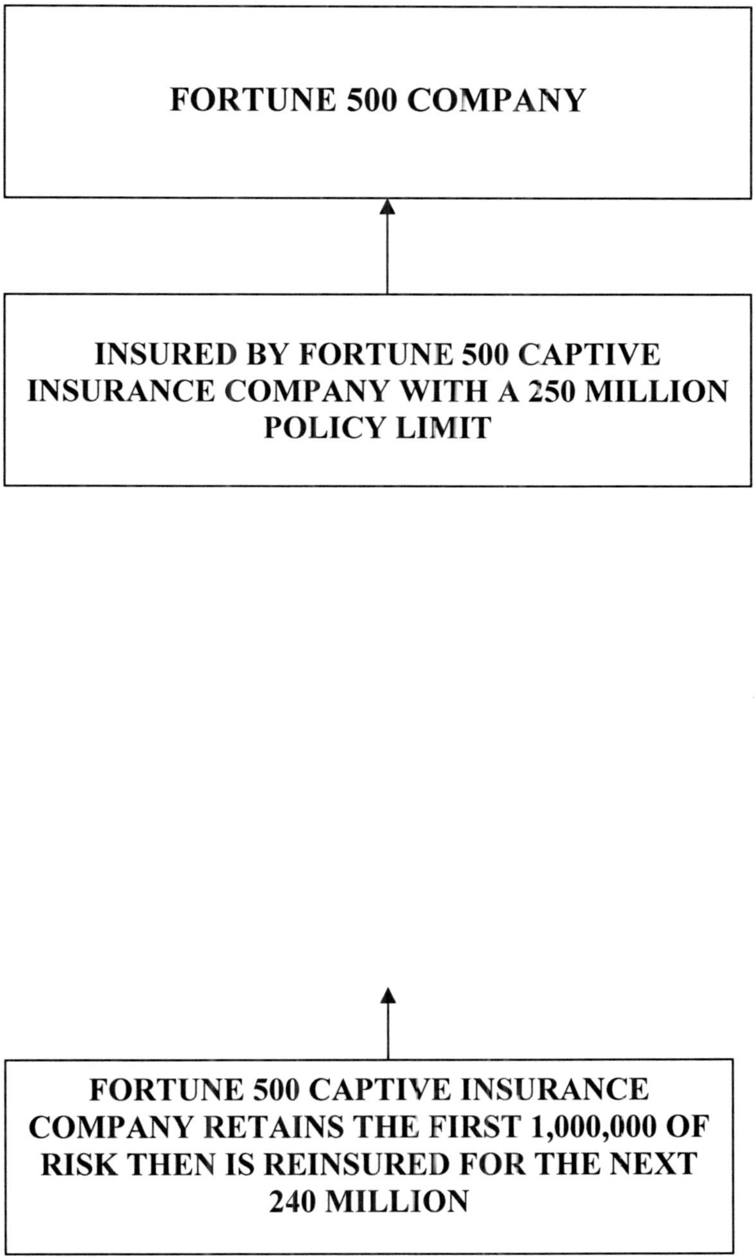

EXAMPLE OF A FRONTING ARRANGMENT

Parties	Agreements
Managing General Agent or Managing Underwriting Agent	Underwriting Agreement
Front Insurer	Fronting Agreement & Reinsurance Agreement
Professional Reinsurer	Reinsurance Agreement Letter of Credit or Reinsurance Trust Account Escrow Account

Section 40

PLACEMENT SLIP / SAMPLES

A placement slip is a document providing a quick way to review terms, rates, and conditions of a reinsurance treaty. It's often used by reinsurance intermediaries with the more lengthy and detailed contract following at a later date. Direct reinsurers will also use a format similar to a placement slip to provide quotation reinsurance terms.

In this section we provide the following examples:

Placement Slip	Sample A	Casualty Excess of Loss 750,000 x 250,000
Placement Slip	Sample B	Casualty Excess of Loss 500,000 x 500,000
Placement Slip	Sample C	Professional Liability Excess of Loss 1,500,000 x 500,000
Placement Slip	Sample D	90/10 Quota Share Workers Compensation and Employer Liability
Placement Slip	Sample E	Property Per Risk Excess of Loss 600,000 x 400,000
Placement Slip	Sample F	Property Catastrophe Excess of Loss
Placement Slip	Sample G	75/25 Property Quota Share
Placement Slip	Sample H	Aggregate Excess of Loss (Stop Loss) 10,000,000 x 5,000,000
Placement Slip	Sample I	Professional Medical Liability

PLACEMENT SLIP - SAMPLE (A) *Casualty Excess of Loss 750,000 x 250,000*

Our Reference No.: 100-20

REINSURED COMPANY	**Neptune Insurance Company** Carson City, NV
TYPE OF TREATY	First Layer Casualty Excess of Loss – 750,000 x 250,000
PERIOD OF REINSURANCE	Continuous contract effective January 1, 2009
CANCELLATION PROVISION	Any 1/1 anniversary with 90 days written notice. In the event either party cancels, the Reinsurer shall participate in all policies ceded within the scope of this Agreement, and shall remain liable for all policies in force at termination of this Agreement; however, the liability of the Reinsurer shall cease with the natural expiration or cancellation of each policy ceded, but not to extend beyond (12) months after such termination or the requirements of applicable law, if any.
ATTACHMENT OF REINSURERS LIABILITY	Policy attaching basis effective 1/1/09. The reinsurers liability attaches to those insurance policies and their related endorsements that are new and renewal.
LINE OF BUSINESS REINSURED	Business written by the company and classified as automobile liability insurance for commercial trucking companies.
CLASS OF INSURED	Commercial trucking companies
TERRITORY	The reinsurance territory shall be identical with the Company's policies.
ESTIMATED ANNUAL SUBJECT PREMIUM **GROSS NET WRITTEN PREMIUM INCOME (GNWPI)**	6,000,000 (1/1/09 – 12/31/09)
RATE	5.0% of subject premium

ANNUAL DEPOSIT	$250,000 annually, payable quarterly in advance at $62,500 each quarter
ANNUAL MINIMUM	$250,000 annually
REINSURANCE LIMIT	750,000 each accident Excess of 250,000 each accident
REINSTATEMENT OF REINSURERS LIMIT	The first three (3) each are reinstated at no additional premium, the next two (2) each are reinstated at 50% additional premium each pro rata for amount of each limit reinstated, 100% for time.
POLICY FORM ISSUED BY REINSURED COMPANY	ISO commercial automobile policy
ALLOCATED LOSSADJUSTMENT EXPENSE	Proportional to the loss and in addition to the reinsurer's limit.
EXTRA CONTRACTUAL OBLIGATION	Covered in addition to the loss on an 80% basis within the Reinsurer's limit.
EXCESS OF ORIGINAL POLICY LIMIT	Covered in addition to the original policy limit loss on an 80% basis within the reinsurer's limit.
REINSURED COMPANY RETENTION	The company retains 250,000 on each policy, each claim
EXCLUSION	This Agreement shall not cover:

(A) Private Passenger Autos

(B) Taxicabs

(C) Rental Car Agencies

(D) Buses

(E) Hazardous Waste Truckers

(F) Automobile Physical Damage

CONTRACT WORDING To be agreed

PARTICIPATION/ ACCEPTANCE ________________________________

REINSURER AUTHORIZED SIGNATURE

DATE ________________________________

YOUR REFERENCE NUMBER ________________________________

REVIEW OF PLACEMENT SLIP SAMPLE (A)

This is an excess of loss reinsurance treaty written on a continuous basis with the right to be cancelled with (90) days written notice by either the reinsured-company or the reinsurer prior to the anniversary date of January 1, 2010 or any subsequent January 1 anniversary.

WHAT TO WATCH OUT FOR?

- The attachment of reinsurer's liability is based on the insurance policies issued by the reinsured company. The reinsurer is only responsible for losses in the layer 750,000 x 250,000 emanating from policies issued after 1/1/09 that are newly issued or renewed. The reinsurance is *not* covering in force policies; therefore they must be covered by the prior reinsurance.
- The reinsurer's original limit of 750,000 can be reinstated five (5) additional times, therefore the reinsurer can pay a total of six (6) losses each for 750,000. The first three (3) times it is reinstated there is no additional premium. The next two (2) times it's reinstated it's at 50% additional premium each reinstatement. If a limit is reinstated at 50% additional

premium it is pro rated for the amount of limit reinstated, there is no consideration for the length of *time* it is reinstated.

- The reinsurer will pay a loss of 750,000 plus allocated loss adjustment, which will be in proportion to the loss it, pays. For instance, if the reinsurer pays 60% of the loss it pays 60% of the allocated loss adjustment expenses.
- The reinsurer's limit is on an each policy each claim basis. This means it will pay up to 750,000 on each separate insurance policy that has a claim up to the overall limitation of the reinsurance agreement.
- Extra contractual obligation, the reinsurer will pay 80% of an extra contractual obligation within its overall 750,000 limit
- Excess of original policy limit, the reinsurer will pay the original loss and 80% of the loss if there is an award excess of the original policy limit within its 750,000 limit.

PLACEMENT SLIP - SAMPLE (B) *Casualty Excess of Loss 500,000 x 500,000*

Our Reference No.: 200-20

REINSURED COMPANY	**Neptune Insurance Company** Carson City, NV
TYPE OF TREATY	First Layer Casualty Excess of Loss – 500,000 x 500,000
PERIOD OF REINSURANCE	Continuous contract effective January 1, 2009
CANCELLATION PROVISION	Any time with 90 days written notice. In the event either party cancels, the Reinsurer shall participate in all policies ceded within the scope of this Agreement, and shall remain liable for all policies in force at termination of this Agreement; however, the liability of the Reinsurer shall cease with the natural expiration or cancellation of each policy ceded, but not to extend beyond (12) months after such termination or the requirements of applicable law, if any.
ATTACHMENT OF REINSURERS LIABILITY	Policy attaching basis effective 1/1/09. The reinsurers liability attaches to those insurance policies and their related endorsements that are in force, new and renewal.
LINE OF BUSINESS REINSURED	Business written by the company and classified as commercial general liability insurance.
CLASS OF INSURED	Generally will consist of small manufacturing companies and retail stores.
TERRITORY	The reinsurance territory shall be identical with the Company's policies.
ESTIMATED ANNUAL SUBJECT PREMIUM (GNWPI)	10,000,000 (1/1/09 – 12/31/09)
RATE	3.75% of subject premium

ANNUAL DEPOSIT	$300,000 annually, payable annually in advance
ANNUAL MINIMUM	$300,000 annually
REINSURANCE LIMIT	500,000 each policy, each claim Excess of 500,000 each policy, each claim
REINSTATEMENT OF REINSURERS LIMIT	The first one (1) at no additional premium, the next one (1) at 100% additional premium pro rata for amount, 100% for time.
POLICY FORM ISSUED BY REINSURED COMPANY	ISO commercial general liability policy
ALLOCATED LOSS ADJUSTMENT EXPENSE	Proportional to the loss and in addition to the reinsurer's limit.
EXTRA CONTRACTUAL OBLIGATION	Covered in addition to the loss on an 90% basis within the Reinsurer's limit.
EXCESS OF ORIGINAL POLICY LIMIT	Covered in addition to the original policy limit loss on an 90% basis within the reinsurer's limit.
REINSURED COMPANY RETENTION	The company retains 500,000 on each policy, each claim.
EXCLUSIONS	This agreement shall not cover (A) Directors and officers liability written as such (B) Auto liability (C) Errors and omissions liability written as such (D) Marine liability

CONTRACT WORDING

To be agreed

PARTICIPATION/ ACCEPTANCE ______________________

REINSURER ______________________

AUTHORIZED SIGNATURE ______________________

DATE ______________________

YOUR REFERENCE NUMBER ______________________

REVIEW OF PLACEMENT SLIP SAMPLE (B)

This is an excess of loss reinsurance treaty written on a continuous basis and can be cancelled with (90) days written notice given at anytime by either the reinsured company or the reinsurer.

WHAT TO WATCH OUT FOR?

- Either party can cancel at *any time* with (90) day written notice.
- This reinsurance *does cover* in force, new and renewal policies issued after 1/1/09.
- This treaty provides only two (2) reinstatements so the reinsurer will pay only three (3) losses in total.

PLACEMENT SLIP - SAMPLE (C)

Professional Liability Excess of Loss
1,500,000 x 500,000

Our Reference No.: 300-20

REINSURED COMPANY	**Neptune Insurance Company** Carson City, NV
TYPE OF TREATY	First Layer Professional Liability Excess of Loss 1,500,000 x 500,000
PERIOD OF REINSURANCE	Continuous contract effective January 1, 2009
CANCELLATION PROVISION	Any 1/1 anniversary with 90 days written notice.
ATTACHMENT OF REINSURERS LIABILITY	Losses occurring basis. The reinsurer shall pay losses occurring during the period 1/1/09 to 12/31/09
LINE OF BUSINESS REINSURED	Business written by the company and classified as director and officers liability insurance.
CLASS OF INSURED	Corporations, mostly in the Fortune 1000
TERRITORY	The reinsurance territory shall be identical with the Company's policies.
ESTIMATED ANNUAL SUBJECT PREMIUM (Gross Net Earned Premium Income)	20,000,000 (1/1/09 – 12/31/09)
RATE	12.0% of subject premium

ANNUAL DEPOSIT	$1,920,000 annually, payable quarterly in advance at $480,000 each quarter.
ANNUAL MINIMUM	$1,920,000 annually
REINSURANCE LIMIT	1,500,000 each policy, each claim Excess of 500,000 each policy, each claim
REINSTATEMENT OF REINSURERS LIMIT	The first two (2) each are reinstated at no additional premium, the next five (5) each are reinstated at 50% additional premium each pro rata for amount, 100% for time.
POLICY FORM ISSUED BY REINSURED COMPANY	Claims made directors and officers insurance policy issued with various retroactive dates. Defense cost within the policy limit.
ALLOCATED LOSS ADJUSTMENT EXPENSE	Part of the loss, the allocated loss adjustment expense is added to the loss to arrive at the total loss.
EXTRA CONTRACTUAL OBLIGATION	Covered in addition to the loss on an 80% basis within the reinsurer's limit.
EXCESS OF ORIGINAL POLICY LIMIT	Covered in addition to the original policy limit loss on an 80%basis within the reinsurer's limit.
REINSURED COMPANY RETENTION	The company retains 500,000 on each policy, each claim.
EXCLUSIONS	This agreement shall not cover (A) Auto liability written as such (B) Workers compensation and employers liability
CONTRACT WORDING	To be agreed

PARTICIPATION/
ACCEPTANCE ________________________________

REINSURER ________________________________

AUTHORIZED
SIGNATURE ________________________________

DATE ________________________________

YOUR REFERENCE
NUMBER ________________________________

REVIEW OF PLACEMENT SLIP SAMPLE (C)

This is an excess of loss reinsurance treaty written on a continuous basis with the right to be cancelled with (90) days written notice by either (reinsured-company or the reinsurer) prior to the anniversary date of January 1, 2010 or any subsequent January 1 anniversary.

WHAT TO WATCH OUT FOR?

The attachment of reinsurer's liability is based on the *date of loss*. The loss must *occur* (that's why it's called a *losses occurring* treaty)within the period of reinsurance 1/1/09 to 12/31/09,these dates are the looses occurring dates.

PLACEMENT SLIP – SAMPLE (D)

90/10 Quota share
Workers Compensation and
Employers Liability

Our Reference No.: 400-20

PARTICIPATION/ ACCEPTANCE	______________________________
REINSURED COMPANY	Neptune Insurance Company
REINSURER	Carson City, NV
AUTHORIZED SIGNATURE	______________________________
TYPE OF TREATY	90/10 Quota Share
PERIOD OF REINSURANCE	Continuous contract effective January 1, 2009
DATE	______________________________
CANCELLATION PROVISION	Any 1/1 anniversary with 90 days written notice.
YOUR REFERENCE NUMBER	~~In the event either party cancels, the Reinsurer shall~~ participate in all policies ceded within the scope of this Agreement, and shall remain liable for all policies in force at termination of this Agreement; however, the liability of the Reinsurer shall cease with the natural expiration or cancellation of each policy ceded, but not to extend beyond (12) months after such termination or the requirements of applicable law, if any.
ATTACHMENT OF REINSURERS LIABILITY	Policy attaching basis effective 1/1/09. The reinsurer's liability attaches to those insurance policies and their related endorsements that are in force, new and renewal.
LINE OF BUSINESS REINSURED	Business written by the company and classified as workers compensation and employers liability for commercial trucking companies.
CLASS OF INSURED	Medium to large size corporations in various industries.
TERRITORY	The reinsurance territory shall be identical with the Company's policies.

ESTIMATED ANNUAL SUBJECT PREMIUM (GROSS NET WRITTEN PREMIUM INCOME)	10,000,000 (1/1/09 – 12/31/09)

REVIEW OF PLACEMENT SLIP SAMPLE (D)

This is a quota shared treaty written on a continuous basis with the right to be cancelled with (90) days written notice by either the reinsured-company or the reinsurer prior to the anniversary date of January 1, 2010 or any subsequent January 1 anniversary.

PLACEMENT SLIP - SAMPLE (E)

Property Per Risk Excess of Loss
600,000 x 400,000

Our Reference No.: 500-20

REINSURED COMPANY	Neptune Insurance Company Carson City, NV
TYPE OF TREATY	First Layer Property Per Risk Excess of Loss – 600,000 x 400,000
PERIOD OF REINSURANCE	Continuous contract effective January 1, 2009
CANCELLATION PROVISION	Any 1/1 anniversary with 90 days written notice. In the event either party cancels, the Reinsurer shall participate in all policies ceded within the scope of this Agreement, and shall remain liable for all policies in force at termination of this Agreement; however, the liability of the Reinsurer shall cease with the natural expiration or cancellation of each policy ceded, but not to extend beyond (12) months after such termination or the requirements of applicable law, if any.
ATTACHMENT OF REINSURERS LIABILITY	Policy attaching basis effective 1/1/09. The reinsurers liability attaches to those insurance policies and their related endorsements that are new and renewal.
LINE OF BUSINESS REINSURED	Business written by the company and classified as fire, allied lines, inland marine and multi-peril (property only)
CLASS OF INSURED	Mainly small commercial buildings
TERRITORY	The reinsurance territory shall be identical with the Company's policies.
ESTIMATED ANNUAL SUBJECT PREMIUM (GNWPI)	8,000,000 (1/1/09 – 12/31/09)
RATE	3.0%of subject premium

ANNUAL DEPOSIT	$240,000 annually, payable quarterly in advance at $60,000 each quarter
ANNUAL MINIMUM	$200,000 annually
REINSURANCE LIMIT	600,000 ultimate net loss any one risk, any one loss Excess of 400,000 ultimate net loss , any one risk, any one loss Maximum any one occurrence 2,400,000
REINSTATEMENT OF REINSURERS LIMIT	Three (3) each at no additional premium
POLICY FORM ISSUED BY REINSURED COMPANY	ISO commercial package policy
ALLOCATED LOSSADJUSTMENT EXPENSE	Proportional to the loss and in addition to the reinsurer's limit.
EXTRA CONTRACTUAL OBLIGATION	Covered in addition to the loss on an 80% basis within the Reinsurer's limit.
EXCESS OF ORIGINAL POLICY LIMIT	Covered in addition to the original policy limit loss on an 80% basis within the reinsurer's limit.
REINSURED COMPANY RETENTION	The company retains 400,000 ultimate net loss any one risk, any one loss
EXCLUSION	This Agreement shall not cover: (A) Earthquake written as such (B) Ocean marine (C) Animal mortality, livestock, bloodstock

(D) Growing crops as such

(E) Crop hail as such

(F) Flood or water damage written as such

(G) Satellites

(H) Nuclear risks

(I) Warehouses

(J) Bowling alleys, restaurants, retail stores

(K) Boiler and machinery written as such

CONTRACT WORDING To be agreed

PARTICIPATION/ ACCEPTANCE ______________________________

REINSURER

AUTHORIZED SIGNATURE ______________________________

DATE ______________________________

YOUR REFERENCE NUMBER ______________________________

REVIEW OF PLACEMENT SLIP SAMPLE (E)

This is an excess of loss reinsurance treaty written on a continuous basis with the right to be cancelled with (90) days written notice by either the reinsured-company or the reinsurer prior to the anniversary date of January 1, 2010 or any subsequent January 1 anniversary.

WHAT TO WATCH OUT FOR?

Even though this is a property per risk treaty it contains a maximum amount the reinsurer will pay on any one occurrence. In this example it is 2,400,000.

PLACEMENT SLIP - SAMPLE (F) *Property Catastrophe Excess of Loss*

Our Reference No.: 600-20

REINSURED COMPANY	**Neptune Insurance Company** Carson City, NV
TYPE OF TREATY	Property Catastrophe Excess of Loss First Layer 95% of 1,000,000 x 1,000,000 Second Layer 95% of 3,000,000 x 2,000,000 Third Layer 95% of 5,000,000 x 10,000,000 Fourth Layer 95% of 10,000,000 x 10,000,000
PERIOD OF REINSURANCE	Twelve (12) month term agreement January 1 to December 1, 2009
CANCELLATION PROVISION	Any 1/1 anniversary with 90 days written notice.
ATTACHMENT OF REINSURERS LIABILITY	Losses occurring basis. The Reinsurer shall pay losses occurring during the period 1/1/00 to 12/31/00, coming within the scope of this Agreement.
LINE OF BUSINESS REINSURED	Business written by the company and classified as fire, allied lines, inland marine and multi-peril (property only)
CLASS OF INSURED	Mainly small commercial buildings and other property
TERRITORY	The reinsurance territory shall be identical with the Company's policies.
ESTIMATED ANNUAL SUBJECT PREMIUM (Gross Net Earned Premium Income)	10,000,000 (1/1/09 – 12/31/09)

REINSURANCE LIMIT

First Layer
95% of 1,000,000 each occurrence in respect to the Company's ultimate net property retention.
Excess of
95% of 1,000,000 each occurrence in respect to the Company's ultimate net property retention.
Reinsurance Rate 3.50% of Gross Net Earned Premium Income. Annual Deposit $350,000 payable in two semi-annual installments of $175,000 at June 1, 2009 and $175,000 at December 1, 2009
Annual Minimum $350,000
Reinstatement of Reinsurers Limit:
One (1) at 100% additional premium pro rata for amount, 100% for time.

Second Layer
95% of 3,000,000 each occurrence in respect to the Company's ultimate net property retention.
Excess of
95% of 2,000,000 each occurrence in respect to the Company's ultimate net property retention.
Reinsurance Rate 2.25% of Gross Net Earned Premium Income.
Annual Deposit S225,000 payable in two semi-annual installments of $112,500 at June 1, 2009 and $112,500 at December 1, 2009
Annual Minimum $225,000

Reinstatement of Reinsurers Limit:
One (1) at 100% additional premium pro rata for amount, 100% for time.

Third Layer
95% of 5,000,000 each occurrence in respect to the Company's ultimate net property retention.
Excess of
95% of 5,000,000 each occurrence in respect to the Company's ultimate net property retention.
Reinsurance Rate 1.50% of Gross Net Earned Premium Income.
Annual Deposit $150,000 payable in two semi-annual installments of $75,000 at June 1, 2009 and $75,000 at December 1, 2009
Annual Minimum $150,000

Reinstatement of Reinsurers Limit:
One (1) at 100% additional premium pro rata for amount, 100% for time.

Fourth Layer
95% of 10,000,000 each occurrence in respect to the Company's ultimate net property retention.
Excess of
95% of 10,000,000 each occurrence in respect to the Company's ultimate net property retention.
Reinsurance Rate 1.75% of Gross Net Earned Premium Income.
Annual Deposit $175,000 payable in two semi-annual installments of $87,500 at June 1, 2009 and $87,500 at December 1, 2009
Annual Minimum $175,000
Reinstatement of Reinsurers Limit:
None, Reinsurers limit shall not be reinstated.

POLICY FORM ISSUED BY REINSURED COMPANY

ISO commercial package policy and other property forms

ALLOCATED LOSSADJUSTMENT EXPENSE

Proportional to the loss and in addition to the reinsurers limit.

EXTRA CONTRACTUAL OBLIGATION

Covered in addition to the loss on an 80% basis within the reinsurers limit.

EXCESS OF ORIGINAL POLICY LIMIT

Covered in addition to the original policy limit loss on an 80% basis within the reinsurer's limit.

EXCLUSION

This Agreement shall not cover:
(A) Earth movement including earthquake in respect only to the state of California.
(B) Ocean marine

(C) Animal mortality, livestock, bloodstock

(D) Growing crops written as such

(E) Crop hail written as such

(F) Flood or water damage written as such

(G) Satellites

(H) Nuclear risks

(I) Warehouses

(J) Bowling alleys, restaurants, retail stores

(K) Boiler and machinery written as such

HOURS CLAUSE

(A) 72 Consecutive Hours
Windstorm, hail, tornado, hurricane, cyclone including ensuing collapse and water damage.

(B) 72 Consecutive Hours

Riot, civil commotion, vandalism, and malicious mischief

(C) 168 Consecutive Hours

Earthquake

(D) 168 Consecutive Hours

Freeze, Occasioned by Collapse, Breakage of Glass and Water Damage (Caused by Busting of Frozen Pipes and Tanks).

CONTRACT WORDING

To be agreed

CONDITIONS	(1) For purposes of this Agreement the Company's maximum retention each risk shall be 500,000. (2) Two or more policies must be involved before this reinsurer Agreement.
PARTICIPATION/ ACCEPTANCE	First Layer ________________ Second Layer ________________ Third Layer ________________ Fourth Layer ________________

REINSURER

AUTHORIZED SIGNATURE

DATE

YOUR REFERENCE NUMBER ____

REVIEW OF PLACEMENT SLIP SAMPLE (F)

This Property Catastrophe reinsurance is only for a twelve- month term July1 to December 31, 2009.

<u>WHAT TO WATCH OUT FOR?</u>
This treaty is covering the reinsured company's retentions from a series of losses from a single occurrence.

PLACEMENT SLIP - SAMPLE (G)

75/25 Property Quota Share

Our Reference No.: 700-20

REINSURED COMPANY	**Neptune Insurance Company** Carson City, NV
TYPE OF TREATY	75/25 Property Quota Share
PERIOD OF REINSURANCE	Continuous contract effective January 1, 2009
CANCELLATION PROVISION	Any time with 90 days written notice. In the event either party cancels, the Reinsurer shall participate in all policies ceded within the scope of this Agreement, and shall remain liable for all policies in force at termination of this Agreement; however, the liability of the Reinsurer shall cease with the natural expiration or cancellation of each policy ceded, but not to extend beyond (12) months after such termination or the requirements of applicable law, if any.
ATTACHMENT OF REINSURERS LIABILITY	Policy attaching basis effective 1/1/09. The reinsurers liability attaches to those insurance policies and their related endorsements that are in force, new and renewal.
LINE OF BUSINESS REINSURED	Business written by the company and classified as property insurance on commercial buildings
CLASS OF INSURED	Generally will consist of small manufacturing companies and retail stores.
TERRITORY	The reinsurance territory shall be identical with the Company's policies.
ESTIMATED ANNUAL SUBJECT PREMIUM (GROSS NET EARNED PREMIUM INCOME)	25,000,000 (1/1/09 – 12/31/09)
CEDING COMMISSION	27.50% of subject premium

PROFIT COMMISSION	15.0% after reinsurer's expense of 2.50%, deficits carry forward. Calculation 36 months from inception or 1/1/11.
ACCOUNTING REPORTS	Quarterly report within (30) days of the end of each quarter and shall include gross original premium written, unearned premium reserves, earned premium loss reserve, and remittance information. Balance due either party shall accompany quarterly report.
POLICY FORM ISSUED BY REINSURED COMPANY	NAIC workers compensation and employers liability insurance Policy or similar.
REINSTATEMENT OF REINSURERS LIMIT	One (1) free at 100% additional premium pro rata for amount,100% for time.
POLICY FORM ISSUED BY REINSURED COMPANY	ISO commercial general liability policy
ALLOCATED LOSS ADJUSTMENT EXPENSE	75/25 Quota Shared with Reinsurer's
EXTRA CONTRACTUAL OBLIGATION	75/25 Quota Shared with Reinsurer's
EXCESS OF ORIGINAL POLICY LIMIT	75/25 Quota Shared with Reinsurer's
REINSURED COMPANY RETENTION	10.0%
CASH CALL	When the Company pays or expects to pay a covered claim under this reinsurance of 50,000 or more, then upon a written request and supporting documentation showing the Company has paid or expects to pay such loss, the Reinsurer will promptly pay its quota share percentage to the Company.

EXCLUSIONS This agreement shall not cover

CONTRACT WORDING To be agreed

PARTICIPATION/ ACCEPTANCE ______________________________

REINSURER ______________________________

AUTHORIZED SIGNATURE ______________________________

DATE ______________________________

YOUR REFERENCE NUMBER ______________________________

REVIEW OF PLACEMENT SLIP SAMPLE (G)

This is a quota shared treaty written on a continuous basis with the right to be cancelled with (90) days written notice by either the reinsured company or the reinsurer prior to the anniversary date of January 1, 2010 or any subsequent January 1 anniversary.

PLACEMENT SLIP – SAMPLE (H)

Aggregate Excess of Loss (Stop Loss)
10,000,000 X 5,000,000

Our Reference No.: 800-20

REINSURED COMPANY	**Neptune Insurance Company** Carson City, NV
TYPE OF TREATY	Aggregate Excess of Loss (Stop Loss) – 10,000,000 X 5,000,000 In respect to the company's ultimate net retention's for automobile liability, commercial general liability, directors and officers liability
PERIOD OF REINSURANCE	Continuous contract effective January 1, 2009
CANCELLATION PROVISION	Any 1/1 anniversary with 90 days written notice. In the event either party cancels, the Reinsurer shall participate in all policies ceded within the scope of this Agreement, and shall remain liable for all policies in force at termination of this Agreement; however, the liability of the Reinsurer shall cease with the natural expiration or cancellation of each policy ceded, but not to extend beyond (12) months after such termination or the requirements of applicable law, if any.
ATTACHMENT OF REINSURERS LIABILITY	Losses occurring basis. The reinsurer shall pay losses occurring during the period 1/1/09 to 12/31/09.
LINE OF BUSINESS	Business written by the company and classified as commercial auto liability, commercial general liability, directors and officers liability
CLASS OF INSURED	Generally will consist of commercial trucking companies, small manufacturing companies and retail stores, and corporations, mostly in the Fortune 1000.
TERRITORY	The reinsurance territory shall be identical

with the Company's policies.

ESTIMATED ANNUAL SUBJECT PREMIUM (GNWEPI)

AL	4,500,000
CGL	8,000,000
D&O	16,000,000
	28,500,000 (1/1/09 – 12/31/09)

RATE

2.94% of subject premium per the Company's NAIC Annual Statement, Page 7 Underwriting and Investment Exhibit Part 2 – Premiums Earned Column 4

ANNUAL DEPOSIT

$800,000 annually, payable annually in advance

ANNUAL MINIMUM

$800,000 annually

REINSURANCE LIMIT

10,000,000 in the aggregate in respect to the Company's ultimate net retention's for automobile liability, commercial general liability, directors and officers liability

Excess Of

5,000,000 in the aggregate in respect to the Company's ultimate net retention's automobile liability, commercial general liability, directors and officers liability

REINSURED COMPANY RETENTION

The Reinsured Company warrants for the term of this Agreement it shall maintain its reinsurance program consisting of:

(A) Auto Liability
First Layer Casualty Excess of Loss
750,000 X 250,000

(B) Commercial General Liability
First Layer Casualty Excess of Loss
500,000 X 500,000

(C) Directors and Officers
First Layer Professional Liability Excess of Loss 1,500,000 X 500,000

All reinsurance, whether listed above or not, inures to the benefit of this Stop Loss Aggregate Agreement.

It is recognized that all of the Reinsured

	Company's treaties have limited reinstatement provisions. If losses exceed the company's treaty reinsurance they shall also be part of this Aggregate Excess of Loss Agreement. The Reinsured Company warrants for the purposes of this Agreement its maximum policy limits are: (A) Auto Liability 1,000,000 (B) Commercial General Liability 1,000,000 (C) Directors and Officers Liability 2,000,000
REINSTATEMENT OF REINSURERS LIMIT	NONE
POLICY FORM ISSUED BY REINSURED COMPANY	ISO commercial auto liability ISO commercial general liability Directors and officers liability
ALLOCATED LOSS ADJUSTMENT EXPENSES	Not covered by this Reinsurance Agreement
EXTRA CONTRACTUAL OBLIGATION	Not covered by this Reinsurance Agreement
EXCESS OF ORIGINAL POLICY LIMIT	Not covered by this Reinsurance Agreement
EXCLUSIONS	This Agreement shall not cover: (A) private passenger autos (B) taxicabs (C) rental car agencies (D) buses (E) hazardous waste truckers (F) automobile physical damage (G) errors and omissions liability written as such (H) marine liability (I) workers compensation and employers liability
CONTRACT WORDING	To be agreed
PARTICIPATION/ACCEPTANCE	______________________________

REINSURER ______________________________

AUTHORIZED SIGNATURE ______________________________

DATE ______________________________

YOUR REFERENCE NUMBER ______________________________

REVIEW OF PLACEMENT SLIP SAMPLE (H)

This is an aggregate stop loss reinsurance treaty written on a continuous basis with the right to be cancelled with (90) days written notice by either the reinsured company or the reinsurer prior to the anniversary date of January 1, 2010 or any subsequent January 1 anniversary.

PLACEMENT SLIP – SAMPLE (I)

Professional Medial Liability
Excess of Loss 500,000 X 500,000

Our Reference No.: 1000-20

DRAFT SLIP FOR QUOTATION

REINSURED COMPANY	**Neptune Insurance Company** Carson City, NV
TYPE OF TREATY	Professional Medical Liability Excess of Loss 500,000 X 500,000
PERIOD OF REINSURANCE	Continuous contract effective T.B.A. (To Be Announced)
CANCELLATION PROVISION	Any 1/1 anniversary with 90 days written notice. In the event either party cancels, the Reinsurer shall participate in all policies ceded within the scope of this Agreement, and shall remain liable for all policies in force at termination of this Agreement; however, the liability of the Reinsurer shall cease with the natural expiration or cancellation of each policy ceded, but not to extend beyond (12) months after such termination or the requirements of applicable law, if any.
ATTACHMENT OF REINSURERS LIABILITY	Policy attaching basis. The reinsures' liability attaches to those policies that are new and renewal.
LINE OF BUSINESS	Business written by the company and classified as liability insurance (medical malpractice and general liability) for physicians, surgeons, other medical personnel, some hospitals may be written. Coverage can also be extended to the medical entity.
CLASS OF INSURED	Basically all physician groups, with some hospitals.
TERRITORY	The reinsurance territory shall be identical with the Company's policies.
ESTIMATED GROSS NET WRITTEN PREMIUM	10,000,000 1/1/09 – 12/31/09 (12 months)
RATE	TO BE QUOTED

ANNUAL DEPOSIT TO BE QUOTED

ANNUAL MINIMUM TO BE QUOTED

REINSURANCE LIMIT 500,000 Excess of 500,000

This Excess of Loss reinsurance to follow each underlying policy on an excess of loss basis in respect to the limit of liability enumerated in the underlying policy, such as each claim, each loss event, each insured, each physician or other.

POLICY FORM

Separate Policies
Medical liability shall only be on claims made policy.
Commercial General Liability shall be occurrence.

POLICY COVERAGE

Medical Liability…claims made form only
Allocated loss and adjustment expenses can be structured in two ways:
(1) Within the policy.
(2) In addition to the policy.

Defense Cost Within the Policy Limit
Reinsurer shall follow the underlying policy in respect to ALAE. If defense costs are in then the limit, ALAE will be part of the loss.

Defense Cost in Addition to the Limit.
If defense costs are in addition to the policy limit, ALAE will be proportional to the loss and in addition to the Reinsurers' limit.

Multiple ways policy may be structured:
(a) Limit for physician only
(b) Limit for corporation only
(c) Shared limit among physicians
(d) Shared limit between physicians and corporation

General Liability…occurrence form
Allocated loss adjustment expense is in addition to the policy limit.

Reinsurance in respect to ALAE shall be proportional to the loss and in addition to the

	reinsurers limit
EXTRA CONTRACTUAL OBLIGATION	Covered on a 90% basis
EXCESS OF ORIGINAL POLICY LIMIT	Covered on a 90% basis
CONTRACT WORDING	To be agreed
PARTICIPATION/ACCEPTANCE	______________________________
REINSURER	______________________________
AUTHORIZED SIGNATURE	______________________________
DATE	______________________________
YOUR REFERENCE NUMBER	______________________________

REVIEW OF PLACEMENT SLIP SAMPLE (I)

This is a draft placement slip that would accompany a great deal of information needed by the reinsurer to quote on the specific treaty offered in Draft Placement Slip (I). This information would include corporate information, financial statements, actuarial reports, marketing information, underwriting criteria and guidelines, claims data, limit and risk profiles and other relevant information and data specific to the treaty.

CPSIA information can be obtained at www.ICGtesting.com
Printed in the USA
BVOW051301110512

290003BV00003B/16/P

9 781105 229862